American Churches

American

Roger G.

Director of the National Museum of

Stewart, Tabori & Chang,

Churches

Kennedy

American History of the Smithsonian Institution

Publishers, Inc., New York

This book is for Ruth

frontispiece:
The First Congregational Church of Woodbury,
South Woodbury, Vermont.
©Sonja Bullaty and Angelo Lomeo

Acknowledgments

Excerpt on p. 15 from *Collected Poems,
1951–1975* by Charles Causley.
Reprinted with permission of Macmillan London Limited.

Excerpt on p. 265 from "Sailing to Byzantium"
by William Butler Yeats.
Reprinted with permission of Macmillan Publishing Co., Inc.
Copyright 1928 by Macmillan Publishing Co., Inc.,
renewed 1956 by Georgie Yeats.
Canadian rights granted by Macmillan Limited,
M. B. Yeats, and Anne Yeats.

Book design by Nai Y. Chang
Photo research by Sybille Millard
Editorial supervision by Leslie Stoker

Library of Congress Cataloging in Publication Data

Kennedy, Roger G.
    American churches.

    Bibliography: p.
    Includes index.
    1. Church architecture—United States.
2. Churches—United States. I. Title.
NA5205.K46   246'.9   82-5613
ISBN 0-941434-17-6   AACR2

Distributed by Workman Publishing Company, Inc.
1 West 39th Street, New York 10018

Printed in Japan.

CONTENTS

LIST OF CHURCHES

PREFACE

This is not the sort of book that falls neatly within any academic "field." I have been the beneficiary of the generous and patient instruction of such scholars as Laurence Stookey of the Wesley Seminary and Jakob Petuchowski of the Jewish Theological Seminary in Cincinnati, who read the manuscript in a number of stages, corrected my worst errors, and made suggestions for further reading. Professor Stookey, in particular, permitted me to make use of a number of his own ideas with regard to Gothic architecture; these insights are central to whatever virtues may be found in my own text.

Administrators at each of the churches represented here were asked to provide answers to a detailed questionnaire, but many went considerably beyond what was asked of them. I think especially of the kindness of Abbot Dworschak of St. John's Abbey in sending me unpublished materials and homilies, and of the excellent information shared with me by a number of building committees. Of course, the interpretation of this information is my own, and I am grateful to the committees for their tolerance and encouragement in this regard.

I was assisted in research by Carol Frost, Henry Singer, William Braverman, Robert Davenport, and Daniel Sherman. Naomi Glass and Joyce Ramey helped answer innumerable questions, lent their advice and organizational skills, and weathered the wild fluctuations of an administrator who was also trying to be an author. I would have been duller by far without the remarkable team of editors and photo researchers at Stewart, Tabori & Chang.

This book was Andrew Stewart's idea, and he was bold enough to let it grow sizably beyond my original "picture book" intentions, offering good, encouraging counsel all the way. I do not think I would have ventured upon this project at all but for the example and friendship and instruction of James P. Shannon, Charles Taylor, and Joseph Ruff . . . and of my wife.

A Note on the Text

This book has been designed to interweave two components: general reflections on religious life and architecture in America, and essays about specific religious buildings—their history, architecture, architects, and worshipers. The general reflections have been set in one column, while the essays have been highlighted in a two-column format.

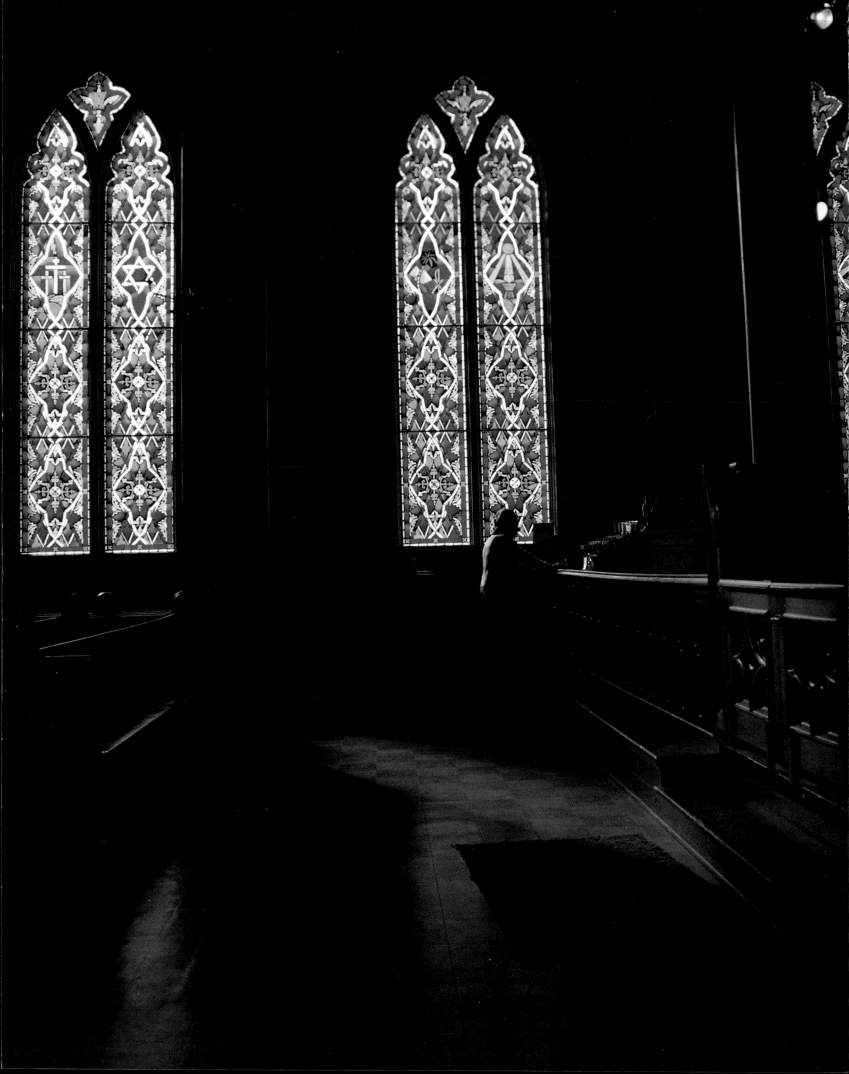

The King of Kings and the Lord of Lords;
who alone is immortal,
whose home is in inaccessible light,
whom no man has seen and no man is able to see:
to him be honor and everlasting power.
Amen.

1 TIMOTHY 6:15–16

INTRODUCTION

This is a book about buildings, but it is not primarily about architecture. It is about religious buildings, but its central idea is that the content, not the container, makes a building religious. The physical style of a structure, the name it bears, even the way in which it is described, may suggest its purpose. But if it is a church, what counts is the degree to which it reinforces religious feelings and actions.

Two stained glass windows in St. Mary's in the Mountains in Virginia City, Nevada. ©Mirko J. Pitner/After-Image

At the end of the second century, that rigorous old teacher, Clement of Alexandria, warned his readers not to be too interested in architecture: "A temple is not a building but a gathering of the faithful," he wrote. We will not be so severe as to ignore the physical appearance of the religious buildings in this book, but we will try to keep in mind what sort of "gatherings" they contained.

Our primary interest is in how churches were, and are, used for worship. We will, of course, pay some attention to their aesthetic qualities and to the chronicles of social history they offer; we will look at them as objects, certainly. But we will attempt to search out as well how they have presented environments for events of the spirit.

The intensity of those events determines the magnitude of a religious building, not its physical dimensions. The human race has been repeatedly reminded that grandeur of setting does not insure grandeur of event, nor do all grand events require grand settings.

History was set upon a new direction, and the religious life of billions of people was profoundly affected, by the birth of a child in an animal shed. From time to time this has been an embarrassment to people who calibrate the significance of a religious space by its dimensions. Anne of Austria, for example, instructed her architect in 1635:

> The church must be a sumptuous and magnificent sanctuary in order to compensate as much as possible for the extreme vulgarity and poverty of the place where the Eternal Word chose to be born.

This book will offer a series of important American buildings, some very grand, some very modest. It will describe the buildings' appearance, but it will try to push further, to offer some information about how they function as religious edifices.

Along the way we will try to tell who built them and out of what materials, how they comported with the taste of their times or the idiosyncracies of their architects. We will try to suggest the economic and ethnic

composition of their congregations. These are all useful things to know—churches, temples, and synagogues are important documents of social and religious history, of politics, of psychology, of economics, and sometimes of artistic genius—but for us these matters are insufficient to a full statement of their meaning. More than anything else we want to know how these buildings have provided for people to assemble for the purpose of coming into a closer relationship to a Mystery.

Mystery is a word that will be frequently found in these pages. According to the *Oxford English Dictionary*, *Mystery* has a precise meaning in the Judeo-Christian tradition: "a religious truth known only from divine revela-

Mennonite meeting house in Lancaster, Pennsylvania—plain architecture, plain dress, and plain living.
©George A. Tice

tion, usually a doctrine of the faith involving difficulties which human reason is incapable of solving.''

God is the Mystery behind all mysteries. Throughout the Old and New Testaments we are instructed not to be too confident that any word or thought of ours is sufficient to encompass Him. We can seek His presence in many ways, in many places. If we cannot presume to set words upon a page and think they can express His nature fully, how much more foolish it would be to think any one form of building could be appropriate to all His aspects! One of the glories of architecture is that it offers multifarious testimony to the boundless variety of His revelations.

This book is about that variety as it has appeared in religious architecture in America. It testifies that there cannot be any final solution to humanity's probing after a mystery. "You cannot see my face," said the Lord to Moses, "for man shall not see me and live" (Exodus 33:20). Later, Saint John reminded his readers that "no man has ever seen God; if we love one another, God abides in us and his love is perfected in us" (1 John 4:12).

It is certain that no one, except, some of us would say, Jesus, has seen God, nor defined Him, bounded Him, explained Him, nor "proven" His existence. Such a "proof" would imply that humankind can comprehend the qualities of God, as if those qualities fit within the experience of humanity.

A major theme of this book is that the very mysteriousness of God invites a great variety in the forms of the buildings created for His worship. Variety (which is the inevitable outcome of experiment which cannot produce any single "solution") and paradox are the fruits of humanity's insatiable desire to state its relationship to the compelling and the inscrutable.

A seventeenth-century Latin poem (translated by Charles Causley) suggests in a succession of paradoxes how various are the results of human understanding repeatedly bouncing off what it cannot ever wholly understand:

> I am the great sun, but you do not see me,
> I am your husband, but you turn away.
> I am the captive, but you do not free me,
> I am the captain you will not obey.
>
> I am the truth, but you will not believe me,
> I am the city where you will not stay,
> I am your wife, your child, but you will leave me,
> I am that God to whom you will not pray.
>
> I am your counsel, but you do not hear me,
> I am the lover whom you will betray,
> I am the victor, but you do not cheer me,
> I am the holy dove whom you will slay.
>
> I am your life, but if you will not name me,
> Seal up your soul with tears, and never blame me.

In the same spirit, we defer to the custom of many people—including the ancient, as well as the modern Jews—of avoiding the use of a name for

Fay Jones's Thorncrown Chapel in Eureka Springs, Arkansas. Reflections in a glass wall make an already open church seem more open still. ©Timothy Hursley/B. Korab, Ltd.

15

deity except in the gravest of circumstances. This book will use the term *the Mystery* both because it seems better to do so, out of respect, and because by doing so we may continue to suggest that a variety of churches, is an outcome of human energy that wishes to find physical means of expression for a very difficult but necessary task, worship of a Mystery.

This is the place to make it clear that we will use the term *church* in its broadest dictionary meaning, to include the diverse places of worship of Christians, Jews, and other religious peoples.

It is probably also the place to make explicit something that you must have already discerned: we affirm that worship need have no single voice, no single theme, no single rhythm, nor need it be housed in any single form. It would be strange if all churches were to look alike, since all worshipers do not, and they worship a Mystery "no eye has seen" nor the sound of which has any "ear heard." Churches are of many forms because that which is worshiped within them takes many forms, perhaps as many as there are worshipers.

The diversity of forms in America, though it has been occasioned by a diversity of ways in which to seek out the Mystery, has invited two large questions. They are the same as those put to architects, patrons, and building committees for thousands of years. They have been expressed with great force, especially since Christians, while professing humility, began to build very grand buildings. If this were not enough, they also kept producing spectacular new forms to surround a faith rooted in very ancient traditions.

The first of these two questions was put forward by the building committee of the Tabernacle Church of Christ in Columbus, Indiana, surely as reflective and wise a group as has ever been assembled for the purpose: "Why," they inquired, "is a monumental building desirable to the practice of Christianity, the humblest of faiths?"

The second is often put with equal vigor but less elegance: "Why don't they build something that looks like a church?"

We should arrange our own thoughts about the first of these two inquiries, because its answer is crucial to understanding the reasons for the creation of the large objects which we will be discussing here, and because our own attitude toward these buildings will color how we respond to them as physical objects. Since it is always good to try to be as conscious as possible of the reasons why we feel as we do about things, we can thank our predecessors for asking these questions directly and providing us with some answers to consider.

The prophets of Israel asked whether it was right to lay up great buildings when the resources thereby invested might better be used to

minister to the poor. Their criticism of what has subsequently been called "the edifice complex" commenced as soon as Solomon persuaded a neighboring king to lend him the skills of an architect and to provide the huge timbers needed to construct a temple. That criticism reached its greatest vehemence at the time Herod rebuilt Solomon's structure and surrounded it with a compound of the most bullying and muscular Roman style. That construction was going on when Jesus was crucified.

Soon after his crucifixion, one of his followers, named Stephen, "was filled with grace and power and began to work miracles." He was brought before the Sanhedrin in Herod's new temple "for making speeches against this Holy Place and the Law." Though Stephen had "the face of an angel,"

Colonial First Congregational Church in Newfane, Vermont, is a handsome example of what many of us consider "something that looks like a church."
©Sonja Bullaty and Angelo Lomeo

17

his words were infuriating. They were seditious politically, an affront to Herod and his oligarchs, and disruptive emotionally because these rulers had accepted subjection under Rome, and their displaced pride and energy had gone into the building of a temple. They did not welcome being reminded of that fact, declared him seditious, and sent him out to be stoned to death. The construction stones came easily to hand. Stephen had insisted that "the Most High does not dwell in a house hands have built," and he quoted from Isaiah:

> *With heaven my throne*
> *and earth my footstool,*
> *What house could you build me,*
> *what place could you make for my rest?*
> *Was not all this made by hand?*

These were the words that provoked his martyrdom in the presence of a young man called Saul, who "entirely approved of the killing." After Saul had experienced his epiphany upon the road to Damascus, he became the Apostle Paul, and he remembered Stephen when he wrote years later that each believer was "God's building . . . you are God's temple and God's spirit dwells in you."

The issue addressed by Stephen and Paul was a narrow one: whether God dwelt, like some nature spirit, in a particular place, which had a proscribed architectural form, or whether He dwelt, instead, everywhere in the hearts of men and women. Their doubts about the efficacy of "religious architecture" rise from new voices each time a great church is planned.

To the question "Does God need such a grand building, indeed, does God need any building at all?" the building committee in Columbus, Indiana, gave the answer that *God* does not, but His *people* may have such a need.

> A costly church can be justified, in our opinion, only so far as it inspires and stimulates people in living better lives . . . people do make Christians of other people and people do help each other to accomplish Christian ends. . . . We are all very sensitive to our surroundings. . . . Great buildings dominate and influence the lives of all who live near them. A church which embodies and illustrates the truths of Christianity should be a monument in which the affection and aspiration of many generations of Christians are centered. That is why we chose to spend our money in this way. We want our labor, in the form of this

building, to continue to influence the lives of our children and of theirs, to remind those who pass of Christ and to renew His spirit among us.

What of the second question "Why didn't they build something that looks like a church?" Much of this book can be taken as an answer. One example of that cumulative response might be the extremely unusual building designed by Marcel Breuer for the Benedictine community at St. John's Abbey, in Collegeville, Minnesota, a masterly execution of Abbot Baldwin Dworschak's charge to Breuer:

> The Benedictine tradition at its best challenges us to think boldly and to cast our ideals in forms which will be valid for centuries to come, shaping them with all the genius of present-day materials and techniques.

That ancient Benedictine tradition required a search for new and appropriate forms in new times, not capriciously, but after that sobriety of reflection which takes into account an intention that they should last. Breuer not only designed a church; he was asked to provide a plan for the next century's construction. New forms developed in this way offer a new crystallization of the needs of the community for solace, stimulus, and reaffirmation. The Mystery presents a different face to each searcher and to each group of searchers. All the forms that come into being in response to a glimpse of each such face will not satisfy all. They are not intended to do so, for their purpose is not to win competitions, but to serve the worshiping group.

The marvelous diversity of religious architecture in America is a statement of the energy and ingenuity with which Americans have clothed the spaces within which they have gathered to search out a Mystery.

Within this diversity there is much that seems grandiose and much that seems so subtle as to appear almost diffident. Within it there is much, as well, that is challenging to our sense of tradition, some which even challenges our sense of fitness; at the other extreme, there is some that appears to be merely an unconsidered expression of architectural inertia. Yet unifying it all is a common thread: all these buildings were built for humankind, to satisfy human needs. Among those needs is a place to seek the Mystery and to associate with others in that search. Some searchers require the affirmation of the past to urge them on; others more easily press toward new insights within new forms.

We are led, therefore, to seek to penetrate further into the psychology of religious architecture in America. We want to know why some people seem

Reflections upon curved surfaces—
light and diversity—a Ukrainian
church in Chicago (right) and The
Mother Church of The First Church
of Christ, Scientist in Boston (far
right). ©Bohdan Hrynewych/Stock, Boston
©David F. Hughes/Picture Group, respectively

to need one kind of building rather than another. We want to know their feelings toward the forms they ask of their architects. Since architects are themselves members of this searching and worshiping group of humans, since they have good reason to try to articulate their feelings, and since they have also had good reason to exchange views with congregations of worshipers, we will start with them.

These are the matters that will be addressed in Part One.

PART ONE
The Architecture of Mystery

1
The Artist and
the Mystery

Does each of the buildings we see in these pages represent an isolated event? Or are there important unifying ideas that are shared by most, if not all, of their architects, ideas which—when articulated clearly—also express the motivation of those who seek to have them built and those who use them afterward? Like most of us, artists begin with themselves, but most of them proceed to include us as well; they define themselves often in terms of their relationship to us. Although it is not as conventional to do so today as it once was, very often artists also define themselves, and us, in relation to the Mystery. The role of the artist is expressed in its horizontal dimension toward the community and in its vertical dimension toward the Mystery. (These directional indicators are not intended, of course, to be taken literally. Few people think they know "where" the Mystery "is.")

There is more to this than finding a location. It is remarkable how often architects speak of a sense of being that is "placed" not only within these "dimensions," but harmoniously as part of a larger scheme. When one reads the personal musings of the greatest architects whose work appears in these pages, and the letters they wrote to their trusted clients, there appear striking similarities in the ways they express their views on the nature of their craft, regardless of their apparently dissimilar artistic personalities. What especially arrests our attention is how often these views occur apparently without awareness that they are similar to those of the others. Often the same metaphors drawn from music were used among the builders of the ancient world and by medieval cathedral builders (as we will observe). Years later, generations of Renaissance designers employed very much the same concepts. They stated that they were seeking the harmonies of number, rhythm, and proportion found in the design of the universe, with which architecture, at its best, joins in an extended harmony.

It is true that most practitioners no longer attempt to express a complete architectural cosmology. Comprehensiveness is out of fashion. But though grand manifestoes or even large interrelated ideas are not to be found tacked on many drawing boards, these ancient ways of feeling are still very powerful. The great architects of our own epoch willingly acknowledge their efforts to find consonance between what they do and what the universe does, despite the rapidity with which both they and the universe change!

They state their cosmology in their work. Great churches represent a harmony between the artist and the community—and at the same time an extension of the liturgy. The entire building becomes an altar, set in the midst of the community.

Louis Sullivan had ample reason for cynicism about an artist's life in the twentieth century, yet he insisted that "an art work" must be "animate

St. Paul's United Methodist Church in Cedar Rapids, Iowa (top)—the interior of Louis Sullivan's "concentric" concept (as completed). ©Gerald Mansheim

A rectilinear masterpiece—the interior of Frank Lloyd Wright's Unity Temple in Oak Park, Illinois (bottom). ©Hedrich-Blessing

with a soul" and be directly, readily, and obviously of use to its community. His commissions to design religious buildings were deeply frustrating—at the beginning, at the Kehileth Anshe M'Ariv Synagogue, and at the end, at his Cedar Rapids church. The designs he intended could not be executed. But in both cases Sullivan was drawn instinctively to a concentric, unifying form, which brought the congregation together as an expression of a living community, and he was animated to put his best energies to the service of that community by a profound, religious sense of the witnessing role of the architect himself.

According to Sullivan, no cool detachment was possible in this quest. While serving its purpose, the structure must also

> stand for the actual, first-hand experiences of the one who made it, and must represent . . . not only . . . physical nature but more especially . . . the out-working of that Great Spirit which makes nature so intelligible to us that it ceases to be a phantasm and becomes a sweet, a superb, a convincing Reality.

The work of an artist, said Sullivan, must be "as real and convincing as is his own life . . . and yet as unreal, as fugitive, as inscrutable, as subjective as the why and wherefore of the simplest flower that blows . . . unless, when he was born, there was born with him a hunger for the spiritual . . . all other craving avails as naught."

The strutting of Frank Lloyd Wright before his clients and—in his writing—before the world, is too familiar a phenomenon to require reexamination here. But one visit to Unity Temple is enough to demonstrate that even Wright was a servant there, humbled by something he knew to be larger than himself.

Wright would have nothing of vaporous theorizing. He regarded the writing of his mentor, Sullivan, as "baying at the moon." But even Wright's insistence that the artist stands alone, requiring the aid of no models except perhaps a set of Froebel blocks, quiets in the presence of the architectural problem itself. Like many other post-Renaissance artists, Wright regarded most of his peers as knaves and fools and professed, on occasion, to disdain his clients as well. But he was a member of the congregation at Unity Temple, and he gave them what many regard to be his most complete and satisfying work of art. Like all artists who achieve anything more than the trickily competent, Wright stood in awe of what is demanded of the artist who serves art—which is one aspect of the Mystery.

Wright would be unlikely to say that ecclesiastical architecture represents the service of the Mystery, but his son John reported: "he was convinced that a Source existed which, by its very nature, produced ideas in

the mind that could be reproduced in the world. The rejection of his work by ignorance did not faze him. He concentrated on the intelligence that accepted it.''

Artists after the Renaissance often felt themselves to be larger than their times and out of harmony with their contemporaries. Nevertheless, it is noteworthy how often even the most seemingly egocentric of them expressed feelings toward the Mystery which, if rendered into Latin, we might take to be medieval.

The great twentieth-century Swiss architect and theoretician Le Corbusier was no more pleased with his century than was his contemporary Wright, but Le Corbusier never tired of exhorting his colleagues to serve it better. He had an enormous influence on younger architects in America, and he brought into their vocabulary of ideas concepts derived from the cathedral builders of his own country and of France.

Le Corbusier opened his book *When the Cathedrals Were White* with this almost Augustinian exhortation: ''I should like to bring to an examination of conscience and to repentance those who, with all the ferocity of their hatred, of their fright, of their poverty of spirit, of their lack of vitality, concern themselves with a fatal stubbornness to the destruction and hindrance of whatever is most beautiful. . . . the invention, the courage, and the creative genius occupied especially with questions of building—with those things in which reason and poetry co-exist, in which wisdom and enterprise join hands.''

Le Corbusier speaks of the participation of the artist, and specifically of the architect, in the ordering of the universe:

> In the immense hubbub of the Middle Ages . . . human beings observed the Hermetic rules of Pythagoras; everywhere you could see the eager search for the laws of harmony. . . . They threw themselves passionately into the reconquest of the . . . axis of human destiny: harmony. The law of numbers was transmitted from mouth to mouth among initiates. . . . The rules of harmony are complicated, intricate. To understand the reason in them you have to have a spirit of some sensibility.

Le Corbusier loathed the self-glorification demonstrated by other artists though he was far from mousy himself, and he was especially irritated by people who called themselves artists and cared more for the grand gesture than for the creation of a work of use to the community. Of them he said that they ''place themselves above things. . . . With them life stops; often there results a fair of vanities—a sect setting itself up over society.''

Christ Church in Lancaster County, Virginia, built in 1732. All great churches are not large, nor are we sure we know the names of those who designed them. ©Robert C. Lautman

29

Forty years after Le Corbusier wrote these words, we look upon an enlarged "fair of vanities." In architecture's many-ringed circus, one "style," one "sect" (according to his use of the term), follows after another, displaying its "amazing feats." The bystanders, unpersuaded by the press agents of this "fair of vanities," are disposed to view it as the architecture of frippery, in which craft is reduced to craftiness, and aesthetic conviction and commitment to community are shriveled into aesthetic sectarianism and trendiness. Deprived of its calling to work in and through community, in the service of something larger than itself, art becomes trivial. When only the acolytes of a particular artist understand or can put to use the work, it is no longer art, but the titillation of the invidious satisfaction of a clique, in which form follows faction.

But with Le Corbusier we can look back beyond all this to an older attitude. With curiosity at first, and then a rush of friendship for those who share our fundamental view of the relationship of artist to the Mystery, we can embrace our predecessors.

This does not mean, of course, that we should turn upon these predecessors and pillage their way of building. Larceny is not a reward for friendship. We do not even need to borrow from them, but instead to participate with them in a point of view toward architecture's place in the universe. That point of view leads to endless inquiry, to continuous experiment, to the abandonment of a fear of novelty, to a steeling of oneself for the

Unity Temple—a genius finds an answer to a problem of design, and answers another requirement as well.
©Robert D. Beard

adventure of leaving the shelter of received forms and easy habits. That attitude commences in awe and dread in the face of the Mystery, but it is not timorous before human incomprehension or sloth. It is reverent and bold, and, at its center, it is deeply committed to serve the best in a community. Sullivan and Le Corbusier were very clear about this. (Frank Lloyd Wright may be more confusing because his prose is so outrageously ego-rampant. But when we catch him unaware at work we see another man, the man his son observed. At Unity Temple, for example, Wright's whole spirit was engaged, not in setting himself apart, but in participation.)

Here is the center point of our inquiry. A great building, when it is designed and built, always manifests at least one of two different modes of the artist's participation. One we can call, with a little explanation, participation in the creation of the world. The other requires no explaining; it is, simply, creation in the service of the community.

Neither of these modes requires dissolution of the artist's ego nor loss of consciousness: art is the conscious application of craft of a very high order to serve powerful forces emerging from the unconscious. Both these modes of participation were required of the medieval artist. Both modes of participation are required, with even greater poignancy, of artists today. And a full understanding of what we mean by them is necessary if the rest of us are to experience fully what all art can provide, and especially that art which is our subject—church building.

UNITY TEMPLE
(now UNITARIAN UNIVERSALIST CHURCH),
Oak Park, Illinois, 1904–6

Frank Lloyd Wright's highly personal style had gained him a measure of fame by the early 1900s. He was living in Oak Park, Illinois, and was a member of the Unitarian Universalist Society of about four hundred members. Its pastor, Dr. Johonnot, asked him to design a new "temple" for his congregation at Lake Street and Kenilworth Avenue. The result was a new form. If any American church justifies the description "masterpiece," it is Unity Temple.

Accepting the constraint of a low budget as a poet might work within the fourteen lines of a sonnet, Wright used poured concrete, unfaced, as the primary material. The material spoke for itself; it was not hidden by brick or stucco. Also to save money, he decided on a precisely symmetrical plan so that the wooden forms for the concrete could be reused repeatedly.

From the start, Wright was determined to design a building without precedent. He later wrote:

> Was not...the church steeple, pointing on high...a misleading symbol perhaps?...Was not the time come now to be more simple, to have more faith in man on his earth and less anxiety concerning his Heaven about which he could *know* nothing?

Wright, the son of an itinerant preacher, raised by other Unitarians and Universalists, had a very narrow view of the function of symbols and a very powerful, if apologetic, religious sense. His churches reflect both his enormous skill and his psychological difficulties in the presence of structures associated with "traditional religion" and with the father who deserted him very early in life.

After explaining his conception to the building committee, says Wright, "I sent them away, they not knowing, quite, whether they were foolish, fooled, or fooling with a fool." He was not good at sharing in a creation, but he gave them all he had.

The form he chose was a cube, with four projecting bays. It presents a combination of plain surfaces and carefully chosen ornament—all integral to the structure. Though the geometry is abstract, the space feels warm. The lighting, which pours through amber skylights and clerestory windows, was intended to "get a sense of a happy cloudless day into the room." The structure appears in interlocking piers and spanning elements; it is enlivened by the variety of heights and planes of the intersections. The congregation enters unobtrusively from a lower level, but exits past the pastor through doorways that provide for a choreography as important to Wright's conception as is a grand Gothic nave intended for Feast Day processions. "This scheme gave the minister's flock to him to greet," he wrote. "Few could escape."

In designing Unity Temple, Wright created a setting for the Unitarian Universalist service, which has no traditional Sacraments and puts its emphasis upon rational discourse and an inclusiveness of theology.

Wright later said, with satisfaction, of Unity Temple: "It serves its purpose well. It was easy to build. Its harmonies are bold and striking, but genuine in melody....Here is one building rooted in such modern conditions of work, materials, and thought as prevailed at the time it was built. Singleminded in motif. Faithful in form." Wright was always generous in his appreciation of his own work, but Unity Temple is a powerful argument that he was, indeed, the genius he claimed himself to be.

The current pastor, Dr. Charles Scot Giles, commented in 1981 that "the square plan...reinforces our democratic understanding of ourselves.... There are no seats of power or prestige, we look at each other as well as at the pulpit."

©Don Kalec/HRCS Reservation Slide Library

©Gerald Mansheim

KEHILETH ANSHE M'ARIV SYNAGOGUE (now *PILGRIM BAPTIST CHURCH*), Chicago, Illinois, 1890–91

FIRST CONGREGATIONAL CHURCH OF AUSTIN (now *THE GREATER HOLY TEMPLE OF GOD IN CHRIST*), Austin, Illinois, 1908

FIRST CHURCH OF CHRIST, SCIENTIST (now *CHRIST FIRST DAYSPRING TABERNACLE*), Marshalltown, Iowa, 1902–3

ST. PAUL'S UNITED METHODIST CHURCH, Cedar Rapids, Iowa, 1910–14

Louis Sullivan and Frank Lloyd Wright were men of genius. Both had enormous early success in periods of economic expansion in the American Midwest. When adversity came, Sullivan broke under it and died impoverished and bitter. Wright survived by a combination of skill and charm, bravado, showmanship, and focused, indomitable energy.

Sullivan's early practice came to him largely through the exertions of his partner, Dankmar Adler, a great engineer and a part of Chicago's powerful entrepreneurial German-Jewish elite. Adler and Sullivan designed and built more than forty buildings, ranging in size from the huge Auditorium complex on the shore of Lake Michigan to skyscrapers, warehouses, and many private houses. They also designed three synagogues. Only one remains in anything like the form they intended. To this they were called by the congregation whose name, in translation, means "Congregation of the Men of the West," founded by Adler's father-in-law and headed by his father. Had the synagogue been executed completely as Sullivan designed, it would surely rank among his most famous buildings, with enormous battered rock walls, heavy mullions and transoms in the windows, and huge "Richard-

Kehileth Anshe M'Ariv Synagogue (now Pilgrim Baptist Church) (top). ©Bob Thall

First Congregational Church of Austin. As originally designed, the Congregational Church derived from the Synagogue, which in turn owed something to the Cistercians (bottom). ©HABS/Courtesy of Library of Congress

sonian" (Syrian) arches. The interior might have afforded the richest display of Sullivan's ornamental skill since the Auditorium building.

As it was built largely of brick, Joliet stone, and pressed sheet metal, it is still extremely powerful. As it has passed from the hands of the Jews into those of a congregation mostly of black Baptists, it still retains Adler's marvelous acoustics, perhaps now at better service to congregational singing than originally. The interior ornament, while no longer shining with gold and rich, dark wood, is still wonderful. A hint of what Sullivan would have done with a larger budget (and did accomplish in his banks) appears in the terra cotta facing the gallery and at the base of the clerestory. When the congregation is all present and the singing resounds under that great barrel vault, it celebrates the continuity of a religious space, which continues to serve a purpose so close to the original that only some shifts of accent and liturgy mark the passage of time. It remains dedicated to serving the Mystery, and the ghosts of Adler, his father, and father-in-law, all men with breadth of vision, must be pleased.

A progression of design, through Sullivan's transforming hands into those of his disciples, can be followed by setting, in the mind's eye, the famous Carthusion church of Pontigny, in France, against the synagogue, and the synagogue against William Drummond's First Congregational Church of Austin, Illinois. The date of Drummond's design is 1908, and the example of Wright's Unity Temple, completed two years earlier (see p.32), is clearly in his mind; but Sullivan's synagogue was an even more

First Church of Christ, Scientist (now Christ First Dayspring Tabernacle). ©Tom Bean/Tom Stack & Associates

powerful prototype. The shape of the First Congregational Church accommodates the hierarchy of schoolrooms on the ground floor and sanctuary above, but it also accommodates (especially in a rendering) the memory of Pontigny and of the synagogue. Wright had shown how to eliminate all ornament and how to build of sheer, simple planes (Drummond's are of the brick the congregation at Unity Temple could not afford). But neither Wright nor, after him, Drummond could have moved so fast without the lead given them by the "master," Sullivan.

The congregation of First Congregational also has changed—from Congregationalist to Roman Catholic. The sociology of the neighborhood has, as well. Austin, once a suburb, has been devoured by Chicago. But in a time when it is fashionable to speak of "adaptive reuse," very little adaptation has been required to sustain the use of a building by one group of Christians that was designed for another. The altar is more prominent, the iconography has been enriched, but the purpose remains much the same.

Another example of the Prairie school at work in the Midwest, and of the influence of Unity Temple, is Hugh M. G. Garden's First Church of Christ, Scientist, in Marshalltown, Iowa. This is a relatively small building in the shape of a Greek cross.

The roof is composed of steep cross gables within which are placed greenish-yellow triangular windows designed by Giannini and Hilgart, frequently the glassworkers for Chicago architects.

Garden was never a whole-souled exponent of the pure Prairie school idiom, with its Wrightian rejection (or ostensible rejection) of past styles. The interior of the First Church of Christ, Scientist shows that he was as willing as Bernard Maybeck (see p. 221) to play with structural ideas derived from the Gothic; it displays heavy exposed struts quite unlike the smooth stucco and masonry foundations of the exterior, although the high pitched roof invites their use.

Iowa would, today, possess the greatest of Prairie school churches, aside from Unity Temple, had the Methodist Episcopal congregation of Cedar Rapids been able to build either the grand cube-and-campanile devised for them by Purcell and Elmslie or had they been able to work with the sick and exasperating Louis Sullivan of 1910 to draw out the full glories of which he was capable. As it is, the Cedar Rapids Church, in his circle-and-campanile design (now St. Paul's United Methodist), is a handsome building whose interior works very well to focus the worshipers upon great preaching. But it is not the masterpiece it might have been.

St. Paul's United Methodist Church. ©Gerald Mansheim

UNITARIAN CHURCH OF ROCHESTER,
Rochester, New York, 1962

©John Ebstel

Louis Kahn, a major architect of the second half of the century, contended that a great building "must begin with the unmeasurable, must go through measurable means when it is being designed, and in the end must be unmeasurable.... When the building becomes part of living, it evokes unmeasurable qualities, and the spirit of its existence takes over." Kahn's modesty toward the "unmeasurable," toward what we have called "the Mystery," was harmonious with the theologically diffident —but socially assertive—history of the remarkable congregation of the First Unitarian Church of Rochester. Kahn sought to learn what he called the "flavor" of that congregation, attending many of its services before he commenced the design for their church. "From what I heard...I realized that the form aspect...of their activity was bound around that which is Question...Question eternal."

So when he began his diagram of the church, he "made a square center on which I placed a question mark...the sanctuary." The center offered inquiry, not certainty. But that did not mean the place was to be treated as merely another laboratory or school-room: the questioning was holy questioning. The center was to be approached as carefully as the sanctuary that Eero Saarinen prepared for the Christians at North Christian Church in Columbus, Indiana (see p. 247). Kahn encircled the central space "with

an ambulatory for those who did not wish to go into the sanctuary. Around the ambulatory I drew a corridor which belonged to an outer circle enclosing a space, the school. It was clear that School which gives rise to Question became the wall which surrounds Question. This was the form expression of the church, not the design."

The congregation had been asking questions of itself, of the Universe, and of its own society for a century and a half. It was founded in 1829, during an evangelical outburst in western New York. Its motto was "Here be no one a stranger." Its first leader, Myron Holley, had been commissioner of the Erie Canal and was one of the founders of the abolitionist Liberal party. Arson, probably politically inspired, destroyed the church building in 1859. The congregation gathered again after the Civil War and plunged again into controversy. In the 1870s Newton Mann was the first American clergyman to "proclaim from his pulpit the doctrine of evolution." During his pastorate the local rabbi occupied the pulpit regularly, and joint Thanksgiving services among the Unitarians, Jews, and Universalists commenced.

Many fashionable churches moved out of the neighborhood in which the church was located, but the Unitarians began providing school and social facilities to its neighborhood, increasingly composed of immigrant families. Many of the immigrants were

is an essential component in Kahn's work. At Rochester, his windows are positioned within deep niches; the butterfly roof is surmounted by a clerestory. The intention is to modulate, to sculpt and vary the light, which was to Kahn not only the essence of architecture but of life itself.

All material in nature, the mountains and the streams and the air and we, are made of Light which has been spent, and this crumpled mass called material casts a shadow, and the shadow belongs to Light.
So Light is really the source of all being. . . . When the world was an ooze without any kind of shape or direction, the ooze was completely infiltrated with the desire to express, which was a great congealment of Joy.

The Abbot Suger would have understood completely. Working with light is one of the joys of being an architect; trying to find answers to serious questions—eternal questions—is one of the joys of theology.

Jewish and, as a consequence, were often called either "Jew-natarians" or "Gannetarians" after William Channing Gannett, one of the nation's leading exponents of the social gospel who occupied the pulpit from 1890 to 1910. As a national figure he was followed by David Rhys Williams, who told the trustees, "If there is anything you don't want me to talk about in the pulpit, let me know about it now, so I can decline the call of the church." Apparently there were no demurers, for Williams began in 1928 fully thirty years of outspokenness.

The church history says that in 1959 they "hired the internationally known Louis Kahn of Philadelphia as architect" for a new church. What they got was one of the great buildings of the century. Its simple masses can be felt as masses, its spaces read as spaces—no tricks, no gestures, no billboards inserted to carry the architect's signature—and verticle stacks articulate a plan of defined, discrete spaces. Kahn reacted against slick, mechanistic architecture, preferring something more direct, more primitive. Not all should be done through simply "functional" design: "Of course, steel is a marvelous material. You can do wonderful things with it, build great machines, but in architecture you're not building airplanes after all, are you? A Building should be a more stable and harboring thing."

And within the shelter, there should be light. Light

2
Participation in Creation and Participation in Community

What do we mean by "participating in the creation of the world?" How does the artist do that? How do we accept the invitation of the artist to join in that creation?

Creation, since Creation itself, has been continuous. So has destruction. Ever since the materials of the universe existed, they have been continually combining and dissolving in new ways. The artist participates in those combinations and dissolvings. They occur differently because of the artist's intentions. Thereby humankind participates in continuous creation.

When a work of art finds itself—when an artist, like Michelangelo, chips away from a block all the marble except the statue, or when the notes on a page of music settle down into their appointed positions, when the words stop squirming about in one's head and acquiesce to being tacked into place on a page, or when the lines on the drafting paper seem to form as if tracing something invisible—artists know they are participating in creation. If they were in the neighborhood of Chartres during the thirteenth century, that participation might be experienced as an act of restoring the harmony of the cosmos, coming into consonance with immemorial patterns of number, expressed in rhythmic patterns and intervals of sound or in appropriate architectural proportions.

Even after the Renaissance, even after the Romantic movement endorsed a neurosis—indeed, a madness—called egomania, even in the twentieth century, it is a sense of participation in a larger order of things (another aspect of the Mystery) that imports the deepest satisfaction to the artist. If this statement seems extreme, the language of philosopher Carl Gustav Carus may express the same meaning more comfortably:

> Strange are the ways by which genius is announced, for what distinguishes so supremely endowed a being is that, for all the freedom of his life and the clarity of his thought, he is everywhere hemmed round and prevailed upon by the Unconscious [note the deifying capital letter], the mysterious god [note—no capital] with him; so that ideas flow to him—he knows not whence; he is driven to work and to create—he knows not to end; and is mastered by the impulse for constant growth and development—he knows not whither.

Another philosopher and psychologist, Carl Jung, described artists as often appearing to be, and indeed regarding themselves as being, "ruthless and selfish" in the grip of "an invincible egoism." In fact, according to Jung, artists may actually not be very much in control of themselves. Far from expressing their will, artists may be victims of another will. Their creativeness demands all their energy, monopolizes them by its demands, and makes them "cranks" in the eyes of their community. (The Romantic movement welcomed any crank as a superman and, thereafter, antisocial behavior as a sign of something called "the artistic temperament." We have learned since that while all artists may appear to be cranks from time to time, all cranks are not artists.)

We need to understand this strange relationship between creative energy and the artist if we are to move past our irritation at "artistic behavior" toward a full participation in the works of art. This helps us understand that religious buildings are often the products of the relationship between artist and community, in which the other relationship to which we have referred, between artist and the Mystery, participates but often in a very inexplicit way. We can miss the joy of participation if we do not feel a kinship with the artist, and we can miss the point if we do not understand that we are examining sacred activity, touched by the spirit of the Mystery and activated by its intervention.

Though artists, in their sometimes tormented lives, may seem to be at war with society, they are, in a deeper sense, its unbidden and unrequited servants. The irritability of Le Corbusier or Wright arises from their functioning as pickets or skirmishers for society, exploring its frontiers. They lived at the fringe of the consciousness of their time. Nobody asked them to step beyond the consensus—"nobody" but the necessities of the members of the consensus. And the worship of the Mystery is among those necessities, not just in building churches, but certainly including that work.

When artists are provided an opportunity of working on a project that serves the community, even though this opportunity requires them to pull that community well beyond its intentions, they serve its most profound unspoken needs. Actually, what seems to happen when a masterwork is being conceived is that both its parents, the artist and the client, are surprised by the other. This appears to have occurred in Columbus, Indiana, between the building committee of the Tabernacle Church of Christ (now called First Christian) and Eliel and Eero Saarinen. The committee, of which J. Irwin Miller was the most forceful member, had theological reasons "to discard all their inherited beliefs and to go to the New Testament with open and unprejudiced minds." The architects took up this theme and replied: "You must feel instinctively that any development of form must be a true expression of

St. John's Abbey. Twentieth century materials serve a Benedictine community. ©Hedrich-Blessing

the best endeavors of the life that it represents . . . we . . . have been using the dead styles of alien cultures until the last drop of expressiveness has been squeezed out of these once so expressive styles.'' The building they created together was a new thing, expressing not just the style of the architects but also the style of the community.

The abbey church of St. John the Evangelist, in Collegeville, Minnesota, arose under similar circumstances. Its architect, Marcel Breuer, and the Benedictine Community represented by Abbot Baldwin Dworschak, corresponded with each other in very much the same cadences as did the Saarinens and the citizens of Columbus. ''Plans and details,'' said Breuer, ''were based upon a meticulously re-examined liturgical tradition.'' To crystallize this tradition was the job of the devoted monastic community. ''Although the church may be a new sensation to the eye, its architectural concepts resemble those of . . . the Middle Ages. . . . I merely put a shell around the sacred space designed by the monastic community.''

Breuer's sense that ''style'' is a mere ''shell'' came out of his own transforming experience at St. John's. We should pay attention to what his statement suggests to us about the relative significance of ''shells'' and ''sacred'' spaces before dividing the churches in these pages too

First Christian Church in Columbus, Indiana. Another belltower to serve another kind of midwestern community—a masterpiece by Eliel and Eero Saarinen. ©Balthazar Korab

mechanically into clumps distinguished only by the appearance of their shells.

In all those interchanges that have led to the creation of living buildings, something seems to occur in the life of their architects. This *something* led Breuer, some years later, to say "to build . . . is not to play a role . . . to give an opinion; it is a passion . . . the bread we eat." And at another time: "How much we will be affected by the building . . . will depend on the courage it manifests in facing the ancient task: to render the enclosed space a part of infinite space." On the day the abbey church was consecrated, his parting words to Dworschak were: "Father Abbot . . . this is the first building I have ever designed and the first object I have designed which has been made so sacred, or, as you would say, consecrated to God. I am more deeply moved than I can tell you."

It was in the same spirit that a desperately ill Eero Saarinen, twenty years after the completion of First Christian, wrote to his client and, by then, long-term friend Irwin Miller about his fear that he might not finish the designs for their second church together, North Christian. His office was deluged with work, the Athens Airport, the Repertory Theater at Lincoln Center, the CBS Building. He had refused forty or fifty other commissions. But he was trying to "solve" the church as an obligation "to you, . . . to the

North Christian Church, also in Columbus, Indiana, by the younger Saarinen. ©Balthazar Korab

congregation, and . . . to my profession and my ideals.'' He wanted to ''face St. Peter'' and say ''one of the best'' works in his lifetime ''was a church I did in Columbus, Indiana, because that church has a real idea in the way worship is expressed in architecture, and a real spirit that speaks forth to all Christians as a witness to their faith.''

And so what matters is what happens within the building and how the intentions of the builders affect the forms those buildings take. Things do not stop there. As Winston Churchill once commented: ''We shape our buildings, and afterwards our buildings shape us.''

Churchill's phrase appears again in some comments made by Jung about the ways in which we may join, so to speak, in the continuous process of creation which is offered by a building that is also a work of art:

> . . . when we allow a work of art to work upon us as it acted upon the artist . . . we must allow it to shape us as it shaped him . . . he has plunged into the healing and redeeming depths of the collective psyche, where man is not lost in the isolation of consciousness and its errors and sufferings, but where all men are caught in a common rhythm which allows the individual to communicate his feelings and strivings to mankind as a whole.

St. Louis Priory was designed for the Benedictines of St. Louis, Missouri, who wanted their priory to be "living architecture"—to use the methods, style, and materials of the time in which it was built.

©Frank Aleksandrowicz

The churches presented in these pages disclose a range of ways in which builders have addressed themselves to the Mystery. We have chosen our examples in part because of their familiarity and accessibility. We have, therefore, spread out our selections across time, across space, across denominations, and across "styles," seeking to invite as many people as possible into this book. Some of these buildings present more intensely than others the point of view we have expressed. The reader will decide which among them lead most effectively into the contemplation of the Mystery.

If we allow a work of art, such as a great church, "to work upon us as it worked upon the artist," its architect, if we "allow it to shape us as it shaped him," we may experience something far more powerful than mere pleasure in the beauty of its design, its craftsmanship, and the array of fine materials it sets before us. If we exert ourselves to participate in the creative spirit that brought it into being, we may go beyond pleasure into joy. This can occur, however, only if we are willing to experience those buildings reverently and with due attention to their symbolic content. The next portions of this book make a few suggestions about how this may be done.

College Chapels

"After God had carried us safe to New England," wrote the author of *New England's First Fruits* in 1643, "and we had builded our houses . . . rear'd convenient places for God's worship and settled the Civill Government; One of the next things we longed for and looked after was to advance Learning . . . dreading to leave an illiterate Ministry."

To serve the needs stated in the *First Fruits*, John Harvard, a young minister who died in 1638, left his books, together with a small endowment, to a college which had held its first classes in that year. "Harvard College," as it came to be known, required the resignation of its first great president, Henry Dunster, in 1654 for the Baptist views that had led Roger Williams to depart Salem and set forth into the miseries of the "howling wilderness" of Rhode Island. While Williams later abjured Baptism, his followers remained strong in the colony. The first president of Rhode Island College (Brown University), after it moved to Providence from Warren in 1770, was the strict Baptist James Manning.

The first American universities all were founded for the instruction of the clergy. Yale College moved from one parsonage to another for fifteen years; William and Mary, although it spent years as "a college without a chapel, without a scholarship, without a statute; having a library without books," arose from an ambitious plan of the highest Anglican official of Virginia, James Blair. Princeton was founded to train Presbyterian divines. Even the non-denominational King's College (Columbia) and the University of Pennsylvania were led at the outset by Anglican clergymen.

The college chapel is an art form that has always been heavily influenced by secular benefactors whose architectural views tend to predominate over both the educational and ecclesiastical officials of the institutions. But the consequences have not been bad; most distinguished American universities have equally distinguished chapels—they are often the best buildings on campus.

We have presented a group of these, beginning with the first in time, the chapel of Hamilton College in Clinton, New York, whose façade was designed by the remarkably old-fashioned architect Philip Hooker; his design of 1827 could easily have been built a hundred years earlier. The second, Manning Hall at Brown, six years younger, took the fashionable shape of the day, the Classic revival, which might have been expected at Hamilton. Then we leap to the middle of the twentieth century for Frank Lloyd Wright's idiosyncratic and functionally effective Pfeiffer Chapel of 1938 at Florida Southern in Lakeland, Florida. The spirit of Wright persists in Paul Rudolph's remarkable Tuskegee Institute Chapel, which gives appropriate deference to the distinct qualities of the congregation it is intended to serve. Two chapels by world-famous foreign-born architects, Eero Saarinen and Ludwig Mies van der Rohe, show utterly different ways to create spaces to serve the religious life of schools of engineering, the Massachusetts and Illinois Institutes of Technology. Then, in its superb setting, appear the folded wings —or folded hands—designed by Skidmore, Owings and Merrill for the Air Force Academy Chapel at Colorado Springs. Finally, another chapel designed for another kind of community is that for St. Louis Priory in St. Louis, Missouri.

HAMILTON COLLEGE CHAPEL,
Clinton, New York, 1827

The chapel stands on the Hamilton College Campus, about a mile west of Clinton, New York. Completed in 1827, it is constructed of local gray stone which, being rich in iron, has oxidized into a soft orange, while its mortar joints have acquired a pale blue. It stands upon a hill, and, accommodating the building committee's injunction that it have "three tier [sic] of windows...33 feet in height above the watertable" (not the usual two-story structure of the time), its height is emphasized by a steeple of four superimposed temple forms in the eighteenth-century manner of Gibbs and Wren.

It was designed by Philip Hooker, a carpenter from central Massachusetts who became the favorite architect of Martin Van Buren's "Albany Junto," the ruling politicians of the state before Van Buren's ascent to the vice-presidency under Andrew Jackson and then to the presidency. Hooker was the architect of at least seven churches, and by 1833, "as seen from the river...the skyline was crossed by seven buildings: on the right, by the belfry of the Academy and the modest steeples of the First Lutheran Church and St. Mary's; in the centre, by the lofty spire of the Second Presbyterian and the dome of the new City Hall; and on the left, by the steeple of St. Peter's and the circular cupola of the State Capitol." Every one of these buildings (with the possible exception of Second Presbyterian) was by Philip Hooker.

His work was as profoundly conservative as were his clients. Albany's ruling merchants and landowners did not welcome the intrusion of the contemporary styles of the time, the Greek and Gothic revivals. Neither did the building committee at Hamilton, which eschewed as well any stress upon the liturgical uses of the building. They were practical, hard-fisted men. Their instructions were to plan a building "for other purposes, beside, Religious and Classical exercises...to be completed as soon as practicable consistent with due economy." Hooker replied, offering "a Steeple with a proportionate Spire" but suggesting "Something of the Style of a cupola with two Sections finished with a dome....The tower I presume ought to Contain a clock and a College bell as a matter of course." They agreed that a dome, clock, and bell would be "more proper for a chappel than a lofty spire."

By the late nineteenth century the chapel's interior had taken on a heavy Victorian atmosphere, resulting from the introduction of golden oak woodwork and stained glass windows. After World War II, however, a decision was made to restore the building to the spirit and style of the original chapel and to dedicate it to alumni who had died in the service of their country. Victorian darkness was banished to make way for colonial simplicity, and gleaming white became the primary interior color. The ponderous chancel arch was replaced by a simple, square opening that framed a new Palladian window behind the altar, and a new high pulpit faced neatly boxed pews. Stained glass gave way to plain glass of the kind originally used. The grace of the chapel's exterior was again matched by an austere inner beauty. Today the chapel continues to be regularly used for religious services, as well as a host of other purposes, from meetings and lectures to concerts and theatrical performances.

©Jon Cashen

MANNING HALL,
Brown University, Providence, Rhode Island, 1833

The first European settlers of Rhode Island were Baptists under Roger Williams. Williams led a dissenting band of his followers out of the Massachusetts Bay Colony, itself dissenting from the Church of England. From the outset, these Puritans were distinguished by their tolerant love of learning, but Rhode Island had to wait two centuries thereafter to assemble wealth enough to begin to rival the educational entrenchments of Massachusetts or Connecticut.

When Manning Hall was dedicated on February 4, 1835, Brown University had fewer than 100 students and a faculty of less than a dozen. Standing between University Hall, the first college building, and Hope College, the second, Manning Hall was built to include a Baptist chapel on the second floor above the library on the first. Today's chapel is available for worship for any denominational group at the university, which numbers approximately 6,600 students and 530 faculty members.

The building was financed by Nicholas Brown, of the family of benefactors for whom Rhode Island College was renamed Brown University in 1804. He requested that the building be named after his instructor and friend, Reverend James Manning, the first president of the college. Manning Hall is one of a group of interesting examples of Classic revival buildings in Rhode Island, many of them designed by Russell Warren of Bristol.

There is some scholarly dispute about whether Warren or James C. Bucklin was principally responsible for Manning Hall's Doric form. They were associated in the Arcade, in Providence, and other buildings. They probably collaborated in laying out and constructing the hall, which measures 90 feet in length and 42 feet in width, with walls 40 feet high and built of rough stones from neighboring hillsides and covered with plaster. The floors and the roof are constructed of wood. The temple front of the building presents a porch with four fluted Doric columns, architrave, frieze, and cornice, and the windows and two entrances are ''correct,'' unornamented rectangles.

A flight of stairs from the entrance vestibule leads to the chapel on the second floor. The chapel floor is supported by a double row of fluted columns within the library. At the west end of the chapel is the balcony, which houses the organ and the organ console; at the east, a raised platform with two pulpits and an altar.

Upper Manning Hall has not always been a chapel. For more than forty years it served as a lecture room until, in 1958, it was reconverted into a chapel. The building's return to its original function recalls the last stanza of the ode sung at the original dedication of Manning Hall:

To Thee, pure RELIGION, to thee,
We have built the fair temple, made sacred the shrine:
And ever, blest faith, may it be
Kept holy to thee and thy service divine;
It is learning's—'tis Freedom's—'tis Thine.
Through ages unborn, let its altar still be
Thou God of our fathers, kept holy to Thee.

ANNIE PFEIFFER MEMORIAL CHAPEL,
Florida Southern College, Lakeland, Florida, 1941

©Walter Smalling, Jr./for HABS

The entire campus of Florida Southern College was designed by Frank Lloyd Wright in 1938 to be constructed in steel-reinforced concrete. The Annie Pfeiffer Memorial bears no surface indication of being set aside for religious purposes, but inside it serves the student community very effectively.

A complex, irregular building, the chapel consists of a hexagonal tower superimposed over a rectangular ground floor and supported by four major structural columns. Wright, hearkening back to his early experiments in cantilevered construction, enabled the walls to serve not as load-bearing masses, but to tie this building into the rest of the campus. The campus is tied together with beige-colored concrete, wood, pools, and plants. Inside the chapel, skylights contribute natural illumination. A balcony flows continuously around the room, screened on one side by concrete openwork, which relieves the

©Walter Smalling, Jr./for HABS

eye with patterns of shadow. The chancel and pulpit complete an implied central focus with the seating of the congregation, giving a strong sense of unity.

Over seventy years old when he designed the chapel, Wright was still full of fresh ideas. He applied himself with a religious fervor to what he called "the Cause of Architecture." "Architecture is life," he said, "... the truest record of life.... So architecture I know to be a Great Spirit.... Architecture is that great living creative spirit which from generation to generation, from age to age, creates."

He was very chary of explicitly religious sentiment, perhaps in recollection of his embarrassingly effusive father, an itinerant preacher. But his own son, John, has helped us to decipher his guarded language and to recognize him as a profoundly religious man (see p. 26).

53

54

TUSKEGEE CHAPEL, Tuskegee Institute, Alabama, 1969

Ezra Stoller ©ESTO

Religion has always been an integral part of Tuskegee Institute's program. When its old chapel was struck by lightning and burned down in 1957, college administrators chose Paul Rudolph to design its replacement, in collaboration with Louis Edwin Fry and John A. Welch. Rudolph's Tuskegee Chapel almost achieves the spiritual intensity of Le Corbusier's Ronchamp, to which Rudolph gave explicit reference, and the vigor of Frank Lloyd Wright's ecclesiastical work. And it achieves more—it is itself serving its community's special aspirations and liturgical needs, as a "meeting house": placing religious observance in the midst of the community—and, achitecturally, vice versa.

Completed in 1969, the chapel is constructed of steel frames supporting brick cavity walls. The mechanically produced bricks, 850,000 of which were used to build the edifice, are light pink, a contrast to the darker color of the hand-produced bricks of the older Tuskegee buildings. The contrast is positive: the chapel is a daring, imaginative structure that competes with the earlier, humbler buildings. The exterior is composed of curved brick walls, interlaced with cubic offshoots and openings: there is no real front or back to the building, and it looks different from every angle. Some openings push out like periscopes, sealed with colored glass, to provide

shafts of light to the interior. The roof rises upward on its bent axis like that at Ronchamp.

To provide good acoustics for the famous Tuskegee Institute Choir, the huge asymmetrical auditorium was designed. But it is also a powerful religious hall. The ceiling is a long plane curving in two distinct directions. Its joists are placed to appear to curve, like the ribs of a fan. Skylights, parallel to the wall, emit changing shafts of light, while brick-sheathed ducts on both sides of the chapel provide air; the total effect is kaleidoscopic. Steplike forms break up the smooth surface of the side walls and direct one's attention to the pulpit and chancel. The pulpit is the focus of the interior, its brick form jutting out into the congregation. Beside the large auditorium is a much smaller meditation chapel, a narrow, perpendicular room, sprinkled with shafts of light from skylights and colored-glass cavities high on the wall. The remainder of the building is used by the Tuskegee Music School.

The chapel stands at the top of a ridge near the graves of Booker T. Washington, the institute's first principal, and George Washington Carver, its first great scientist. As an integral part of the campus, the chapel not only serves all faiths but is also a popular assembly hall. It is a means of continuing the institute's original purpose of helping the community.

ST. SAVIOUR'S CHAPEL AT IIT, Chicago, Illinois, 1952

MIT CHAPEL, Cambridge, Massachusetts, 1955

Two chapels for technical institutes, built after the Second World War, present radically different approaches to church architecture, illustrating the conflicting philosophies and aesthetics within the architectural profession in the postwar era.

For a time it appeared that the old romantic Frank Lloyd Wright and his acolytes stood alone against a "modern movement," which held that design should be a no-nonsense deployment of industrial materials like steel and glass. Buildings were to be machines. References to the past were taboo. It was not easy, however, to apply this orthodoxy to the design of churches. Machines for worship were they to be?

During this period, the almost interchangeable parts of the architecture of Ludwig Mies van der Rohe were more influential upon American architecture than those of any other artist. Given the opportunity to design the campus of the Illinois Institute of Technology in 1939, Mies drew up a plan composed of repeated, regular, precise square modules of which the chapel was a participating group of modules. Mies was as fervently committed to clarity and precision as any maker of machine tools. Saying, "God is in the details," he compared the technological age to "the religious movement of the Middle Ages."

The IIT chapel is an austere building of brick, glass, and steel, created for an institution by an architect who felt it should avoid "the spiritual association or a traditional fashion in architecture, such as Gothic." The building is not recognizable as a chapel; Mies did not want it to be. At the dedication he spoke of it with restraint: "There is nothing spectacular about this chapel. It was meant to be simple....In its simplicity, it is not primitive, not noble; and in its smallness it is great, in fact monumental." Perhaps. But the building was "only reluctantly" accepted by the Episcopal diocese, which anticipated, sadly, what has occurred since—it is very poorly attended.

Eero Saarinen's chapel at MIT is another story. The building is as daring in its use of light, to create an atmosphere and to focus attention upon the altar, as any Baroque church. From the altar, ascending to the circular skylight, is a Jacob's ladder of shimmering prisms or, perhaps, a tree of life. The circular chapel is dimly lit, focusing attention on the service. The simplicity of forms—circles and cubes, unadorned wood, brick, stone, and concrete—are not the product of the "machine aesthetic." They are chthonic but not barren. This is a building created not for an institution, but for people. The undulating brick walls contain no windows; the place is intended to shelter, to afford a refuge from the secular qualities of an engineering education.

St. Saviour's Chapel at IIT (top).
©Robert D. Beard

MIT Chapel (bottom). Ezra Stoller
©ESTO

AIR FORCE ACADEMY CADET CHAPEL,
Colorado Springs, Colorado, 1956–62

©Owen Franken/Stock, Boston

The Air Force Academy Cadet Chapel crowns the military college which educates and trains officers for the United States Air Force. Designed by Walter A. Netsch, Jr. of the firm of Skidmore, Owings and Merrill, it was built during 1958–63 to provide a focal point for cadet religious activities. It sits at the base of the front range of the Rocky Mountains at an elevation of nearly 7,200 feet. The soaring aluminum tetrahedrons that form the outer shell of the chapel evoke both the shape of the mountains and a person's hands pressed together in prayer. The spaces between the tetrahedrons are filled with colored glass. Reinforced concrete buttresses topped with

hinges lend support to the spires but permit the metal structure to flex with temperature changes.

The upper level houses a 1,100-seat Protestant sanctuary, graced with a 47-foot tall aluminum cross symbolizing a bird in flight and a pipe organ with more than 4,300 pipes.

On a lower level are Catholic and Jewish sanctuaries. The Catholic chapel, with seating for 500, has a basilican nave with three aisles, vestibule, font, confessionals, altar, and sacristy. Next to the Catholic sanctuary is a Jewish one, circular in shape, with seating for 100.

©Balthazar Korab

ST. JOHN'S ABBEY, Collegeville, Minnesota, 1961

©Hedrich-Blessing

There have been frequent references in the main text of this book to St. John's Abbey, which occupies a unique place in the architectural history of the twentieth century. It is the only major religious building by a Bauhaus architect. It is, of course, much more than that, for its architect, Marcel Breuer, rose to his highest creative level at Collegeville and produced a building and a master plan that far transcend anything his training or his other work might lead us to expect.

The Bauhaus was an academy of the arts and crafts, a laboratory for standardization, a studio, an atelier, and a workshop all in one. It flourished under Walter Gropius in Germany between the First World War and the onset of the Nazi terror. It emphasized modern design, by which most of its constituents meant an embrace of new industrial materials and of the machine. The Bauhaus was the central power-house of "the International style," sleek, smooth, metallic-glassy, geometric, modular, and ostensibly anti-Romantic.

Yet at Collegeville Breuer produced a warm, reverent, almost passionate set of buildings, of which the church, with its bell tower, is the most important, the most powerful, and the least to be anticipated within the precepts of the modern movement. Perhaps it would be more accurate to say that those precepts were mysteriously enlarged and animated in the presence of other, older, broader ideas, derived from the Benedictine tradition.

The famous "banner," a slab of reinforced concrete 112 feet high, contains the bells of the old monastery church and is held upward by two huge concrete parabolic clamps. It was "made possible," as Breuer asserted, "by our technology, by new building methods, new materials, and modern engineering." It was also made possible by "eternal laws of geometry, gravity, space" and, more subtly, by very ancient example.

It is like the "westwork," the fortress tower which was the primary facade of many Benedictine churches of western Europe, a fierce statement of permanence. In Collegeville it is a proclamation of the presence, upon the great prairie, of a religious tradition that had built masonry towers—almost slabs in their severity—at the entrances of its churches for a thousand years; "in the old days, stone on stone held in place by the weight of the parts; now, one flowing line of concrete held in place by the continuity of steel bars," said Breuer. As when entering a Romanesque Benedictine church in Europe, one walks through and under the westwork, through what had been the vestibule or narthex of the church, passing, thereby, through a defensive structure, into the sanctuary. There, at the center, in the protected place, at the focus of vision, is the altar.

Breuer's church places the altar at the center, surrounded by seating for 1,600. The members of the monastic community, including the teachers of the school and the university, are seated around one segment of the circle, the townspeople and the students around the other segments, leaving space for the choir—itself split in two parts to provide for antiphonal singing of the Benedictine plainsong. This coming together around the common liturgical center, for the central unifying liturgy in which all participate, the looking across the Sacrament to the other participants, unites clergy and laity, teacher and student. In many churches the clergy face each other in the choir, behind the altar, catching sight of the congregation of laity only through a screen, out of the corners of their eyes. In such churches the clergy sing and speak responsively to each other, not to the congregation. The church at St. John's deploys all the marvelous dexterity of twentieth-century technology to unite the worshiping community, cantilevering the huge balcony overhead to avoid even the disruption of columns, suspending a baldac-

chino, porous to the light, over the altar, so that prisms divide that light just as the huge stained-glass wall transmutes the "natural" light of the outside into a special light, in which humans have participated.

The primary liturgical elements are ordered in the sequence in which they are experienced in the life of a Roman Catholic—baptismal font, church door, confessionals, Communion tables, and altar, along the central axis of the building. Someone, perhaps Breuer, perhaps one of the congregation led by Abbot Baldwin Dworschak, conceived of the whole space as being like a bell, with the choir at its throat and the nave at the mouth, as if to enlarge the sound of prayer, of songs of praise.

The setting is a 2,400-acre monastic center on the high Minnesota prairie in an area primarily settled by Germans. It is the largest Benedictine monastery in the world, containing both a school and a university. The atrium, inside the door of the church, is covered by glass; the "banner" reflects the sunlight, which strikes its south side into the church through the stained glass.

The church appears to be built like an accordion-folded paper file. Concrete plates compose the wall and roof and provide a vast, clear span inside. All these elements are held aloft on concrete piers, keeping the ground level free, airy, and open. From the outside these folded concrete walls assume the aspect of a fortress. Like the "westwork banner" (which, as it happens, is on the north side), these sturdy walls remind us that while the interior feels "open," this can occur because it is safe there. In a harsh climate—in a harsh world—a community can gather there to share prayer and song.

Finally, it may be noted that the prisms of the north wall of the sanctuary, which hold the stained glass and act as a backdrop to the "banner," are of the same hexagons that dominate Eero Saarinen's design for North Christian Church in Columbus, Indiana (see p. 245). It is as if the hexagon had become a twentieth-century, postindustrial mandala.

SAINT LOUIS PRIORY, Saint Louis, Missouri, 1962

Dom Columba Cary-Elwes, former prior of the Saint Louis Priory in Saint Louis, Missouri, once spoke of the relationship of theological tradition and innovation:

> Strange as it may seem, the very fact that the Benedictine spirit is so deep in tradition made it unlikely that any of these expressions of the past would be the expression of the present-day members.... Tradition in theology is not sticking to the letter of a primitive text, but rather an intrinsic growth, a repeated restatement in new terms, intelligible to each age. So, too, in architecture, tradition is not static but living.

Like the Benedictines at St. John's Abbey in Collegeville, the Benedictines of St. Louis decided their priory should be of "living architecture"—that is, architecture that used the methods, style, and materials of the time in which it was built. They chose the firm of Hellmuth, Obata, and Kassabaum, architects then untried in church design. Gyo Obata was famous as the principal designer of the "radical" St. Louis airport. But, like Marcel Breuer at St. John's, he did not impose a designer's ego upon a church; rather, the energy seemed to flow in the other direction:

> As we studied the building and the program, the design evolved from our deepening awareness of the needs of this particular church. The church is designed as it is not because we wished to be daring, but rather because it came to seem to us the only way for this church to be.

The priory lies on a beautiful wooded site in Saint Louis, and the church itself stands on the highest ground of a grassy ridge overlooking the entire priory enclosure, the centerpoint and the beacon of the complex. (One thinks of St. Michael's, Charleston—see p. 113.) The design is simple: two successively smaller circles of twenty thin, reinforced-concrete parabolic shells on top of one another, topped by a third, of ten "shells," ending in a central cross. Each circle defines and contains a part of the church. The lowest, 22 feet high, defines the ambulatory and the several entrances. The middle, 18 feet high, defines the six-hundred-seat nave and the monks' choir, while that at the top, 30 feet high, serves as a lantern and bell tower and features a skylight that provides direct natural light to the central altar. Fiberglass window-walls fill out the parabolas, appearing black from the exterior, in contrast to the white concrete.

The atmosphere of the interior of the church is one of light, visibility, and serenity, though only 6 percent of the walls are of glass. Light, which also comes from the skylight, is central to the monks' and architects' program. They wished to create a space of maximum visibility for all participants to encourage "participating, not watching." The altar is encircled by seating for the congregation, originally to be largely schoolboys and monks, now serving a parish community of five hundred as well. Only six pews separate the furthermost seat from the sanctuary, gathering "all into a central unity."

All the aisles lead straight to the altar, whose importance is enforced by the apex of the ceiling that soars above it. Twenty private chapels, formed by the bays of the parabolic arches, adorn the side of the church. The floor is ceramic, and the altar, lectern, and pews are of Georgia granite and red oak—simple, strong materials.

The petallike form of the priory church complements its natural setting. The church is part of the monastic enclosure, which includes a library, administration buildings, and living quarters for the monks. The buildings are sprinkled with courts and gardens and have glass sides to complement their location. Their quiet, flat roofs do not jostle the silhouette of the church. Near the enclosure is a boys' school, maintained by the priory.

The priory church, which was the gift of one family, transcends the label "contemporary," and the prior, Luke Rigby, O.S.B., reports that he finds "many traditionalists except it from their dislike of modern architecture."

3
Pleasure and Joy

There is a difference between pleasure and joy. Pleasure is a response to the senses. Joy does not require experience transmitted by the senses. One could feel joy suspended in space, if that were the sort of place in which one felt joyous. But one could not, so suspended, feel pleasure.

The essential paradox of most Christian architecture is that its sensual pleasures may be impediments to joy unless those pleasures are enveloped in fear and dread.

Like many paradoxes, this one can be untied if one knows the secret, and with the untying comes a deep satisfaction. *Fear* and *dread* are terms that seem very forbidding to most people in the modern world. This is true though innumerable theological works have sought to sustain in them their old meanings, which were not so terrifying. The paradox begins to unravel if we substitute for them the word *reverence*, which is not nearly so strong or so encompassing but indicates a way toward joy. As a practical people, disposed to action rather than contemplation, and as a people indisposed to recognize that a search for joy is the impulse which leads to liturgy (which is religious choreography), we want to know what to "*do* about it," how to *act* in order to find joy. *One Hundred Ways to Find Joy*? No, this is not that sort of book. *One Hundred Ways to Understand Church Architecture and Thus to Find Joy*? Closer, but too long for a title and too ambitious a program. How about just one modest, conventional suggestion?

Let us pray.

And, since we are so disposed toward action, let us fall on our knees first. Let us do what many others do when they enter a church; let us kneel down for a moment, bow our heads, and try to enter into the spirit of the place. That is what architects try to do before there is any space, before it is formed of its materials. We come afterward and enter a finished building, but we will miss its point if we do not take some liturgical action to do what the architects were doing at the moment it formed itself in their consciousness.

Christians might find it useful to recall that traditionalist Jews, when entering a synagogue, recite Psalm 5:8:

As for me,
through the greatness of thy loving kindness, O Lord,
I enter Thy house;
in reverence of thee,
I bow down towards thy holy temple.

Even if the knees do not bend easily, even if the words of prayer do not come in convenient time, this small personal liturgy is one right way to enter church. Noisy tourist peregrinations or a chatter of gossip demean the labors of the architect and affront the worshiping community, even if that community is no longer physically present.

Saint Paul spoke of fear and trembling. Saint Bernard found in Genesis the words of appropriate prayer of entry: "How dreadful is this place! this is no other but the house of God, and this is the gate of Heaven." Twentieth-century people unaccustomed to such prayers may be led to them by the statement of a contemporary, Carl Jung, that "God may be loved, but He must be feared." It might be added that unless He is approached in fear, His sacred places may remain locked against us, though we may physically penetrate their every cranny. The purpose of a ritual of bowing or kneeling is not to placate God's presumed need for such choreography, but to induce some of those feelings suggested by such words as *fear* and *dread.*

A story from the Middle Ages may help those who have not yet the habit to escape any tremor of embarrassment which may pass down stiff backs at the thought of something so strange. We are, after all, no more suppliant by nature, no less arrogant, no more timorous, no less cruel than that pack of wolfish barons who stood with Henry I of England at the door of the new choir of Canterbury Cathedral at its dedication. It was in the year 1130, very long after Christ, not very long after the Norman Conquest.

At the door, among his fierce and very successful followers, stood Henry, youngest son of the Conqueror. Some of the men about him had ridden with him to London thirty years before, when he seized the throne, "wasting no time in mourning" the murder of his eldest brother, King William Rufus. Twenty-four years had passed since he had defeated his other brother, Duke Robert of Normandy, whom he kept thereafter in lifelong imprisonment. The whole panoply of Britain stood at that door in Canterbury, seeming "more splendid than any other of its kind 'since the dedication of the Temple of Solomon.' " They were not disposed to awe, the tough lot of ennobled brigands. They had seen too much, survived too much. Yet, as they entered, they fell silent before the grandeur of the space within, "ablaze with innumerable lights." The procession entered, and the chant was heard: "Awesome is this place. Truly this is the house of God and the gate of Heaven." Then the hard old king, his voice breaking, "swore with his royal oath 'by the death of God' that truly the place was awesome."

A feeling of awe is one of the preconditions to entry into a religious building, though no such feeling need precede mere physical ingress. There is a difference—and in this context a crucial difference—between entering and entering in. We sometimes employ the latter term with the customary

66

St. John's Abbey Church in Collegeville, Minnesota—a place of
contemplation. ©Eric Sutherland/
courtesy of Marcel Breuer Associates

irony of moderns in the face of emotion. But if one can suspend irony long
enough to be respectful of a far longer and deeper set of experiences with
the Mystery than those immediately accessible to us, we can prepare
ourselves to experience another emotion that can succeed it—joy.

Many people—not all, but many—find the worshiping spirit of awe or
dread comes more easily in old places than in new. They feel greeted there
by guides from the past who offer a thousand quiet inducements to enter
with them a space in which they have worked and worshiped.

It is true that most of us feel some very eerie things happen when we
move into a space inherited from another. We feel some of the emotions the
space evoked when it was young. Spaces do accumulate experience. They
will impart those experiences if we are attentive. They can teach us; in fact,
they will teach us, willy-nilly, because we cannot avoid the messages they
send to our unconscious. They speak from the walls; the very stones have
tongues. We are wise to listen.

The newness of America deprives most of us of these place-guided
tours. Americans cannot, in their own country, experience ancient churches
which have sustained their liturgical life and have accumulated experience
over many centuries. What has been built here is not only new, but comes
from a period of history in which newness itself was important. We came into the modern world with a bang—indeed, with a series of bangs.

The United States began simultaneously with the industrial revolution.

Our continent was settled during an explosion of the population in western Europe and a concurrent explosion of ideas. We were born amid changes the scale and pace of which were unprecedented in the life of our species. Those changes have shifted the earth between us and former times as if a geologic fault had appeared. As a result, we know much about the art history of old ways of building, but we feel cut off from the life of spirit contained in those old ways.

We may congratulate ourselves in our cool, scholarly approbation of Gothic, Romanesque, or Byzantine buildings. We can, in another mood, maunder about their gloomy vastnesses in a vague, nostalgic blur. But it is difficult for us to enter in a thoughtful, natural, and unself-conscious way into the world view that brought them into being. We find it hard to catch the rhythm of the world that existed before the "triple revolution": the Renaissance, the Reformation, and industrialism. The metronome of our lives has been set to a different beat.

Though they are very distant from us, we can learn much from our predecessors in the time before the triple revolution. They knew much that is powerfully relevant to us today. We can learn from them how to enter a religious building, ancient or modern. But it must be reiterated that as we approach them for instruction, we come not to copy them, not to collect their crockets and finials out of a foolish fondness for antiquity. The Mystery requires more of us than to collapse into the arms of the past.

The Brothers' Chapel at St. John's Abbey. ©H. Witzman/courtesy of Marcel Breuer Associates

69

We need not be so timorous in creating fresh religious forms as were some nineteenth-century people who mistook an effort to understand the spirit of building for a restless, acquisitive, yet deferential need to pillage the past. Much has happened since the critic and traveler Théophile Gautier intoned his view that "Byzantine architecture is most certainly the necessary form of Christianity" and the Cambridge Camden Society proclaimed "gothick the only Christian architecture."

Nor should any among us be slack and sentimental, like that Anglophiliac who pronounced that "we of the Saxon race feel always a home-whispering voice when we gaze upon some crumbling beauty of Gothic Art in our nation's birthplace across the ocean." The genuine beauty of Gothic art, crumbling or not, is that it can teach us how to think about building, not how to build. That is a lesson requiring much exertion to learn, but we can learn if we try.

What is to be learned is more than just art appreciation. That may help lead the way to pleasure, but it is not our business here. We are seeking something quite different, something that helps us find in places ways to join others who have gone on ahead in creating spaces that solicit from humans an appropriate response to the Mystery.

A very rare example of the iconography of Christ in Majesty in St. Vincent Ferrer in New York City (far left). "Awe" has its ancient meaning amid complexity and subtlety.
©Joseph Kugielsky

Awe and dread are not only found in dark interiors or in ancient stone buildings. There was plenty of reverence in New England and in Renaissance England itself, though there was also, it may be said, a boldness and confidence that the horrors of the subsequent years have somewhat enshadowed. But it may be easier for us to go all the way back, beyond the fathers to the grandfathers, so to speak, to recapture the unalloyed awe of the Middle Ages than to feel again that strange mixture of boldness and fear present in many meeting houses and Renaissance churches. The clear, uncolored light streaming into these buildings, their balance and clarity, and their absence of bright color, were natural to English Puritans and sons of the Enlightenment. While religious architecture elsewhere in Europe quickly moved beyond the tautness of the Renaissance into the wilder complexities of the Baroque and the Rococo, and in England the older Gothic tradition soon returned with new force, the group of settlers who went to Britain's American colonies not only embraced the Renaissance coolness, brightness, and clarity, but many of their descendants have kept on building that way ever since, though it may be fair to suggest that much of the awe and fear that was originally there may have been bleached away in all the subsequent sunlight.

It is a fair guess that when most Americans speak of "something that looks like a church," they think first of a "colonial" structure of white painted wood or of brick; and even when they run toward the Gothic, it is only part way, to another brightly lit, rectangular space, with a steep roof added and pointed windows. Right through the nineteenth-century revivals, we have kept on building this way, accepting a few tags and tatters of older styles, but keeping to our confident brightness all the while.

Perhaps there is a psychological truth about us to be found in this pattern. Perhaps, originally, this proud architecture was a celebration of the colonists' invidious good fortune in coming to a place where the Native Americans—their only competitors for a profusion of natural resources—were at an enormous technological disadvantage, and were vanquished relatively easily. Perhaps it celebrates, too, an apparent conquest over nature itself. Perhaps it was their sense of dominion over nature that enabled them to reduce to a thin skin those barriers from the outside that had shielded most earlier worshipers. Clear glass windows and white painted wooden walls—very thin membranes—felt sturdy enough to such a proud people. The availability of such materials, of mass-produced nails and milled, standardized lumber, may merely have confirmed a preference for a kind of architecture that began in confidence and came, in time, to be something like defiance.

The settlers of America set forth from Europe when the Renaissance

Avondale Methodist Church in Colorado—serenity and clarity. ©Robert Adams

and, later, the Enlightenment were in full vigor. The rationalism and confidence of those movements was thereafter reinforced here, with amazing good fortune. We are not, as a consequence, a notoriously humble people. Our ears are unaccustomed to listening, with metronomes set too fast to pause very long at the entry of sacred space.

Churches need not be built in old forms to justify kneeling, listening, pausing, reverence. Some old forms are now dead. Some new forms do, it is certain, evoke "awe," "dread," and an appropriate reverence in the face of the Mystery. We are not, in this book, primarily interested in the style of a building or in its art-historical provenance. We are interested, instead, in what happens to people who enter and participate in a space.

In the next section we will examine one ancient form of building, the Gothic, as a proxy for all those created before the triple revolution. We do so not because we propose to analyze it structurally, to write of its ways of carrying loads or distributing forces, or because we wish to discourse upon the wonders of Gothic ornamentation, but because its builders were the first in the Western world to develop, consciously and explicitly, a way to build churches. They built plenty of secular buildings, too, but to their churches they brought a set of ideas which, if we seek to listen to them, can help us understand not only why they built as they did but why we build as we do.

Iconography and stained glass in the Church of St. Vincent Ferrer in New York City. ©Joseph Kugielsky

75

THE CHURCH OF ST. VINCENT FERRER,
New York, New York, 1916–18

St. Vincent Ferrer Parish, at Sixty-sixth Street and Lexington Avenue, was established in 1867 in the midst of a predominantly immigrant neighborhood. When a second parish proved unable to accommodate the large congregation funds were raised for a third church. Several architectural firms were commissioned to design plans for a house of worship that would incorporate the contemplative and apostolic spirit of the Dominican Order, whose members founded the parish and continue to serve it.

Finally, after a decade of search, they chose Bertram Goodhue, who had been a partner of Ralph Adams Cram, the eminent Neo-Gothic architect of the day. After consultation with the pastor, Father Fitzgerald, Goodhue began work on the present St.

Vincent Ferrer, his first Catholic church.

Begun in 1916, the building was opened for services in May 1918. However, funds were not available to complete the original plans. Rather than omit what they believed to be essentials of a beautiful church, the Dominicans decided to prolong the project, adding furnishings, ornamentation, etc., as funds became available.

Goodhue died suddenly in 1924, at the age of fifty-three. Nonetheless, all later work on the church was carried out according to his design. The result is one of his most powerful reworkings of the Gothic style, and has been declared a landmark of the City of New York. Many believe its stained glass to be the most beautiful in the United States.

4
The Cathedral Builders

Any visitor to New York who stands on Fifth Avenue between Rockefeller Center and Fifty-seventh Street can see that, in the glassy shadows of the skyscrapers, there lurks an older way of stating reality. There are two great churches that state that older way, even amid that domain of high contemporary fashion—St. Thomas and St. Patrick's. Not far away, in fact, is St. Vincent's amid its active monastic community.

The spiky presence of the Middle Ages is still felt in the most "developed" real estate in the world, competing for space with the quintessential forms of modernity. These three New York churches sturdily stand off their surroundings; they happen to be expressed in Gothic, but it is what they say, not how they dress, that is important. We must not be put off by the architectural trappings but, in accordance with our task, must try to listen, not just to look. Looking may provoke admiration. But admiration is a dry pleasure. Something much more, a joyous encounter, is possible if we try to converse, in imagination, with the cathedral builders.

We should enter that conversation respectfully. The medieval cathedral builders were a very sophisticated lot. Among other things, their knowledge of the correspondences among music, architecture, and mathematics was deeper than ours, in part because it is nobody's profession today to seek such correspondences. So we should begin by being deferential toward them. They knew many things we do not know.

Among other things they knew the true use of the word *symbol*.

They lived in a time when the word was still alive. It had not been diminished by academic overuse. When they spoke of a church as a "symbol of the architecture of the universe," they did not mean that church to be merely a model or maquette, nor a miniature like a child's toy car. They did not mean that the church merely suggested something vague about the universe. For them to speak of a symbol was to speak of something specific, literal, and very large in its scope.

In our own century, Carl Jung has helped us to restore the full power of the term *symbol* to its etymological meaning: something that participates in and connotes a larger group of not-fully-disclosed meanings. A symbol in this sense is always more than what we can understand of it at first sight. It is an assemblage of various things, thrown together in a complex way; an assemblage that is ambiguous, ambivalent, and likely to surprise us at second and third examinations. In fact, a symbol is something that will continue to surprise us. It will always radiate new meanings because it participates in the unconscious. It lies at the frontier of what we know consciously.

Now we are getting closer to what a medieval person might mean by saying a church is a symbol of God's creation. But we have further to go. To take the next step we must abandon the art-historical way of looking at an

St. Patrick's Cathedral (left)—a commanding presence on New York's Fifth Avenue. ©Lisl Dennis

Another urban church that has set the atmosphere for its environment is St. Bartholomew's in New York City (above). ©Andrew Stewart

icon or at a cathedral. Instead of presuming that we can identify it, analyze it, assign to it a place or station in some grand artificial taxonomy of style or influence, we must abandon ourselves to it, to the thing itself. We must relinquish a critical stance. We must let it lead us into its own intention for us, not the other way round. In the seventh century, Maximus the Confessor offered us a way to do this, a way he called "symbolic contemplation."

If we contemplate an icon (or a cathedral) with sufficient intensity and fixity, we may be able to grasp the invisible reality lying behind it. One then discovers that the holy object is important not truly as an object but as an aperture. It is a surface that, under fixed, rapt, devoted, and fearful attention, dissolves to provide a window into another world that has no surfaces, but only substances.

Thus a window of stained glass becomes an icon, an image which can be seen and then seen through as it becomes insubstantial. The architecture surrounding such a window is a frame about a dissolving icon. Then, in turn, under symbolic contemplation, the whole wall dissolves to become an hallucination of heaven.

Medieval architects did not insert stained glass in windows as we might, to make them pretty or to throw colors against the motes of dust in the shafts of sunlight within. Instead they expected those who looked out toward the sun through those dissolving, transparent walls to be engaged in symbolic contemplation of an eternal tabernacle. These architects built as much with light as with solid materials.

What a dreadful undertaking! Building with light is to participate in the Creation itself. And that is precisely what the cathedral builders believed they were doing. There was no doubt that God had created the world in stages. First, He set out the materials, and then into that chaos He provided light and, simultaneously, order. Much later, according to Christian belief, He incarnated Himself in human form, providing, in another way, the Light of the World. Christ, too, and thereafter the Holy Spirit, became architects as well: they were restoring the harmonious structure of the world disrupted by Adam's fall and by humanity's persistent obstreperousness.

Now we can see why the medieval builders felt so proud to work on cathedrals, and at the same time why they were in such fear and dread. Saint Augustine had informed Christians that the universe had once been in "unison" with God; wherever humankind had not yet been disruptive, harmony still prevailed. There, as Abelard put it, "the ineffable sweetness of harmonic modulation renders eternal praise to God." The task of architecture, of music, and of mathematics is restoring that harmony. "Thou

hast ordered all things in measure and number and weight"—and now humanity must build to redeem the world from its disharmony, its disproportions, and its loss of balance.

The cathedral builders, especially those of the late Middle Ages centering around Chartres, used a language partly derived from the Scriptures and partly from Neoplatonic philosophy. It was not very different from that of twentieth-century analytical psychology in whose terms the matter might be put this way: architectural symbols derive their potency from participation in the energy provided by archetypes. These archetypes exist beyond the reach of language, but aspects of them present themselves through the laws of music and proportion, which are related, in turn, to architecture.

The mathematical proportions of many medieval cathedrals were deliberately and painstakingly derived from the same cadences of harmony and order that appear in medieval music and poetry. They are not familiar to us, as a part of our education, but we feel them in satisfaction and joy nonetheless. As we do so, we participate in the work of people who

Stained glass in Willibrord Roman Catholic Church, Chicago, Illinois (pp. 82 and 87). ©Regina Kuehn

Stained glass in the Cathedral Church of Bryn Athyn, Bryn Athyn, Pennsylvania (pp. 83–86). ©Michael Pitcairn

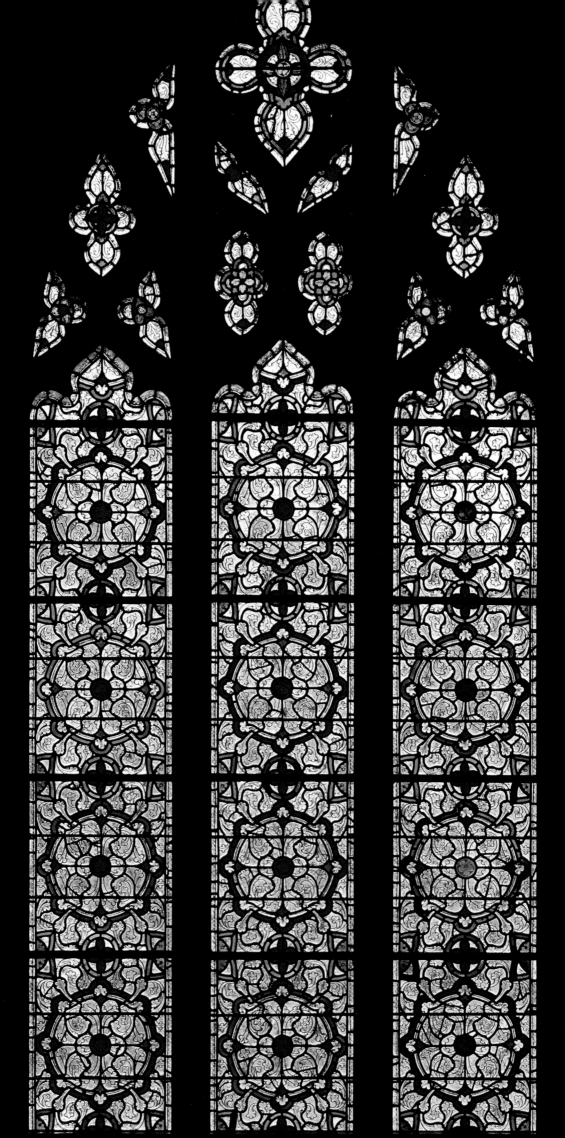

believed that those who shared the experience of these arts shared also in the restoration of the harmony and order of the universe.

We are not here just describing the medieval people upon whom our attention has fallen in these past few pages. As the curtain of our own history opens, we find that we have, in fact, been introducing a much larger cast than they. The stage contains most of the architects and builders and craftspeople who have built churches in America. They have not lived in a world in which it was conventional to state their aspirations in such ambitious terms, but they have, over and over again, invited us to share in their feelings, and those feelings are the same as the feelings of those who have been building churches anytime, if they believed in what they were doing.

It is a joyous thing to go about a building with those who have worked on it in such a spirit. Earlier in these pages some great twentieth-century architects invited us to see their work in this way, and in this section we have sought to bring into the discussion some more distant voices. But the guides agree: begin in reverence, listen for larger harmonies, and participate in the joy of creation.

Overleaf left: Stained glass in the Cathedral Church of Bryn Athyn, Bryn Athyn, Pennsylvania.
©Michael Pitcairn

Overleaf right: Stained glass in St. James' Episcopal Chapel, Grosse Isle, Michigan.
©Richard Rushin

ST. PATRICK'S CATHEDRAL, New York, New York, designed 1853–57, constructed 1858–88

St. Patrick's Cathedral in New York is a product of the Gothic revival of the mid-nineteenth century, an architectural style that then largely served Anglican, not Roman Catholic, congregations. It is a magnificent building; yet it is a poignant reminder of the difficult position of American Catholicism in the 1850s, at the high tide of the "Know-Nothings," who looked with distrust and disdain upon all Roman Catholics, especially the Irish immigrants to whom St. Patrick's was the most important symbol of a proud presence in America. It was designed by a Protestant architect, James Renwick, whose reputation had largely been established in parish churches for the Anglicans, or Episcopalians in their American syntax. These were derived from the Gothic of modest English parish churches, which the Anglicans regarded as mystical (but not "papist," or "Roman," as they saw Gothic cathedrals). Among Protestants, therefore, the Gothic revival was originally an insistence upon small churches of Gothic design.

American Catholics had had few opportunities to build churches during the colonial era. They were an embattled minority, without even a bishop of their own. When they were accorded their first bishop, John Carroll of Baltimore, they very promptly began a cathedral—but not a Gothic one (see p. 256). The Cathedral of the Assumption, begun in 1804 in Baltimore, was the largest church in America, intentionally grand as a symbol of papal authority. A cathedral for the new diocese of New York was begun in 1808, dedicated in 1815 to St. Patrick. By 1850 the diocese of New York had been elevated to the status of an archdiocese, and Archbishop John Hughes became determined to build something befitting that eminence as well as, what he felt to be, the appropriate status for Catholics in general.

Funding for such a project was, of course, a problem. Hughes solicited contributions from wealthy parishioners, explaining that his goal was to erect a cathedral "that may be worthy of our increasing numbers, intelligence and wealth...and...worthy,

as a public architectural monument...of this metropolis." By 1853, contributions were sufficient to acquire the site, which was criticized at the time as being too far uptown (it was referred to as "Hughes' folly"), and to engage Renwick. His design was completed in 1857, and in August 1858 the cornerstone was laid.

Between 1853 and 1857 Renwick made an extended tour of Europe, where he was exposed to a Gothic revival quite independent of that of his former clients, the Anglicans. The Cologne Cathedral had rested unfinished for centuries; only the choir and west façade remained from medieval times. Since most of the Gothic cathedrals were, in one way or another, unfinished or else completed in different styles, Cologne, alone, could, with the propulsion of Bismark's Prussia and Germany's imperial ambitions, "fulfill" its "architectural destiny." Marvelous engravings of the cathedral's interior and exterior could make that completion possible.

Cologne's thirteenth-century magnificence was achieved by completing its symmetrical, twin-towered façade, the only such façade in existence. Later France would follow suit, completing a twin-towered façade at Rouen. Entirely new churches were also being built in Gothic revival twin-towered form. All over Europe the craze for Gothic—especially for Gothic derived from the example of Cologne—was resulting in huge projects, and St. Patrick's benefited from the same impetus.

At the same time, the technology of iron was changing construction techniques. While Renwick designed a visually Gothic building of the Cologne style, he intended to use iron systematically in its construction. In choosing a twin-towered façade, Renwick not only separated the design for St. Patrick's from the tradition of American (Protestant) Gothic—which called for a single frontal tower—but also ran counter to the Anglican Ecclesiological movement (see p. 224)—which insisted on asymmetry.

Budgetary limitations required eliminating major

92

parts of Renwick's plan: flying buttresses, a rounded apse with radiating chapels, a Lady chapel, and an octagonal tower over the crossing.

Construction was interrupted by the Civil War, but when work resumed in 1868, Renwick and the archbishop fully intended to vault the building in stone. But stone vaulting required skilled stonemasons and was vastly expensive (as the Washington Cathedral has demonstrated); by 1875, plans were altered to provide a lath and plaster ceiling. Although the interior view of a plaster "vault" is indistinguishable from one of stone, the consequences to the building's exterior appearance were enormous; the absence of stone vaulting necessitated the omission of flying buttresses, lest their "counterthrust" (without a thrust to counter) push in the walls. The huge buttress piers had already been built, and so they remained.

Work progressed slowly. One reporter wrote that "one has an almost irresistible inclination to lie down and go to sleep somewhere about the place." Nevertheless, the workers doubtless felt that they were creating a building for history; some craftsmen even inserted a preserve jar containing their names in one of the bosses as a "time capsule." (The jar was found during the 1973 interior restoration.) By 1879, the main body of the church had been completed. The completed spires crowned the façade nine years later.

The interior of the building, though small in comparison to European models, was and is immensely impressive. Unlike the exterior, it is in the English style. Most Americans are awe-struck by its vast, soaring spaces, by its bright but exotic forms, and with the richness of the marble and stained glass, though many Protestants grumbled at its opulence. Many non-Catholics first saw the interior of the cathedral in 1878, before it was formally opened, when the nave was the site of a grand fair. A direct consequence was a determination by New York's Episcopalians to build something bigger, St. John the Divine, in Morningside Heights (see p. 94).

St. Patrick's still dominates the pedestrians who pass by; but seen from above (as Gothic architecture was never meant to be seen), amid the skyscrapers, which both echo and mock its spires, St. Patrick's seems strangely lost. Once inside, however, the worshiper knows the nature of the church—grand, ceremonial, but alive.

THE CATHEDRAL CHURCH OF ST. JOHN THE DIVINE, New York, New York, begun 1893

When the spires of St. Patrick's Cathedral were finally completed in 1888, the Catholic cathedral became the dominant church in the United States. Not to be outdone, the Episcopal diocese of New York became determined to build an even more impressive monument to the power and glory of their faith.

The original design was, in keeping with late Victorian Protestantism, vaguely Romanesque in style. The competition that preceded that choice generated some of the finest architectural draftsmanship ever produced in America, especially the magnificent (though losing) submission by Harvey Ellis for LeRoy Buffington. Monumental is not the word for the project; gargantuan might be closer to the truth, for at a planned size of 600 feet by 200 feet, the building would be not only twice the size of St. Patrick's but would be among the largest in the world.

With the turn of the century came a shift in taste, however, and in 1911 the commission was switched from Heins & Lafarge to the preeminent Neo-Gothicist of the day, Ralph Adams Cram. Construction had begun in the Romanesque mode, and the crossing remains, its huge stone blocks implying (as often was the case with transitional churches of the Middle Ages) a curved resolution, and the piers rose toward a cusp. The Gothic nave, begun in 1913, not only exceeded St. Patrick's in size but in authenticity

well, for the vaulting was built, with the help of modern technology, in stone. (St. Patrick's "vault" is of plaster and is not structural.)

Not surprisingly, a project of this magnitude required enormous sums of money; and in 1941 when war broke out, work came to a halt. The project was resumed in the late 1970s as part of the New York economic comeback. Stonecutters went back to work; the immediate goal is to complete the towers. St. John's was conceived in confidence and in competition (both American qualities). It may never be finished in its revised form. But the leaders of the cathedral, nearly a century after it was begun, are fulfilling the promise of the church—speaking of the institution, not the building—in a multitude of ways as they serve not only its immediate, and often troubled, area, but, in some ways, as the conscience of the city and of the Episcopal denomination.

Like Riverside Church, not far away, St. John the Divine is more important for what it does than what it is. Both have attracted great churchmen of broad vision and an alert sense of the needs of society. Their masonry masses perform a symbolic function of calling attention to the long tradition of Christian service to the community and to the stability of that commitment despite the ebb and flow of population or of architectural fashion.

CATHEDRAL CHURCH OF ST. PETER AND ST. PAUL (WASHINGTON CATHEDRAL), Washington, D.C., begun 1907

Pierre L'Enfant, when planning the city of Washington, wrote, "A church should be erected for national purposes, such as public prayer, thanksgiving, funeral orations, etc.; and be assigned to the special use of no particular denomination or sect; but be equally open to all." Leery of any connection between church and state, however, the founding fathers scrupulously avoided any provisions for a "national church."

By 1893, however, popular sentiment had so changed that an act of Congress was passed, empowering a corporation to "establish and maintain within the District of Columbia, a Cathedral and institutions of learning for the promotion of religion and education and charity." In 1850, a Sunday school teacher who used the chapel of St. John's Church School for Boys, had died, leaving forty gold dollars for the construction of a "free church" on Alban Hill. With this fund a parish church, St. Alban's, was built, thus preserving the land upon which the Washington Cathedral would one day be built.

At the time, the "City Beautiful" movement was sweeping the country, espousing the use of Classical/Renaissance architecture and urban planning. Nonetheless, for the cathedral, Episcopal bishop Henry Yates Satterlee insisted upon a Gothic design. "Beyond any doubt," he said, "the Gothic style of architecture is far more conducive to the thought of prayer and of worship than that of any other period, and unlike other styles, owes its development entirely to Christian influences."

To accommodate Satterlee's directive, an advisory board, which included non-Gothicists Daniel H. Burnham and Charles F. McKim, chose an English architect, George F. Bodley, and (to give an American perspective) a Bostonian, Henry Vaughan, to come up with a plan. In 1907, the scheme was completed and the cornerstone laid. At the ceremony, both President Theodore Roosevelt and the bishop of London spoke.

The cathedral construction has been proceeding by fits and starts since 1907, at about the pace and within the precedents of English Gothic cathedrals. There is a full Gothic structural system of ribbed vaults (built of limestone) and flying buttresses, and the decoration includes finials and crockets, stained-glass windows, carved bosses, gargoyles, and grotesques, in addition to angle-softening molding terminations. The resulting juxtaposition of dizzying height and minute, human detail appeals on a variety of levels.

The cathedral is a monument both to the grandeur of its purpose and to the specific human events of its construction. A carved tribute to stonecutter Joseph Ratti, who died in a fall from a scaffold while working on the cathedral, is a poignant reminder of the affection his co-workers felt for him and of the fragility of the lives of all men. The Children's Chapel is responsive to children's feelings: the wrought-iron gates are surmounted by various fanciful animals; the ceilings are low and fan-vaulted; an intimate and comforting air pervades the chapel, in contrast to the awesome nave.

In 1974, a further link between the earthbound and the celestial was forged when a sliver of moon rock was encased in a stained-glass window. It was, said Dean Sayre, a memento "of man's primordial urge that requires him to trace out with his stubby finger the wondrous shape of creation."

Though modern technology has accelerated the processes of building such a cathedral, modern circumstances have diverted attention and funds from those processes over the seven decades that have passed since the start of construction. After an intensive building drive, the nave was completed for the Easter 1976 services, but the towers of its west façade remain to be built. Nevertheless, one can feel the years of care and love that have gone into the building and into the vigorous presence its leadership has provided in the life of the capital city.

©Irwin Wensink

©Morton Broffman

©Robert C. Lautman

©Robert C. Lautman

©Jonathan Wallen

©Jonathan Wallen

EPISCOPAL CATHEDRAL,
Philadelphia, Pennsylvania, begun 1932

©Courtesy of St. Mary's-at-the-Cathedral

In the 1920s, when money seemed unlimited, the Episcopal diocese of Pennsylvania decided to build a cathedral bigger than both St. John the Divine in New York and Washington Cathedral. The Philadelphia cathedral would then be the largest Gothic cathedral in the world. The chief sponsor, Samuel F. Houston, had made a fortune in real estate and diverse other interests, and was determined to create something "big."

Construction began in June 1932, but was stopped by the Depression; only the Lady chapel behind the high altar and two side chapels had been completed. The project was abandoned until the early 1970s, when new federal and state regulations required large sums for the renovation of church-sponsored facilities in the diocese, and some resolution of the use of the land reserved for the cathedral also became necessary. The energy of the Episcopalian community turned the problem into an opportunity. Using the land as collateral, an $11-million bond issue was sold to build housing for retired people, sponsored by the church, on the land. The Reverend Thomas L. McClellan engaged Edward R. Watson of Mirick Pearson Batcheler to redesign a chapel, called St. Mary's-at-the-Cathedral, out of the remnants of the anticipated chancel—a process that, on a much smaller scale, recreates the experience of the cathedral at Beauvais, which is composed of only a portion of another huge, projected building. The chapel is the hub of the entire complex, a structure, like Beauvais, taller than it is long, seating a congregation of about one hundred largely local residents.

Ten apartment complexes spread out from the chapel: an "ambulatory" for elderly people, including a commons with dining rooms, kitchen, and office facilities. The entire project, begun in 1977 and taking three years to complete, cost $22 million.

101

CATHEDRAL CHURCH OF BRYN ATHYN,
Bryn Athyn, Pennsylvania, 1913–29

At a glance the Bryn Athyn Cathedral might seem to be a nicely executed but typical Neo-Gothic building like many others erected during the early twentieth century. A closer viewing, however, reveals beauty of proportion and detail that are unusual—the result of a unique process of construction carried out for nearly two decades, not according to an immutable plan but rather through a less fixed system.

All the craftsmen involved with the construction were ensconced in workshops on the site, the better to preserve the intimate link between creator and creation that was deemed necessary to produce ''the same exquisite detail, the same unerring sense of beauty as the great cathedrals.'' Hence a gradual evolution of the building, based on the cooperation of many, took place.

John Pitcairn donated the money for the building in 1908; ground was broken in 1913. Although the Neo-Gothicist firm of Cram & Ferguson acted as architects until 1916, for the remaining years Raymond Pitcairn took over architectural direction. John's son, Raymond was an architect by avocation only, his profession being that of attorney and business executive. However, he was an enthusiastic art collector and evidently had a remarkable eye for design.

Though constructed in accord with ''Arts and Crafts'' principles (which were derived from the medieval guild system), the cathedral is not decorated in the traditional Gothic manner, but rather according to Swedenborgian tenets, which seek to establish a new symbolism. Another unusual characteristic of the cathedral is the use of curved lines, familiar enough in Periclean Doric architecture but only discovered early in this century to have been built into French and English cathedrals of the Middle Ages. For instance, bowing horizontal lines upward corrects the eye's tendency to see straight lines as sagging. Though less rectilinear, the curved lines at Bryn Athyn lend a vibrant quality to the structure that would otherwise be lacking.

''Bryn Athyn'' means ''hill of cohesion.'' In its cathedral the cohesion of efforts by scores of individuals has resulted in a unique blend of old and new.

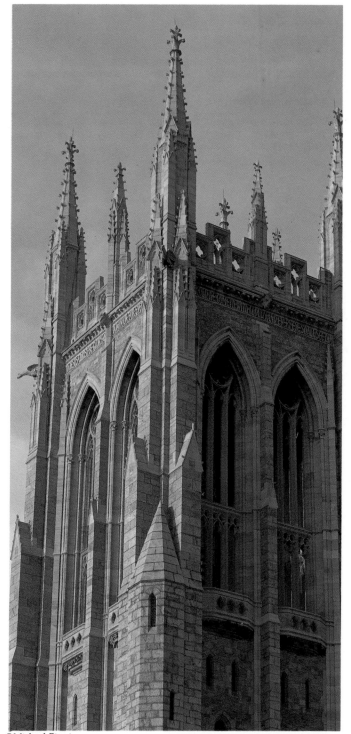

©Michael Pitcairn

PART TWO
The Children of Light

1
Renaissance and Reformation

If we had seen nothing of American architecture and knew only that many and various were the religious sects of the country, we might suppose that we could sort out the sects by looking at their buildings. We might think, for example, that the Anglicans would build in English Gothic, the Catholics in the Baroque (the architecture of the Counter Reformation), and the Puritans and their innumerable offspring only clean, clear, unembellished buildings.

We would not be completely disappointed in such an expectation, but we would be risking many losses if we were to invest much upon it. Much larger determinants overwhelmed sectarian questions. The Renaissance and the Reformation, which were simultaneous but distinct movements, convulsed Europe, while at the same time both were being exported to a new world during the greatest migration in human history, as millions of Europeans and Africans moved across the Atlantic.

The Renaissance spread northward out of Italy, while the Reformation was working its way out of the north of Europe, affecting many of the same people. The Reformation left Italy almost unchanged. There, Renaissance architecture—clear, clean, symmetrical, balanced, and orderly—evolved into the muscular, dynamic Baroque long before Italians in any numbers followed the example set by Columbus, Verrazano, or the Cabots and took an interest in America.

In Spain, the Renaissance came later, and the first Spaniards who went to America continued to build there the forms preceding that architectural revolution: although there are no Spanish Gothic churches in the United States, some do remain in Latin America.

The British, like the Spaniards, were more than a century late in accepting the new forms of the Renaissance. In their case this was largely because they had very little energy for architectural change. They were busily engaged in their religious wars and in the social insurrections of the fifteenth, sixteenth, and seventeenth centuries. They also were not yet the beneficiaries of the riches of their colonies and were, therefore, still relatively poor. Not until West Indian sugar, African slaves, and cotton from America and India had enriched them could they mount the great architectural campaigns that ornament their gentle countryside with great houses and lovely parish churches in the style of Christopher Wren and James Gibbs.

The first Englishmen who came to America were the entrepreneurs of Virginia, who built in Gothic; but very little of their work is left to us, unlike the profuse legacy of the first to settle in New England. They, too, built first in Gothic forms, but none of their churches has survived. We possess examples only of a later period, when finally there was enough prosperity and tranquillity in Britain to nurture the Renaissance, when that style was reex-

The Renaissance comes to Ramah, Colorado. ©Robert Adams

Unity Church in Colorado Springs, Colorado (right)—the Gothic endures. ©Robert Adams

St. John's Catholic Church in Stoneham, Colorado (far right) —another Colorado example of the persistence of the Gothic. ©Robert Adams

ported to the colonies. To that reexport we owe both the simple white clapboard churches of New England and the "Southern colonial," which, under its brick sheathing, is not very different.

In France, the Renaissance and the Reformation wrought their transformations simultaneously. But the French emigrants to America concentrated their larger architectural accomplishments in their headquarters in Canada and, much later, around New Orleans. Time has been cruel to their smaller communities along the Mississippi, which have largely disappeared. As a result, the United States can offer nothing like the continuous Baroque tradition of Canada (or of Mexico, for that matter) to represent the official architecture of the Catholic Church and monarchy. The two French cathedrals of St. Louis and New Orleans will be described in these pages, but they remained almost without companions until, in the twentieth century, Neo-Baroque began to appear as a style among Roman Catholic churches.

Catholics and Protestants, Anglicans and Puritans built much the same kind of buildings at the same time and of the same materials. Yet there are subtle differences among the works of these people arising from religious practice, ancestral habit, available materials, and the personalities of individual architects. One could trace the history of American ecclesiastical structures by following any one of these threads, but (not surprisingly, perhaps, in light of the discussion in the foregoing chapters) we will try to work our way outward, from the worshiping community. We will try to describe how each of the groups of persons who assembled in these buildings expressed themselves, drawing upon all these factors. We will divide our discussion into the rough groupings in accordance with the primary attitude toward religious architecture that seemed to dominate each.

110

ST. MICHAEL'S CHURCH,
Charleston, South Carolina, 1752–61

After 1750, the major churches in the British colonies in America emulated, to the extent they were able, the style of James Gibbs's St. Martin-in-the-Fields in London. St. Michael's Church, on Broad Street in Charleston, South Carolina, was probably the grandest and most complete of these colonial monuments. Its powerful steeple records that affinity—and much more.

Although Samuel Cardy is named as the architect, the influence of James Gibbs on the building's design is substantial. As plans were being made for the church, an article in the local gazette stated that "this church will be built on the plan of one of Mr. Gibson's designs." Since no architect named Gibson is known who could possibly have done the work and, since architectural reporting was a little vague at the time, it is generally assumed that the reporter was referring to James Gibbs's *A Book of Architecture* (London, 1728), which contains plans that had been used or rejected for many churches in London. Many parts of St. Michael's are similar to the plates in Gibbs's book, so it is apparent that the local builder (probably Samuel Cardy) borrowed some of Gibbs's ideas and added some of his own.

As construction began, some of the material such as slate, glass, and iron had to be imported from England and Holland. Molded bricks were made for the portico's Tuscan columns. The brick walls were rough-cast and painted. It was found that the beams would support the slate roof, so the planned interior support pillars were omitted.

Gibbs's influence can be seen in St. Michael's huge entrance portico, its double-tiered arched windows, and the octagonal, triple-tiered tower topped with a triangular spire. The Gibbs tower is not attached, as it is in the earlier churches, but rises instead from the body of the main building. The simple masonry, white wooden porticos and towers, and smooth white stucco exterior reflect South Carolina's taste and materials.

The windows display the sumptuous taste of the early plantation owners. The richly carved pulpit is found in the southern corner of the nave; the ceiling is decorated with carved cypress and cedar. The

©Tom Jimison

chancel had a semicircular apse with a Palladian window. A cannon shell destroyed much of the chancel in 1865. It was rebuilt in 1866, and additional renovations were executed by the Tiffany studios in 1905.

Sir Christopher Wren once said that "handsome spires, rising in good proportion may be of sufficient ornament to the town." The spire of St. Michael's has been more than an ornament. In 1787, five years before the building was completed, the General Assembly of the province needed a beacon in the harbor to help guide ships. The assembly was having difficulty in finding a safe place to construct the building. "Whereas," the statutes read, "it has been found impracticable and unsafe to build or erect a beacon... and it hath also been found that the spire... of the church of St. Michael's parish doth in a great measure answer the end and purpose of a beacon. Be it therefore enacted ... that out of ... the said tax imposed...on the first purchasers of negroes and other slaves imported...shall be...paid...for building the said church steeple and spire of St. Michael's parish." A church has often been a lighthouse, but seldom so literally.

©Ron Anton Rocz

CHRIST CHURCH, Philadelphia, Pennsylvania, 1727–44

Christ Church, at North Second Street, was the first Anglican religious building to be erected in Philadelphia and the Pennsylvania province. Among its organizers were many people who played key roles in the founding of the United States and of the Episcopal Church there.

The land for the building was part of the grant by Charles II to the Quaker William Penn in 1695. The church was founded by thirty-six laymen, one of whom was the attorney general and two of whom, it is said, were pirates. Construction of the present building began in 1727 and was completed seventeen years later in 1744. The architect is reputed to have been Dr. John Kearsley, a physician and amateur architect; he may have been the one to organize the work for Alexander Hamilton, architect for Independence Hall, who was on the vestry during the construction. Robert Smith and a "Mr. Harrison" of the Carpenters Company are credited with the design and construction of the steeple, completed in 1754.

William White, who played a large part in the formation of the Episcopal Church in the United States of America, was baptized in Christ Church. White, unlike other clergy from Christ Church, joined the American cause during the Revolution. Jacob Duché, rector of Christ Church, was the first chaplain to the Continental Congress, but then declared himself a Loyalist and asked George Washington to desert the cause. His successor, Thomas Cooke, was also loyal to the crown. Both resigned and returned to England.

White returned to Philadelphia after the British occupation and served as chaplain of the Continental Congress, first bishop of Pennsylvania, and then presiding bishop of the Episcopal Church. Since the Revolution had put an end to the archbishop of Canterbury's sovereignty over the Anglican Church in America, White had drafted the Constitution for the Episcopalians. It was adopted and the Book of Common Prayer amended at a convention held just after George Washington's inauguration in 1789. The meeting was held in Christ Church and later was moved to Independence Hall, which provided more space.

When constructed in 1727, Christ Church came closest of all the colonial churches to duplicating the Anglican churches designed by Christopher Wren and James Gibbs. In its final form it is very similar to Gibbs's St. Martin-in-the-Fields, London. The heavy Baroque masonry with double-tiered arched windows separated by pilasters reflects his style, which is also apparent in the huge Palladian window which dazzles the eye directed to the altar on the east wall.

The window stresses the importance of the major liturgical focus—the Communion table. It was surrounded by elaborately painted and gilded panels. The center panel over the window had a representation of the Holy Spirit in the form of a dove. The barrel-vaulted ceiling in the chancel was similarly decorated with a "glory" in the center of five panels. The Decalogue, Lord's Prayer, and Apostle's Creed can still be found on side panels. This complies with the 1604 church canon that orders that they "be set upon the East end of every church and chapel where people may best see and read the same." The transition was complete from the stained-glass illustrations of the pre-Gutenberg world to the assumption of literacy on the part of at least part of the congregation.

The placement of altars in chancels was a controversial subject in the seventeenth-century. Reformers wanted the altar brought out from the east wall to be accessible to the people. Christ Church followed the pattern of Gibbs and of the "Laudian churches," returning the altar to the east wall and enclosing it in rails. People could kneel there to receive Communion, as it was felt to be protected from irreverence or profanation.

A distinct Philadelphian flavor can be sensed in the design and craftsmanship of much of the work. Its wealthy merchants liked heavy, serious Flemish

©Jonathan Wallen

bond brickwork. The "wine glass" pulpit built by Philadelphia cabinet-maker John Folwell, was the design of Batty Langley. The simple wood font (one of two fonts in the church), however, was brought from England in 1697. High-backed box pews were replaced box by slip pews in 1835.

In 1754 a peal of eight bells were enclosed from the London company of Leston and Pack. They had been purchased by funds raised by the "Philadelphia style lottery," operated by Benjamin Franklin. They rang with the Liberty Bell to celebrate the signing of the Declaration of Independence on July 4, 1776. They were carried, and hidden, with the Liber-

ty Bell and the bells from St. Peter's Church through British lines before the occupation of Philadelphia. These were the bells that, in 1876, inspired Henry Wadsworth Longfellow (who was visiting for the Centennial Exhibition) to pen these lines:

Distant and soft on her ear fell the
*   Chimes from the belfry of Christ Church,*
While intermingled with these, across the
*   meadow were wafted*
Sounds of psalms, that were sung by the
*   Swedes in their church at Wicaco.**

---

*Wicaco is the Philadelphia Swedish Lutheran Church.

115

©Howard Millard

©Howard Millard

©Howard Millard

ST. PAUL'S CHAPEL OF TRINITY CHURCH,
New York, New York, 1766

St. Paul's Chapel stands on Broadway in downtown Manhattan, with its 219-foot spire dwarfed by skyscrapers, a continuing link between the United States and Great Britain from the colonial days until the present. The superb scale, proportions, and ornamentation make St. Paul's, with Christ Church, Philadelphia (see p.114), the chief examples of high Georgian—one could say British Baroque—architecture in the United States. It is the oldest public building in Manhattan in continuous use, established as an offshoot of the older Trinity Church and intended to be located beyond the wall (now called Wall Street), in the suburbs of the port city of New York at the tip of Manhattan. The cornerstone for the chapel was laid May 14, 1765, and the building was opened October 30, 1766.

The architect was Thomas MacBean, who may have been a student of James Gibbs in England or may simply have used the latter's *A Book of Architecture*. The steeple, which was built in 1794, was designed by James Cromelin Lawrence, but both church and steeple are close adaptations of Gibbs's London church, St. Martin-in-the-Fields.

The large rectangular building is made of Manhattan mica schist with brownstone quoins. The large east portico fronting on Broadway has Ionic columns and a triangular pediment that contains an oak statue of St. Paul. The wooden steeple makes subtle transitions between three octagonal levels with opulent Baroque ornamentation.

The interior of the church presents eighteenth-century elegance in basilican form. Fourteen chandeliers, all but one of original Waterford cut glass, hang from the barrel-vaulted cerulean-blue ceiling. The columns seem to support a complete vaulting system, even though it is false. The gray and white marble paving was very fashionable in English churches.

In front of a Palladian window is the high altar, designed by Pierre Charles L'Enfant. It is the first "mausoleum altar" known to have been built in an American Anglican church. The French Baroque "glory," over it, represents Mount Sinai in clouds and lightning, and upon it the Hebrew letters for *Yahweh* symbolize the continuity of the Old and New Testaments. The gold and white pulpit carries out the themes of the altar.

The church had, and has, many ties to England, yet it is very much an American church. Many of its members were Loyalists; St. Paul's was the church of the British governor, and seats were given to the legislature. The first commencement of King's College (Columbia University) was held there in 1754. St. Paul's was closed at the beginning of the Revolution, then used by the British who had taken over New York City. The victorious revolutionaries held a special Thanksgiving service in the chapel just after the inauguration of George Washington. The new president continued to attend services there while the capital was in New York. On the wall above his pew, on the north aisle, is an oil painting of the Great Seal of the United States. Probably the oldest oil depiction of the Great Seal, this painting hung in the pew during Washington's inauguration.

©Howard Millard

©David Halpern

CHRIST THE KING CATHOLIC CHURCH,
Tulsa, Oklahoma, 1926

©David Halpern

Built in 1926, Christ the King Catholic Church in Tulsa, Oklahoma, is the largest and most complex of many designed by Barry Byrne. Byrne was a member of the Prairie school, the American architectural movement of the Midwest before World War I. This church is clearly a reworking of Gothic motifs in the hands of a man trained by Louis Sullivan and conscious of the work of Frank Lloyd Wright and his contemporaries. As such, it bears a family relationship both to Bernard Maybeck's playful use of Gothicisms in his Christian Science Church in Berkeley, and to Sullivan's own remarkably serious adaptation of Cistercian massing in his Kehileth Anshe M'Ariv Synagogue in Chicago.

The church of Christ the King features solid rectangular brick walls that clearly enclose a large auditorium within. The corner design that Byrne had used in his earlier churches is further developed here: bricks run up at a 45-degree angle to the walls to produce spearlike bodies. The corners themselves are chambered (blunted at a 45-degree angle). Similar spears, bunched together to protrude, rise through the center of the façade. The angular theme continues with the window openings: most have triangular tops; the two on the façade also have triangular bottoms. The ornament of the church was designed in collaboration with Byrne's frequent partner, Alfonzo Iannelli.

TUALATIN PLAINS PRESBYTERIAN CHURCH (OLD SCOTCH CHURCH), Hillsboro, Oregon, 1878

Because of its simplicity of construction, flexibility of form, and low cost, the board-and-batten church spread throughout rural America during the nineteenth century. An example of the enduring appeal of the style can be found in Hillsboro, Oregon. Constructed in 1878 by a dozen men and women from Glasgow, Scotland, Tualatin Plains Presbyterian Church is a relatively late example, for the Gothic revival reached its zenith in the 1850s. Undeniably, the church is the product of a frontier culture, conservative in style, plain in execution, and remarkably inexpensive: it cost less than $2,200. The architect, recorded as a ''Mr. Balantyne,'' probably worked from a ''pattern book,'' but the unusual hexagonal tower must have been the product of his own talent. Little detracts from the sharp vertical form of the church; there is no applied ornament, no ''gingerbread'' or tracery. It needs none. It stands in mountain country, amid great firs, which supply their own tracery.

Known locally as the ''Old Scotch Church,'' the building and recent additions house a lively and growing congregation.

Tualatin Plains Presbyterian Church.
©Floyd Schrock/Tom Stack & Associates

UNITED CHURCH OF CHRIST
Bath, Maine, 1843

United Church of Christ.
©H. K. Barnett

Built in 1843, the United Church of Christ on Winter Street in Bath, Maine, is a free and cheerful hybrid of the Gothic and Greek revivals. Its white exterior features lancet windows (grouped and single), applied panels, and Classical pilasters. The steeple, composed of three stages and a spire, recalls the Wren-Gibbs type of earlier Congregational churches. It replaces a tower blown down in the "Great Gale" of 1861. St. John's Church in nearby Bangor, designed by Richard Upjohn, architect of the Gothic mode, may have inspired Congregationalists in Bath to build the Winter Street Church. "Going Gothic" in this way is a clear example of the evolution of architectural ideas within the Congregational Church. The present church building was erected after the former church was found too small; it then passed into the hands of the Roman Catholics, an unpopular minority in Bath, and was burnt during Know-Nothing riots in 1854.

The population of the town continued to change character during the nineteenth and early twentieth centuries; two Congregational churches were merged, and rather than rebuild the old church to accommodate changed needs, the merged congregations determined to build a new one. Their union was the latest of a series of earlier mergers, each of which led to the building of new structures and the relinquishing of older ones in America: the United Church incorporates the Congregationalists, the Christian Church, the Evangelical Church and the Reformed Church.

In 1972, the last service in the Winter Street building was held, and it was transferred to the Sagadahoc Preservation Society, Inc.

2
The First Americans

In the year of Colombus's first landing, a population as great as that of Europe inhabited the Western Hemisphere. The ways in which these peoples were organized ranged from huge cities to agricultural villages. In the fringe areas like those now occupied by most of the United States, bands of people were scattered, people who hunted, gathered nuts, fruits, and berries, and fished to sustain life. Generalizations about the religious practices of these vastly diverse peoples are no more easily summarized than those of their contemporaries in Europe or Asia.

In our own day citizens of the United States can observe in the Southwest a few remaining structures of that time. These structures were built at extreme distances from the great population concentrations of Central and South America, and they were as radically different architecturally as the European outposts at Iceland or Greenland were from Paris or Rome. Native American temple compounds dwarfed anything to be found in northern Europe. It happens that none of these vast, complex temples was built within the geographical limits set for this book. If this means our vision is limited to the surviving kivas of the American Southwest or to the earthworks of the Ohio Valley Mound Builders, we must be careful not to perpetuate the misimpression that these were the most advanced and complex religious buildings of the ''Indians.'' This woul be tantamount to basing one's impression of European religious architecture on Skellig Michael or a Norwegian stave church. We must also be careful not to be confused by words like *primitive* in appreciating Native American religious structures.

A previous chapter appropriated, without proper thanks, some aspects of the anthropologist Levi-Strauss's term ''participation.'' This appropriation was left unattributed because it was used a little freely and because its customary association with ''primitive peoples'' would have gotten in the way. ''Participation'' was used instead in discussing twelfth-century and twentieth-century architects. Now, again for the purpose of provoking thought, this chapter will defy the discipline of another group of anthropologists who have nobly labored to purge the profession of beguiling juxtapositions wrenched out of cultural context. In an earlier era too many such trophies were hung as baubles on the same Golden Bough. But we need some metaphors now to jostle preconceptions; we need present objects and utterances in their unexpected likenesses despite their unlike places of origin. There is so small a danger that any reader will be led to believe that Black Elk and Carl Jung or Seneca and Red Cloud thought alike merely because they find themselves as neighbors on a page, that the risk is probably worth running.

Medieval ruins at Canyon de Chelly in Arizona (left) and at Mesa Verde in Colorado (above). ©Howard Millard ©Michal Heron, respectively

123

In an unfettered analogic spirit, never professing to being encyclopedic, we might suggest that there have been and are today important and perhaps surprising similarities in the way Native Americans and some Europeans address the Mystery. If, for example, we consider the common view of the natural world of many Native Americans and compare this view to that of the dramatist Seneca in ancient Rome, of Saint Basil in the fourth century, of Saint Bruno in the eleventh, of Irish hermits throughout the Middle Ages, and of saints as dissimilar in other ways as Bernard and Francis, we may more clearly see the religious buildings deriving from this view. It does not force humankind apart from animals or even from the non-"animate." It sees humanity as continuous with the rest of the world.

So considered, the iconography of Native American religions is not so different from that employed among Europeans, though superficially each may seem as very exotic to the other. Images half animal, half human crawl about the great temples of Mexico and persist under the eyes of the friars in the Southwest, perhaps because half-human, half-animal figures also crawl about the column capitals of half the monasteries of Spain, France, and Germany.

Native Americans spoke of thunder beings as grandfathers, of spiders as grandmothers, of a corn mother as if not only animals but the very elements themselves were personal in the same wondrous way that a traditional Scottish-Gaelic prayer says "greeting to you, sun of the seasons . . . you are the happy mother of the seasons . . . greeting to you, new moon, kindly jewel of guidance! I bend my knees to you, I offer you my love." Saint Francis commenced his most beloved prayer with "Hail, Brother Sun!" And the Greeks did not accidentally say "he rains" and "he thunders" rather than "it rains" and "it thunders." The instruction in these ways of speaking is that they remind the listener of humankind's relationship with the natural world. This recollection struggles with a modern obsession with dominance, with causality, and with control.

A sense of the intimacy of our relationship to nature appears in the architecture of buildings like Fay Jones's Thorncrown Chapel. The chapel participates in its setting, employing modern materials to serve Gothic structural principles, demonstrating reverence, not mere virtuosity. Those who pause in that chapel feel no sudden sense of the exclusion of the piny hillside or of the rocks underfoot, of the sky and the scents of the land. They have simply moved into a quieter and more sheltered space, where some additional and familiar symbols direct their attention to other reflections.

This heightened feeling of humankind's relationship to nature is a necessary corrective to the frantic insistence upon control that imbalances contemporary consciousness. There are themes in Gaelic verse that echo

Old Narragansett Church in
Wickford, Rhode Island—natural
light and simple materials.
©Bruce Whyte

the animal iconography of the Anasazi in New Mexico. The mandalic forms
of monastic buildings in Europe are the same in their essentials as the post-
hole patterns at the Cahokia Mounds in Illinois and the ceremonial circles of
central Kansas. Contemporary Pueblo ritual aligns well with the Great
Medicine Wheel in Montana and with what we can deduce from similar ar-
cheological remains of the Etruscans and the Romans. Those familiar with
the cadences of Native American religious expression may hear a familiar
beat in the famous passage by the ancient Roman dramatist Seneca from a
letter that might have been written in North America at the same time:

> We worship the sources of great rivers. We erect altars at the place
> where a sudden rush of water bursts from the bowels of the earth,
> warm springs we adore, and certain pools we hold sacred on account of
> their somber darkness or their immense depth.

Speaking very generally, there are great similarities between Native
American religious expressions and those of Europeans, but these
similarities lie beyond the range of perception easily accessible to Euro-

Grave markers in La Cienega, New Mexico.
©John Running/After-Image

peans—and to their descendants—in the grip of obsessive rationalism. In addition, access to the values to be gained from learning from other cultures has been made physically difficult by the bulldozing and vandalizing of Native American religious buildings by descendants of Europeans, who have thereby deprived themselves of experiencing this architecture as a living expression of faith.

One of the religious attitudes shared by Europeans and Native Americans is a reverence for light, especially natural light. Both cultures revere the sources of light—flame, sun and moon—and also apparently lustrous objects in general. In their usually perverse way, certain folk tales invite our interest in these matters. Take, for example, the Dutch-American fable about the crafty Dutch hornswoggling the natives out of Manhattan Island with some "worthless glass beads." In the story we are told of the "childish delight" with which these natives regarded the beads—objects glowing with light. Their faces, we may assume, were suffused with joy, perhaps the kind of joy Saint Thomas Aquinas and Saint Bonaventure experienced when they regarded such things.

For Saint Thomas luminosity was one of two necessary aspects of beauty (the other being harmony of parts). To Saint Bonaventure light (in a pearl, an opal, an emerald, or a glass bead) is a mediator between its gritty material found within, as trapped within the transitory, and all nature's part in eternity. He pointed out how light is inherent in all things: how glass comes of sand and ashes; how fire is born of black coal. An object from which light glows is no trinket. It is no accident that the great age of stained glass was one in which the value of an object was determined by the amount of light it held or displayed.

This is not to imply that Saint Thomas Aquinas and the Manhattan Indians saw things in exactly the same way. Nor does it imply that Saint Thomas's European contemporaries could pursue his extraordinary mind as it sprinted from common perceptions into those complexities that only he could penetrate. Most people on both continents delighted in shining objects for their sheer sensual pleasure, not as symbolic objects.

Shining objects, like this gold cross from the Ukrainian Church in Meacham, Saskatchewan, have a symbolic importance beyond their obvious visual appeal. ©John de Visser

Shimmer has been enough to gladden the faces of bankers and brokers, of cardinals and kings, of all those who have rejoiced atchest, or from jewel-encrusted books and reliquaries. Gold hath charms for all. Although a love of radiance is universal, all continents are inhabited by some who regard light and shining objects in a more subtle and symbolic way. To such people light is a mediator of the Mystery. They especially revere natural light, the light coming from fire, from the moon and the sun in their seasons, bringing warmth and growth and some order to the events of life.

Recent and laborious inquiries into the Great Medicine Wheel, erected far above timber line upon the arid shoulder of a Montana mountain, yield the same persuasive hypothesis as researches accomplished at Stonehenge: light is the key to their architecture, natural light coming from the sun, light appearing at the same time in the same place at regular cycles. Man found his "orient," his compass bearing, in the universe by marking out those repeated patterns of light with stones upon the earth.

Native American religious practices are not completely beyond the ken of Americans of European descent and vice versa. Elements of the religious history of both have been represented in very similar symbols.

Those Native Americans surviving, after four-fifths of their number were exterminated by warfare or disease, were driven out to the extremities of habitable terrain more ruthlessly than the Celts were driven to the extremities of Britain. In those barren places they had few resources to build religious edifices even if their religious practices had, in fact, demanded them. Some ancient kivas continued to be used, but in the places where the Europeans and Africans came to predominate, even the memory of using such places as the Great Medicine Wheel faded.

We are left with mysteries about mysteries: mounds and wheels of stone, cairns and rooms on the face of a cliff, most of them empty. However, based upon what we know about the liturgy of present-day Indians who practice their old religions, one thing can be said about these places: they may, in some ways, offer more immediate access to the great Mystery than the splendid architecture of the Europeans. Many grand European churches have been wrenched—by their elegance, artifice, and mechanical dexterity—out of the frame of the natural world and thus have exacerbated the disharmony between mankind and the rest of creation. Older traditions—some of them apparently primitive—sought instead a harmony. In those traditions, as today, respect for nature is sometimes expressed in an architecture that cooperated with nature and in an iconography that presents humankind as a part of nature.

Silver icon from Notre Dame
Cathedral in Montreal. ©John de Visser

Above the pulpit of St. Paul's Chapel
in New York City. ©Howard Millard

THORNCROWN CHAPEL,
Eureka Springs, Arkansas, 1980

Thorncrown Chapel in Eureka Springs, Arkansas, is a work of art as well as a place of worship. Designed by E. Fay Jones and Associates, it has little precedent in American architecture. Jones was an apprentice at Frank Lloyd Wright's Taliesin in 1952, but his work has only his earlier designs as its real antecedents. Thorncrown Chapel fulfills its aim to be an unobtrusive place of pilgrimage, comfortable in its mountainous setting.

The chapel lies on a steep slope in the Ozark Mountains, nestled among oaks, maples, and dogwoods. Jones has created a setting with no open space, save the narrow gravel path to the entrance.

The chapel is built with the sparest means, which float, almost weightless in the light. Two workers carried to the site all the materials, the most numerous of which were 2-foot-by-4-foot pine slabs and the heaviest of which were the 2-foot-by-12-foot slabs used for the corner columns. The building lies on two stone walls which permit air to enter the interior through invisible gaps in the mortar joints. Warmth during the winter comes from the flagstone floor beneath the roof's large skylight.

The most arresting part of the chapel is the overhead structure, a delicate geometric spiderweb made up of essential elements. Despite its elegance,

130

almost every part has a structural function. At the central crossing, steel truss connectors, made of four limbs, produce crisscross patterns through whose empty centers rays of light slant into the interior. The worshiper sees the valley below through one glass wall and, through the opposite walls, the wooded hillside. Behind the altar is a window opening to a small group of trees and a steel cross. The cross, which stands a little off-center, is painted a metallic blue, as are the truss connectors, the lecterns, the pew supports, and the door pulls. The wood throughout the church is shaded by a gray stain, the only bold color within being the blue of the speaker cloth and pew upholstery.

Thorncrown Chapel was commissioned by James Reed, an Arkansas native, who, upon returning to his home state after years in California as a schoolteacher and real-estate investor, wanted to provide something for wayfarers passing through Eureka Springs and for the town itself. He financed the pilgrimage chapel and the eight acres that surround it. The nondenominational chapel is often used for weddings, and there is a service every Sunday morning during the summer.

3
The Exarchs

The first Europeans to come to these shores were Catholics, not Protestants. And they came not to escape persecution of their religious beliefs, but to *propagate* those beliefs. They were not driven, they were drawn—drawn by the prospect of saving souls; drawn, too, but not so obsessively as some historians insist, by the prospect of saving the exchequer of Spain by sustaining its immense military budget with colonial gold.

The title of this section is intended to do honor to the leaders of the French and Catholic missions, among them great men who labored for a century before such famous latecomers as Junípero Serra of California, Eusebio Francisco Kino in Arizona, Père Marquette and Louis Joliet along the upper Mississippi. By presenting the earliest arrivals to the New World, we also mean to contrast them to even *later* comers, those "exiled fathers cross the sea," the Pilgrims. The Spanish and French fathers were not exiles; they were not fugitives. These great missionaries of Florida, the Southwest, Canada, and the Mississippi Valley were like exarchs, deputies of patriarchs, proud representatives of the metropolis extending into new lands. There is nothing tentative in the architecture they constructed when they had the tranquillity and resources to build. Their architecture is intended to shelter, but it is also intended to awe. The king-emperor and pope are never out of mind in these spaces.

In Spanish America, as in parts of British America later, avarice and evangelism marched together. But often the missionaries were far ahead of gold seekers as the Spaniards explored the new continent. Thirty years after Columbus's landfall in 1492, Ponce de León was ashore in Florida, and priests traveling with him were attempting to convert Indians. Dominicans said Mass in a chapel near the present site of Jamestown, Virginia, three generations before the British settlement there.

Three of the friars in Coronado's train remained in New Mexico after 1540. Before that century—in America, the Spanish century—had passed, the Franciscans had established there the earliest permanent European settlements within the present boundaries of the United States. These Franciscans found themselves at the farthest extremity of the Spanish Empire, where only the saving of souls justified imperial expenditure, for the hope of gold had gone by then. Soon thereafter, at the other extremity of the continent, the French began two activities that Count Frontenac described as the conversion of souls and the conversion of beaver.

Some of those whose souls were to be converted were recalcitrant. A series of revolts in the Spanish possessions culminated in 1670 in what can be called the First American Revolution, when the Native Americans drove the Spanish, clerical and military, out of New Mexico largely because their own religious sensibilities had been affronted by the Christian exarchs. The recalcitrant convertees of Florida had risen several times earlier.

The mission of San Francisco de Asis in Taos, New Mexico.
©Walter Smalling, Jr./for HABS

After a passage of years, Spanish military technology prevailed again. The missionaries and the riflemen returned and rebuilt the missions. The oldest of these missions to survive is at Acoma, originally constructed in 1627. It is the oldest church of European construction in the United States. Just how it looked when it had been abandoned again in the early nineteenth century is described in *Death Comes for the Archbishop* by Willa Cather:

The top of the mesa was about ten acres in extent—and there was not a tree or a blade of green upon it; not a handful of soil, except by the churchyard, held in by an adobe wall, here the earth for burial had been

carried up in baskets from the plain below. The white dwellings—huddled together in a close cluster, with no protecting slope of ground or shoulder of rock, lying flat against flat, bright against bright—both the rock and the plastered houses threw off the sun glare blindingly.

Acoma Pueblo in Acoma, New Mexico—the oldest Spanish mission still standing in the United States.
©Richard Erdoes

The glare described here is not just the sun, not just the heat, not just the impenetrable surfaces of the rock and the rocklike sky: the glare is harsh physical reality. Strongholds like this mission and like its predecessors in Europe provide, in their depths, the grace of shadow. They offer surcease from the battering of the sun and the brutal realities it discloses. The ar-

Acoma Pueblo in New Mexico—
sanctuary. ©Karl Kernberger

chitecture of the mission churches of Texas, New Mexico, and California is an architecture of protection from a dangerous world. It is like Albi, the fortress-cathedral of France, and other fortified sanctuaries in Europe.

Stylistically, the twin towers and massive façades of mission churches, unornamented except about the doors and windows, seem to present a kind of provincial Baroque. Their spaces, as has been suggested, feel as if they were Gothic, and their west façades feel like stern "westworks" of the Romanesque—those great fortresses behind which the church itself extended itself warily in times of peace. The architectural forms are not those of the Romanesque, but similar uses sometimes overwhelm dissimilar details when we yield to the general sense of a place.

Light is very sparingly admitted to these mission churches. Windows are few. Light is deployed in this kind of architecture not to remind the worshiper of what awaits him just outside, but of what awaits him inside himself or in another life. In the great, opulent medieval churches in Ravenna, Constantinople, or Sicily, brilliant mosaics or frescoes on curved surfaces often were arranged to force the worshipers to tilt their heads up to behold the Pantocrator or some other powerful image brooding down upon

136

Murals within Santa Inez Mission in Solang, California (top). ©Eric Sanford

A twentieth century mass celebrated in San Xavier del Bac in Tucson, Arizona (right). ©Glenn Short/ Bruce Coleman

them. This is how it is also in the Spanish mission churches. The placement of light on figures of the Virgin or Christ, saints or martyrs is intended to draw the eye upward, as it is in the much older Byzantine and Romanesque structures.

There is no calculated ambiguity of wall plane as there is in the Gothic and in the Baroque. The surface is there set clearly before us. It bears the message that there is another kind of reality and that this building is the gateway to this reality.

It is important to recognize, too, that while the little struggling English colonies of New England were just daring to penetrate the Berkshires and the Blue Ridge, the sway of the Catholic sovereigns had already reached Wisconsin and Colorado. The energies of the French Protestants, ironically, had been responsible for the presence of the first Catholic missionaries in America. The Catholic missionaries accompanied Huguenot settlers to the New World as a part of an agreement under which Protestants were permitted to settle in New France while their Catholic king insisted that the Indians at least should benefit from his Catholic missionaries.

Thereafter the French, led by the Jesuits, colonized the shores of the St. Lawrence, the Great Lakes, and the Mississippi and were already converting among the Hurons before the British established their colony on

Massachusetts Bay. The old cathedral at St. Louis and the larger one at New Orleans testify to these extraordinary feats of faith. French and Spanish missions were the most important Europeanizing forces over stretches of American terrain, far broader than those touched by the hand of Britain.

Many Catholic Germans sustained the same emotional relationship to the kings of Baden, Württemberg, and Bavaria as their Spanish predecessors had to the throne of Spain. Their religious leaders were, in this sense, also exarchs (though it would be difficult to find a political parallel to Spain: Baden and Bavaria had no imperial ambitions). They were not exiled, forced from their homes. They chose to "repot" in a new place. And they were encouraged by their rulers to do so.

King Ludwig of Bavaria pleaded with emigrants from his country "stay German, stay German! Do not become English!" The so-called Cahenslyite* movement among Germans in the United States was intended to help them do just that. The Germans of this group kept themselves separate from the swirl of "Englishness" about them by remaining in their own parishes, by heeding a clergy speaking German in the non-Latin portions of their religious services, and by relying upon financial and moral support from German and Austrian princes and prelates. The German church, St. Alphonsus' in Baltimore, is a very early example of this German Cahenslyite strain, which lasted as late as the First World War.

How did this proselytizing spirit express itself in architecture? The peculiarly geometric quality in German Gothic, a love of ornament composed of lines, does seem to affect German Catholic architecture in America. In the "German triangle," the area of dense German settlement between Cincinnati, St. Louis, and Milwaukee (with a salient running all the way to Stearns County, Minnesota, by way of New Ulm), there are Catholic parish churches of this "Cahenslyite" style, with twin towers and brick façades. But it is probably true to say that they are German first and Catholic second.

The wonderful, nature-celebrating German Baroque does not appear in America, but something very close to it in a Gothic format does. This is strange because "the triangle" was largely settled by people who came from the areas of south Germany, which possessed a Baroque tradition of singing the Gloria architecturally in exuberant, earthy colors used against white and gold, with column capitals of cattle and sheep's heads, in a wild, passionate Counter Reformation fantasy of faith. How different this is from the contemporary dourness of north European Protestantism! Yet the closest approximation to this kind of celebratory architecture to be found in America is not among the German settlements, but among the Spanish and Mexicans in the Southwest.

---

*The reference is to Peter Paul Cahensly, who spent a lifetime trying to keep German immigrants to the United States from being assimilated or "mongrelized."

SAN JOSE Y SAN MIGUEL DE AQUAYO MISSION CHURCH, San Antonio, Texas, 1768–82

San Jose y San Miguel de Aquayo Mission is located in a valley near the modern city of San Antonio. Mission San Jose was founded in 1720 by Father Antonio Margil, a Franciscan pioneer, and the church was completed in the 1780s, only a decade before the missions were removed from the control of the church, their animal herds expropriated, and their power broken. Briefly, therefore, the mission church was the center of its almost self-sufficient, prosperous community and conveyed an imminent sense of the power of the church in alliance with the Spanish crown.

Mission San Jose forms a large enclosed quadrangle, covering eight acres of land. The church itself is a partially developed example of the New World Hispanic Baroque, built, unlike most of the adobe missions constructed in the Southwest, of rough tufa (porous limestone) masonry and surfaced with stucco. Unfortunately, the mission was never truly completed as a unified design; originally, the walls of the church were covered with an abstract floral motif of red, blue, and yellow, fragments of which remain on the southeast tower of the mission. The effect of this decoration was once described as that of a "sparkling set of tile surfaces." This style of natural forms and abstract geometry may be testimony to the Moorish influence in art and architecture in Spain, but it could just as well express a fusion of Spanish, Moorish, and Native American motifs.

Set between the two towers at the entrance façade is a two-storied sculptured portal, unique in the United States. It is utterly unlike the classical doorways of its contemporary English churches or their American counterparts designed by men like Peter Harrison. In the American colonies the Puritan aversion to sculpture was strong; sculptured figures had been the target of fury among the Puritan armies of Oliver Cromwell in England. Sculpture is one element of the grandeur of the Hispanic Catholic style, which is at the opposite pole of much colonial church architecture, which is intended to serve both a religious and a secular function in the community.

The portal of the San Antonio mission is made of light brown sandstone. It is a great celebratory stage curtain for the interior. Instead of the terrifying scenes of the Last Judgment found at the doorways of many medieval churches, here the Virgin appears in glory in the midst of a choir of saints and angels.

The portal is set between two flanking towers topped by sculptured belfries, only one of which was completed. Originally the belfries were to be surfaced with stucco and painted in quatrefoil patterns of alternating red and blue, but today they appear in more demure ashler masonry and dressed corners. The remaining southeast belfry was intended to have been made of dark sandstone and embellished with carved ornament. This was never completed, but the intention is visible in the blocks of stone and the pier that project from the belfry.

The first three bays of the nave and the sanctuary have a groined-vault ceiling. Above the fourth bay is a dome 60 feet high, supported by an octagonal drum. The windows were few and set high, not for defensive reasons so much as to enhance the association of dim light and the Catholic liturgy. More light is cast below the dome in the sanctuary than reaches the nave, so the worshiper is led from darkness into light in the Baroque style.

In the nineteenth century the mission slowly decayed; the vaults and dome collapsed. The tower followed in 1928. Three years later the Franciscans returned to care for the parish and began restoring the church. The WPA, the diocese, the county, the San Antonio Conservation Society, the National Park Service, and the Texas State Parks Board have contributed to preserving the mission, and the church is actively used to serve the parish.

©John de Visser

143

©Ken Biggs/After-Image

San Xavier del Bac is located on the northern out-skirts of the Sonoran desert, southwest of Tucson, in what is today the state of Arizona. The words "del Bac" are a Spanish adaptation of an Indian place name signifying "where the water runs into the ground." Even today, seen against the dry moun-tains, it seems to stand in a bleak and barren terrain, though it is only nine miles from a great city.

Missionaries first challenged this area in 1700, when a Jesuit priest, Eusebio Francisco, founded the original Jesuit mission of San Xavier del Bac. "Anybody might have found it," he said, "but His whisper came to Me." In 1767 the Jesuits were expelled from the mission by the Spanish crown, opening the way for the Franciscan friars, who began construction of the present church in 1783. It was completed in 1797. Today, San Xavier del Bac remains an impressive Spanish Baroque monument, inspired and designed by Franciscan friars operating with the support of the crown, at the farthest reaches of its Latin American empire.

San Xavier del Bac appears to be more European than the other Spanish mission churches and less molded by American conditions. It has a Latin-cross plan, enclosed by several shallow, oval domes. All appear to have great depth (such illusions are an ele-ment of the Baroque style). Above the crossing, a taller circular dome rests on an octagonal drum. Win-dows in the drum allow light into the great space below the dome, flooding the crossing, transept, and chancel with Arizona sunlight, in contrast to the dimmer recesses of the nave.

Brick, faced with stucco, was used in construction of the walls and vaults. In contrast to the austerity of the nave walls, the dome is painted with frescoes, and the transept and chancel sculpture are brilliantly colored. A wooden reredos, exuberantly decorated with paint and gilt, heightens this contrast.

The exterior of San Xavier del Bac is another study of contrasts. On the one hand it is simple, dominated by its undecorated, massive, white-painted stucco walls. The twin towers and the dome over the cross-ing continue this effect of simplicity and stolidity. But San Xavier's overall effect is not one of heaviness but of lightness, almost of translucency. The sunlight upon white walls is overpowering; the walls seem to dissolve in the shimmering heat.

The western portal of San Xavier is a crescendo of color and carving. It, too, plays tricks with the chang-ing sunlight, cooperating in a celebration of the wonders of creation—perhaps of survival in a distant desert land. The entrance anticipates the reredos in-side; both present images of abundance in a country-side that, to visitors accustomed to greener pastures, seems to be only grudgingly fruitful.

Although legend has it that the Goana brothers were the architects, obviously many persons of wide-ranging talent and skill were involved. Certain-ly an architect trained in mathematics and engineer-ing was responsible for the building. San Xavier is solidly, as well as beautifully, built.

SAN ESTEVAN DEL REY MISSION CHURCH,
Acoma, New Mexico, 1629–42

©John de Visser

Begun in 1629 and completed in 1642, San Estevan del Rey Mission is located sixty-five miles west of the modern city of Albuquerque. San Estevan is the oldest church to survive in its original form in the United States. It was one of the first of the Spanish missions in New Mexico, and, like the others, it has also served as a fortress.

Constructed on a mesa 365 feet above the valley floor, the mission faces east to catch the early desert sun. Local Indians have lived on the mesa since the thirteenth-century, when the Europeans were perfecting the Gothic style. Some of Acoma's foundations are as old as the chancel of King Henry I at Canterbury.

The construction materials for San Estevan had to be brought from the valley floor; ponderosa pine for the altar and roof was cut on Mount Taylor, forty miles away. The legend is that the Indians who bore the 40-foot beams were forbidden by the Spaniards to let the wood even touch the ground; it is said they shifted their burden from shoulder to shoulder as they fell, exhausted. In the front of the mission is a cemetery 200 feet square, enclosed by a mud wall 40 feet high.

On the east façade of San Estevan del Rey, two squared-off bell towers rise above a "battered," inward-slanting wall. Like a fortress, they are broken only by one small rectangular window and a wooden double door.

The walls of the church itself are 9 feet thick and support pine crossbeams—some of which are original—12 to 19 inches in diameter and 40 feet long. The roof, 50 feet above the mud floor, is covered with a mud plaster. The thick walls and high roof create a retreat, protected from the desert's hot days and cold nights. The mud floor covers the entire area, except near the altar. Two small, very high rectangular windows on the south wall (and the one on the east wall) permit a few beams of sunlight to reach the interior. The only row of pine pews is in the front of the altar, for today the Indians still sit on the mud floor. The altar, said to have been designed by the Spanish artisans and friars, was constructed by the Indians. It stands 3 feet high and has four wide wood steps above the mud floor. On the altar itself are two large vertical pine beams, each 15 feet high and carved in spirals, painted red and white. Stretched between the beams are painted canvases. Five depict scenes of the life of Christ and of San Estevan—Saint Stephen.

On September 2 of every year a fiesta is held in Acoma to celebrate the feast of Saint Stephen. The mission is open to the public only on holidays and for special events. It is the property of the local tribal council.

SAN FRANCISCO DE ASIS, RANCHOS DE TAOS,
Taos, New Mexico, 1805

©Chad Slattery/After-Image

Seven thousand feet above sea level the mission of St. Francis of Assisi was built in Taos, New Mexico, between 1805 and 1815. It is the result of a synthesis of the cultures of the Spanish Franciscans and the local Indians.

Most Spanish missions were "designed" by the Franciscans, who directed an Indian labor force. Since the Indians had a tradition of their own, these forms of the Spanish Baroque substantially accommodated both local images of architecture and local materials.

Native American architecture was largely of adobe construction, wherein clay mixed with straw was molded into bricks. Mud was used as mortar, and wet clay, smoothing over the façades, produced the final seamless and "aged"-looking finish.

©Steve Lambert/Tom Stack & Associates

At the Taos mission, wall buttresses support the side walls while the twin-towered façade, reminiscent of a Romanesque "westwork," accents the front. Hidden windows spotlight the altar inside, a device commonly found in contemporary Counter Reformation churches in Europe.

Although they have some devices in common, each of the Spanish missions in the American Southwest differs remarkably from the others. St. Francis of Assisi, in Taos, bears little resemblance to San Estevan, Acoma, or to San Xavier del Bac in Tucson. The intersection of the two cultures occurred in different ways in each of the three.

BASILICA OF ST. LOUIS THE KING (OLD CATHEDRAL), St. Louis, Missouri, 1831–34

On January 27, 1961, the "Old Cathedral" in St. Louis, located on Walnut Street, became the Basilica of St. Louis the King. In canon law, the term *basilica* is a title of the highest honor achieved by a church either through ancient custom or papal decree. This was a historic moment for a place of worship that had originally been a cathedral church in a small frontier community.

Priests from Quebec settled the area around St. Louis as early as 1699. As St. Louis and Louisiana developed under Spanish, French, and finally American governments, the Catholic population burgeoned. In April 1830, the bishop of St. Louis, Joseph Rosati, decided that a cathedral was necessary for the parish. In 1831 the cornerstone was laid; in 1834 the cathedral was consecrated. In his report to Pope Gregory XVI, Rosati described the consecration's effect on the inhabitants of St. Louis:

> Meanwhile everything was in motion, both in the city and in the neighborhood, without distinction of sex or religion in view of contributing to the preparation for the feast or of being present thereat.

The old cathedral is 136 feet long, 84 feet wide, and 40 feet high. The entire façade and sides near the façade are of sandstone, in Rosati's words "of beautiful polished stone, much like marble." The projecting portico, also of sandstone, is Doric, in the style of the ruins of Paestum. An inscription in relief on the frieze of the portico and façade proclaims that the church is "in honor of St. Louis" and dedicated to the One and Triune God. Louis IX, saint and king, is an important figure in the memory of the French nation, and as late as 1834 St. Louis was ruled by a French elite of merchants and fur traders who had been there for nearly a century and a half.

The interior of the old cathedral is divided into three aisles, separated by two rows of five columns constructed of brick covered with stucco. The capitals, the frieze, the architecture, and the cornice decorating both sides of the nave are Doric. The vault of the nave is 40 feet above the floor and is made up of eighteen panels, each decorated with ornaments imported from France. The ceilings of the two side aisles are stuccoed and painted to imitate panels. A balcony holding the organ rises over the entrance door. In the most recent restoration, the architects used pewter and silver leaf, French blue, and a white and magenta carpet. It is an interior that breathes the air of pre-Revolutionary France. The sanctuary is four feet higher than the rest of the church, in the full basilican format (see p. 251).

The old cathedral has survived a number of crises, including a fire in 1849 that wiped out most of the river-front buildings, and an assault in 1854 by a Know-Nothing mob. These "Native Americans," as they called themselves, were European settlers who opposed later immigrants and ravaged St. Louis during the 1850s. Their ire was directed most fiercely against the Irish and the Catholic Church. In the attack of 1854, it is said, the Know-Nothing mob set out to burn the old cathedral, but it was dissuaded by a gray old Irishman armed with a large brass cannon.

ST. ALPHONSUS' CHURCH,
Baltimore, Maryland, 1842

St. Alphonsus' Church in Baltimore, Maryland, built in 1842, can name the Redemptorist fathers, Robert Cary Long, Jr., Reverend Alexander Czvitkovics, C.Ss.R., and King Louis of Bavaria, among its fathers. The Redemptorist fathers, a group of German and Austrian Catholic missionaries in Baltimore, provided Long with his first major architectural commission. He was assisted by the Reverend Czvitkovics, a priest with an interest in church design. Czvitkovics raised funds for the project from such organizations as the Munich Ludwigs Missionen Verein and the Leopoldinen-Stiftung of Austria. He personally solicited money from King Louis of Bavaria. Because Long used English Gothic resources, despite the preferences of his clients for a German Gothic church, St. Alphonsus' became a blend of the two.

The brick exterior has been painted, in accordance with Long's design. Long felt that there was "an honesty" to brick, but found that repairs necessitated by chipping were unsightly. A frontal tower which rises 200 feet is topped by a tiny spire of cast iron.

Unlike the interior of most Gothic cathedrals, St. Alphonsus' has a very open nave, having no gallery or triforium level to obstruct sight lines. This is typical of the German "hallenkirche" (hall church), built to accommodate large crowds on pilgrimage roads. The bundled columns appear to be marble, but are actually "marbleized" plaster over an iron core; similarly, the vaulting (of the English style, using a multiplicity of ribs) is not true stone vaulting; like the columns, it is plaster. A ridge rib runs down the center of the nave, unifying the central space as well as providing additional focus on the altar.

Long launched his architectural career with the building of St. Alphonsus', a career that melded historicism with experimentation. St. Alphonsus' is an example of this synthesis.

©Robert C. Lautman

CATHEDRAL OF ST. LOUIS THE KING,
New Orleans, Louisiana, 1850

The third church on its site, the Cathedral of St. Louis the King on Jackson Square provides a visual exclamation, pointing upward amid the low-lying buildings of the French Quarter in an area quietly resonant with history. The previous buildings, under Spanish and French dominion, held memorial services for Napoleon and Lafayette and provided a greeting place for Andrew Jackson. By the late 1840s, however, the second church, which had been built in 1789–94, had deteriorated to the point where almost total reconstruction became necessary.

The new design, by the French architect J. N. B. DePouilly, called for expansion of the nave in both length and width, a higher façade, and a new openwork cypress spire over the existing central tower, which had been built by Benjamin Latrobe in 1819. The only portions of the 1784 church to be retained were some of the lower portions of the front façade and of the flanking hexagonal towers.

In January of 1850, while under construction, the central tower collapsed. DePouilly and the builder were both dismissed and replaced by Alexander Sampson. Construction proceeded, and the cathedral was dedicated on Christmas Eve, 1851.

St. Louis's had been the parish church for French Catholics since 1727. After the Louisiana Purchase in 1803, the English-speaking population increased; they built their own Catholic church in 1833 (St. Patrick's), where services were held in English. St. Louis's, now the cathedral of the diocese, clung to its French heritage.

While its three spires dominate Jackson Square as well as the view from the Mississippi, the church is not very large. It complements its surroundings, one of the most beautiful and harmonious urban spaces in America. The interior of the church, a conventional basilican plan with vaulted ceilings, is enlivened by frescoes which have been repainted several times since 1851. The building has continuously served its parish, and two major restorations were undertaken in 1918 and 1960. The only apparent change in DePouilly's design is the slate enclosure of the openwork spire, completed in 1859.

©Tom Jimison

4

The
Entrepreneurs

The little brick church of St. Luke in Smithfield, Virginia, is the only Gothic church of the British colonies to survive intact. Only the tower is left of the church at Jamestown. Together these two Gothic survivors represent the triumph over privations of a group of immigrants to America who came neither to proselytize, as had the exarchs, nor to escape religious persecution, as exiles. They were the most numerous class of Europeans in the seventeenth century, and they can be grouped together as entrepreneurs. Many of them were very brave, but our admiration for their hardiness should not make us sentimental about their motives.

They were not there to save souls, either those of the natives or their own. These entrepreneurs were there to make money. Their villages were established at first to be mining towns. Disappointed in that expectation, their proprietors converted them into trading posts. Their occupants took to agriculture grudgingly and so ineptly that despite the technical assistance of the natives, who possessed appropriate technology, these Britons nearly starved.

Churches were neither more nor less central to the lives of these folk than they had been at home; unlike the Spanish or the New England settlements, those in Virginia did not center around the church as the central symbol of community. An examination of the countryside of the middle colonies, where entrepreneurs predominated, shows that there were few village greens and meeting houses, few of those clerical compounds attached to parish churches which can be found along the St. Lawrence, the Mississippi, or the Rio Grande. Instead, one finds the crossroads church, often of brick, at a convenient intersection. Except in those rare and much later villages of Mennonites or Moravians, there is little huddling together in professing communities. This difference of architectural expression is significant because the sociology and national origin of the people of Virginia and of New England were very much the same. (Regional differences of origin are interesting and important in explaining some difference in the preferred use of materials, but they are not the chief explanation of the differing roles of the church structure in the community.)

As we will see in a later section, one colony—New England—hastened more rapidly to abandon the use of steep-roofed "Gothic" houses as meeting places for villagers, building instead symmetrical, rectilinear, relatively lower-roofed buildings for community meetings and for worship, buildings that can, without much stretching, be associated with a preference for similar proportions found in the grander buildings of the Renaissance. Apparently, there were no Gothic churches built northeast of the Hudson, as there were in those areas we call, for provocative convenience, the entrepreneurial colonies.

King William County, Virginia —a crossroads church. ©Arthur Rothstein/FSA–courtesy of Library of Congress

St. James Church in Goose Creek, South Carolina—British Baroque of 1713. ©Ron Anton Rocz

There were, of course, plenty of entrepreneurs in New England, but the chief impulse for settlement had not been the search for economic advantage (such a statement may seem sentimental to some economic determinists, but I think it true). We can see how the rectilinear meeting house expressed a difference from the main spirit of seventeenth- and early eighteenth-century New England from that of the more entrepreneurial colonies if we note that part of the "liturgy" of such meeting houses, their way of expressing religious views architecturally, was a rejection of the Gothic. Gothic was a form associated in the minds of the Puritans with the established church, from which they wished to remove themselves (having failed to reform it to their satisfaction). By contrast, in the Middle Colonies and in Virginia the Gothic still came naturally to the minds of people who had no doctrinal reason to eschew it.

Only the first grudging touch of the Renaissance can be seen upon the pedimented lintel at Smithfield. There and at Jamestown the intent is steadfastly Gothic, holding on for a revival. This is Anglican country; and while the Middle Colonies and the South did contain little enclaves of dissenters—among them Mennonites, Moravians, and Shakers—these communities of the like-minded were not the primary nuclei of growth south of the Hudson. Individuals or family groups were the particles composing a social order that tended to prefer traditional religious architecture, although their social organization may have been fluid and although they may have been in radically new circumstances.

The Episcopal Church was established and organized into parishes very early in Virginia and South Carolina, but these were not integrated Anglican "peaceable kingdoms" comparable to the Puritan towns of New England.

While it would be an exaggeration to say that the crossroads church and the parish church were the same thing, it would be fair to say that they are more similar to each other than they are to the meeting house/church located at the center of a village of the homogeneously pursuaded. The "purity" (in a chemical sense) and "density" (used as in physics) of the theological grouping around the meeting house is higher than it is likely to be in the more disparate and diffuse collection of people who happen to find themselves within a parish or within range of a crossroads church.

The early New England meeting houses did not have towers, and in Virginia the earliest parish churches built of permanent materials did. This was not just happenstance or a result of the unresisted persistence of Gothic forms into the Anglican colonies. It is something considerably more interesting; it tells us about the function of towers, and it gives us an occasion to deal with the cliché that "aspiring" Gothic pinnacles represent an architecture engaged in some sort of assault upon heaven.

The exarchs had built towers atop their missionary outposts. The entrepreneurs built towers because they had been accustomed to doing so at home, and they had no reasons of conscience to cease doing so. They were radical economically but conservative architecturally. The exiles to New England, as we shall see, were not very much interested in converting others; they were inward-looking. Their churches, at the outset, were not invitations, nor were they statements of continuity. These people were, after all, in revolt from a continuity they regarded as diseased. All this changed by the eighteenth century, but there was, for a while, a genuine distinction in religious significance between the towered Gothic and the towerless meeting house of very early New England. (The absence of adequate resources or skills at that time keeps us safe from the temptation to further complicate matters by expiating upon the symbolism of domes.)

These distinctions dissolved in the interactions of the colonists, in new waves of colonization, and in the softening of the Puritan spirit of distinction from mainstream Anglicans during the eighteenth century. But those towers that rose above some churches in the American colonies and not above others presented an opportunity to inquire why people trouble to build church towers at all.

Seen from a distance, the spire of any church is a sign. It leads the way to the church. The tower may provide a perch for a watchman to spy out trouble on the horizon, but essentially it is intended to *be* seen, not for seeing. The spire is also a symbol, inviting the mind to consider a complex of ideas of which one is continuity. At a glance the spire offers reassurance that something remains the same despite the travails of pioneering or, later, urbanization. From that tower toll the bells, solemnly sounding the same refrain on the hour, every day, every year, every decade.

Inside the Gothic church the message is the same: reassurance, reaffirmation. The rhythm is from above downward, as much as it is the other way around. From the outside it appears as if the spire were seeking the light; inside, one sees the light coming through the colored glass of the windows to seek out the worshipers. Like all shadowy church interiors, Gothic spaces admit only a few shafts of direct sunlight. Something intervenes almost everywhere, glass or a reflecting surface, so the light comes from unexpected angles, many-colored. In the nave of New York's St. Vincent Ferrer, Bertram Goodhue's masterpiece, as in Tulsa's Church of Christ the King, designed by Barry Byrne, the light, broken into varicolored shafts emerging from unexpected angles, gives an impression of a density of hovering spirits. One sometimes feels, as one does in other Gothic churches, an assembling of the heavenly host, "coming down out of heaven from God" (Revelation 21:2).

This light is not the direct statement of the sun, but a light in which humanity has participated. Human craftsmen have intervened to offer a light conditioned by their craft. It is as if they were asking, thereby, for a reciprocal intervention in their lives by nature's God.

Something of this feeling is invoked even in very simple spaces like that of the seventeenth-century St. Luke's, Smithfield—which was then upon a very uncertain Virginia frontier—and in other "frontier Gothic" churches at Tualatin Plains, Oregon, or at Taylor Park, Colorado. When, in the nineteenth century, the Gothic style was "revived" (its spirit needed no revival), more than symbols of continuity were provided. It was also an impression of the active intervention of the Mystery into the daily lives of people that the architecture was intended to suggest. The axis was, indeed, "vertical," but as much energy passes downward as upward.

The entrepreneurs of colonial America built places for worship that can be very moving to us when they seem to connect us in an unbroken association with the Middle Ages. But we should not confuse them with religious pilgrims or let sentimental tales of recent invention bleach out the character of the people who built them. They were like us: their motivations were mixed. They were certainly energetic. Up and down the seaboard, then up the river valleys, these entrepreneurs built straggling villages and homesteads. Furs and fish were their first crops, then a little corn and mixed small grains.

Until now, we have found it convenient to treat all New Englanders as if they were Puritan exiles, quite different in their motivation from the entrepreneurs. It is time to thrust this artifice aside. There is a story, probably true because it appears in so many versions, of a service held in a New England fishing village in which Cotton Mather, the great preacher, was reaching a paroxysm of nostalgia for "our forefathers who came here seeking religious freedom," when he was interrupted by a voice from the back of the hall commenting dourly: "They came for fish." In spite of their difference, religion was the companion of them all, ineradicable from human personality. The primary orientation in the entrepreneurial colonies may have been finding fish, furs, or grain, then indigo, tobacco, or cotton, but religious buildings never waited very long to be built after settlement.

Alabama Gothic. ©Earl Young/
After-Image

There were, however, important differences among the architectural patterns of British settlers, related perhaps to the differences in relative importance of religion as a motive for settlement. While the Puritans quickly adopted the rectilinear, brightly but simply lit forms of the early Renaissance—most often with a simple gable roof—they were slow thereafter to budge from that manner of building.

They "identified with it." It was a symbol. Going in and out of it was a part of their liturgy of daily life. They may have been as entrepreneurial as, say, Virginians (a debated point among historians); but for a long time the simple box in which to hear the Word remained their idea of a church, and their idea of a church was more central to their lives than it was to others, regardless of the ebb and flow of fashion.

South and west of the Hudson, the sophisticated English Renaissance styles of Wren and Gibbs, with large sheets of clear glass in Palladian windows, heavily carved woodwork or stucco, and a display of classical learning from architectural pattern books, appeared very early among the entrepreneurs, in small packages like St. James Church, Goose Creek, or in grand ones like St. Paul's Chapel in New York or Christ Church, Philadelphia.

Some people find in these grand, though relatively small, buildings the influence of the Baroque. It is certainly there. But although these churches are not in any sense Puritan, they are restrained nevertheless. These buildings do not attempt those marvelous tricks with light of the south German or Piedmontese Baroque. They eschew the Counter Reformation devices of dazzlement and confusion, which, by a sort of sensual overload, drown out the world and thus distract from sensual reality. Here-and-now Anglo-Saxon architecture is clear, clean, but not stripped. It is proud. It calls attention to the virtuosity of its engineering and the erudition of its architects. The Puritan exiles, farther north, eschewed alike the Gothic, because it was identified with the established church at home, and they spurned any intimation of the Baroque architectural language of the Counter Reformation and of Rome. English, Dutch, Huguenots, and Swedish Puritans were quite similar in their architectural requirements. The

Puritans kept things straightforward and simple. They were averse to color and to images, especially to images made of colored glass. In the place of the altar (or even the wooden table or "the Lord's Board" which, after much controversy, replaced the altar in many places at this time), the Puritans emphasized the Book and the pulpit, from which the Book received its exposition. The elaborate, central pulpit is their great symbol, often with its "sounding board," a disc above, which is the counterpart to the Baroque baldacchino above one altar.

From the onset of the Reformation, differing liturgies expressed themselves in differing uses and arrangements of space. Some of these will be suggested in some detail in a moment, but they did not much affect the shapes and exterior appearance of early American churches. Expressing these differing customs on a grand scale was expensive, and since Americans were relatively poor, extravagant liturgical differentiation had to wait.

In colonial America there were no very large churches by European standards. That meant that they could present no long vistas, and there were no great areas reserved for processions. The church was built to accommodate a congregation, and nearly all such structures had a congregation of only one sort; there was no large division of space between laity and clergy in the Protestant colonies. The chancel, therefore, was small until well into the nineteenth century, when for the first time choirs in some places reenacted the ancient role of the clergy by singing to the congregation rather than with the congregation.

Christopher Wren established in Britain, for the Anglican Church, the kind of interior we call "colonial": a large room, unbroken by screens, essentially uninterrupted by pillars, intended to permit everyone to hear and see the ecclesiastical drama. These churches have no center: their important functions are pressed against the wall, where all can attend to them. The baptismal font is on one wall, most often at the door, the pulpit and reading pew at the side, and the altar in front. They are designed to permit easy traffic flow by communicants who leave their seats and go to the front to receive Communion.

This is not, of course, the pattern of the Gothic or Romanesque church. (Although in Spain, there was a unique group of Gothic churches with very wide naves, intended to permit a large congregation to worship together in full view and sound of the same events.) In medieval churches the teacher sat and learners stood: the bishop, like an ancient rabbi, occupied his seat, the cathedra, and the congregation stood about to hear what he had to say, except when they were kneeling to pray or to receive the Sacraments. The reverse pattern, familiar to many modern Protestants, is one in which the minister stands while the congregation sits. This imparts part of a subliminal message; the other part is conveyed by the bringing of the Sacraments by members of the congregation to the others, who remain seated.

It was the Puritans especially who stressed the seated congregation, though anyone who has sat for long in these seats knows that they did not remain seated comfortably. They emphasized a lengthy discourse upon a reading of Scripture. Here was a paradox: they had insisted, in their attack upon the priesthood, that the clergy had no special role as intermediaries between the Mystery and humankind, even to the extent that a congregation would rise to go to seek Sacraments at the hands of the priests. But Protestants came to substitute salvation through the Word, and the Word was spoken by the clergy.

In the next chapter we will return to examine how Christian churches in the nineteenth century were shaped more plastically to encourage their congregations to focus upon the Word (from the pulpit) or upon the Eucharist (the Communion table) or upon the Covenant (expressed in the baptismal font or pool), or even upon the group itself.

One group of worshipers was especially slow to evidence the unique nature of their liturgy in the exterior configuration of their churches. The Jews did not come to America primarily to proclaim their religious apartness nor to evangelize the natives to Judaism. Like most of the British, Dutch, and Swedes, the Jews came seeking economic opportunity.

There had been Jews, practicing their religion in secret, among the sailors of Columbus. They landed in America in the same year as the expulsion of the professing Jews from Spain. Others had gone to Amsterdam. Pursuing the lines of trade that spread to the New World from Holland, Jews became very important agents of commerce in the West Indies (where the first synagogue in the New World was built) and in those mainland ports that were first engaged in the West Indies trade: Charleston, South Carolina, Savannah, Newport, and New Amsterdam (later New York). In these places the Jewish trading and intellectual community first established itself. These Jews, largely Sephardic (of long ancestral residence in Spain or Portugal), did not put heavy stress upon the buildings where they congregated for study and worship. This is hardly surprising, for—like the Irish—the Jews had had for many centuries a history that did not encourage them to take an interest in architecture. The Irish were systematically impoverished; the Jews were systematically denied permanence.

When for the first time on the mainland the Jews in Newport were sufficiently safe and prosperous to build a place of their own for worship, a place where they could surround themselves with their familiar symbols—the

lights, scents, and tactile instruments of their ancient liturgy—they turned inward, as their forefathers had done.

It is frequently observed that the Touro Synagogue, the oldest in this country, looks very much like the Protestant structures of the time and that its architect was Peter Harrison, a Quaker turned Anglican whose reputation was based on his success with the Anglicans at King's Chapel, the most sumptuous church in the colonies. But while Harrison stayed within his comfortable Wrennaissance* style for the structure of the synagogue, the interior was arranged by Isaac Touro himself. If one looks carefully, one can see that this is no Wrenlike interior, no great white barn of a place, with the sun glaring down through the windows in the fashion beloved only by people who live in misty climates, where the sun is seldom seen.

Unlike any work of Wren or Gibbs, this interior is not pointed toward an altar, certainly not toward an altar set before a huge window that dazzles the eye. As it left Harrison's hands, this was a remarkably skillful example of the crisp, confident classical style of the time. But Isaac Touro and others in the congregation quickly shuttered the windows, filtered the sunlight, and made of it a refuge. The interior of the synagogue was appropriate to a desert people who had gone forth to live in the hot and dry Iberian peninsula and knew the relief one feels in surcease from the sun and also, more profoundly, who welcomed repose from a life of negotiation, of contract, of computation, of bright rationality. Jews, in Newport and elsewhere, followed the stipulation of their law that synagogues should have windows, but they also knew the mercy of the shadow.

While the architectural forms of their synagogues and temples have most often shared the prevailing taste of their surroundings, it is nonetheless true that nineteenth-century Jews in western Europe and in America displayed an unusual affinity for Egyptian symbolism, while Gentiles were busy building structures derived from Grecian forms. The synagogue in Karlsruhe, Germany, had an Egyptian cast as early as 1798. William Strickland freely adapted Egyptian forms in Philadelphia's first large Jewish temple, dedicated in 1825. It was not until twenty-four years had passed that he made use of the style for the Presbyterians of Nashville, though Charles Dakin had designed an Egyptian interior—within a Greek exterior—for the Presbyterians of Mobile, and Minard Lafever had created an Egyptian exterior—with a Greek interior—for the "Old Whalers' Church" in Sag Harbor, New York.

One could dismiss the Gentiles' use of Egyptian motifs as unconsidered and merely fashionable, though it is always unwise to pass too quickly over the reasons people use architectural forms in this breezy art-historical way. (A choice of one symbol over another may not be articulate or even wholly

*The term was apparently invented by Sir Edward Lutyens—lucky man!

conscious, but it arises from a deeper need than merely sharing a fad.) Among the Jews, however, there has been an interesting fondness for architectural symbols associated with the enigmatic qualities of God (some of them Egyptian) and a reluctance to use too much light. Their God, who fixed the sun in the heavens and blinded any man who tried to look upon His face, dwelt ''in deep darkness'' (1 Kings 8:12) and ''made darkness His hiding place'' (Psalms 18:12). His judgments are as deep as ''the great abyss'' (Psalms 36:7); ''He does great things we cannot understand'' (Job 37:5).

Flickering candles, quiet voices, shuttered light, repose, and retreat into the affirming ancient faith have awaited Jews in the Touro Synagogue and in most Jewish places of reverence in Europe, in the West Indies, and in America for two hundred twenty years.

The Jews, like the other early entrepreneurs, were conservative architecturally because they were intent upon having their architecture serve ''affirming ancient faiths'' in established liturgies. The exiles had often been rebels at home, driven into exile because they had sought to reform the liturgy and the architecture forming itself around that liturgy. The exarchs were conservative as well, but they often extended the faith into areas where the materials of physical nature were as exotic to those of the home country as were the materials of human nature. So they became innovators by necessity, creating new forms to serve old purposes out of materials that could not be assembled in the old ways.

The Greek revival interior of First Presbyterian Church (Old Whalers' Church) in Sag Harbor, New York (left) within its powerful Egyptian revival exterior (above). ©William L. Huber

163

ST. LUKE'S CHURCH,
(now *HISTORIC ST. LUKE'S NATIONAL SHRINE*),
Smithfield, Virginia, 1632–38

Built between 1632 and 1638, St. Luke's Church in Smithfield, Virginia, is the oldest surviving church building in the original thirteen colonies. Gothic in style, the church is a testament to early Anglican settlers' efforts to recreate the English parish church in their new world. Many observers see it as the best intact example of Gothic survival in the United States—it is *not* "Gothic revival."

The rectangular body of St. Luke's, its exterior buttresses, windows with pointed lancets, crowstepped gables, and square tower with open porch below are all traditional Gothic motifs. Its steeply pitched roof with small corner turrets also mirrors the seventeenth-century church style in England. Unlike most early Virginia churches, which were made of wood, St. Luke's is built of brick, a further link to English parish churches, which were of masonry construction. The use of masonry may account, in part, for the church's survival.

The interior follows the same pattern of the small English parish church. It has no aisles; chancel rail and rood screen separate the clergy from the congregation. The timber-trussed ceiling, which produces an elliptical profile down the length of the church, was typical of many English churches and secular halls.

But St. Luke's is not a pure example of the English Gothic style; the odd, triangular pediment over the door, included in the first stage of construction before 1657, and the "quoins" (blocks of stone at the corners) added after 1657, are not Gothic in origin, but features of Renaissance architecture that had entered the mainstream of English architectural style by the late sixteenth century. The third story of the tower, added sometime in the last quarter of the seventeenth century, is the most radical shift from the English Gothic style. Corner pilasters and round-arched windows did not appear in the Gothic.

This fact sheds important light on the builders of St. Luke's. The pre-1657 builders, responsible for most of the church, were probably transplanted English provincial masons and carpenters, who, unconscious of architectural fashion, tried to construct their recollections of an Anglican parish church. This explains such inconsistencies as the pediment and quoins as well as the curious blend of styles seen in many colonial buildings. The builder of the third story of the tower, who worked at a later date, knew of more current architectural developments across the ocean.

The history of St. Luke's parallels that of Virginia. For instance, in 1839 (when the church was over two hundred years old) a rumor of a slave insurrection swept the area. (In the wake of Nat Turner's 1831 uprising in which nearly sixty whites were massacred, pervasive fears of a recurrence insured the rapid spread of such rumors.) Fearing looters, the minister of St. Luke's, the Reverend Alexander Morris, went to the church to save the chalice and jewels. He heard a noise out front and, fearing for his life, tried to "escape" through the window in the rear of the church. In doing so, he fell and broke his neck.

Many Americans mistake New England for the oldest part of our country and the most influential source of our culture. St. Luke's in Smithfield, Virginia, a monument older than any New England meeting house, reminds us of the central importance of the American South to our heritage. Its architectural style, stemming from a desire to reproduce the English parish church in the wilderness, hearkens back to English Gothic roots and looks ahead to English and colonial developments. Today St. Luke's is no longer used for church services but is open to the public as an historic shrine.

ST. JAMES CHURCH,
Goose Creek, South Carolina, 1713–19

St. James Church at Goose Creek, thirteen miles north of Charleston, South Carolina, is the earliest and most interesting of a group of Anglican churches near Charleston. It is a colonial building—indeed, it records the period in which South Carolina was in effect a colony of a colony: Barbados.

Planters from Barbados established a congregation at Goose Creek by 1685. This congregation was instrumental in the political "establishment" of the Church of England in the province in 1706 by act of the General Assembly. St. James was appointed one of the nine parishes in Carolina.

Services were first held in a wooden structure, but the settlers started collecting materials for the present church as early as 1707. The start of construction is thought to have preceded the coronation of George I in 1714. Work was slowed by Queen Anne's War and the Yamasee War so that the building was not completed until 1719.

St. James's rectangular mass, elaborately stuccoed interior, light stucco exterior, and jerkin-head roof are derived from earlier West Indian prototypes. Its builders were accustomed to a hot, humid climate and frequent tropical storms. They kept the building low, but it is not stuffy because they had learned in the West Indies to modify the English style with numerous large openings to give needed ventilation to a small building. The walls are smooth, and the windows have semicircular fan lights. But the English Baroque is there, too—cherubs are carved into the keystones of the arches, and the large entrance doors are framed by pilasters and pedimented entablatures.

Inside the front doorway is a vestibule, with a stairway to the gallery. From the vestibule as one looks down the flagstone aisle with its box pews on each side, the eye is naturally drawn to the elaborate ornamentation of the reredos, which looms above the altar and pulpit. There, in bright color and relief, is a heraldic shield, the coat of arms of George I. Behind the center pulpit, where one expects a cross, is a huge Baroque pediment supported by Corinthian pilasters, out of place, and out of scale. Yet one can be grateful for its presence—how very anxiously British! How much a talisman of its time! And how fortunate, for it is probable that the British spared the building during the Revolutionary War (they burned many churches) because of this splendid symbol.

A carved pelican appears in the pediment of the main doorway, as it does occasionally elsewhere in Christian iconography (most notably in mosaic in St. Vincent Ferrer, New York—see p. 74). The pelican, native to South Carolina, is a symbol for redemption; it plucks its own breast to feed its young. It was chosen as a symbol by the Society for the Propagation of the Gospel in Foreign Parts because of a verse from the Psalms interpreted to allude to the Christ: "I am like a pelican of the wilderness."

St. James is one of the few colonial churches with the pulpit located above and behind the altar. This placement was experimental in eighteenth-century architecture but became popular in the nineteenth century. It attempts to create a liturgical unit of word and Sacrament and to give an unobstructed view of the altar and pulpit. The arched tablets found on each side of the pulpit, inscribed with the Ten Commandments, Lord's Prayer, and Apostle's Creed, are a common feature of colonial Anglican churches.

St. James was spared once again during the Civil War. However, the Communion silver was lost at that time. As Charleston grew a few miles to the south and transportation improved, the congregation dwindled. Today, only an annual service and an occasional wedding are held in the building.

CHRIST CHURCH,
Lancaster County, Virginia, 1732

Christ Church, near Irvington, in Lancaster County, Virginia, was built about 1732 at the head of Carter's Creek on the Northern Neck by Robert "King" Carter.

Carter, the wealthiest man in Virginia, owned 300,000 acres and 1,000 slaves. He offered to replace a previous church built in 1669 on the same site to serve the growing community. Carter personally supervised the construction of the new building and of a three-mile, deeply ditched road lined with cedar trees from his mansion, Corotoman, to the church. When the Carters went to church, it was said they made a royal procession in a gilded carriage with finely dressed footmen. Once inside the church, the Carters sat in their great, square pine pew, which could accommodate twenty people. It was shielded from curious onlookers by damask curtains on brass rods. (The governor's pew at Bruton Parish Church in Williamsburg had the same arrangement.) The Carters' pew was in the chancel, diagonally opposite the pulpit, which was against the wall, at the intersection of the nave and transept.

John Carter, Robert Carter's immigrant father, came to Virginia from modest circumstances and prospered mightily as a planter, merchant, and land speculator. He came from a London family of vintners and served as land agent for the Fairfax family. He was very clever and was generous to the church as well.

Christ Church is unusual in colonial America in its plan, a Latin cross. The chancel and transept are of equal length, while the nave is slightly longer. Even though the axes of the cross are 68 feet long, one is not overwhelmed by its size because of the scale of the walls and windows. The high, 3-foot thick walls are complemented by 6-foot-by-14-foot windows; the hipped roof gracefully meets the fine, rubbed brickwork. The pilasters and pediments around the doorways reflect the classical Georgian style.

The masterful design and workmanship of the exterior is matched by that of the interior. The tall, white plaster surfaces are juxtaposed with the dark, walnut woodwork of the reredos, chancel paneling, altar, rail, and pulpit. The barrel-vaulted ceiling is 33 feet high. The font was imported from England and is delicately carved out of marble with cherubs' heads and acanthus leaves.

Christ Church shows more clearly than any other ecclesiastical structure the ideals and the style of the Southern colonial landed gentry. Its isolated location has helped to preserve it.

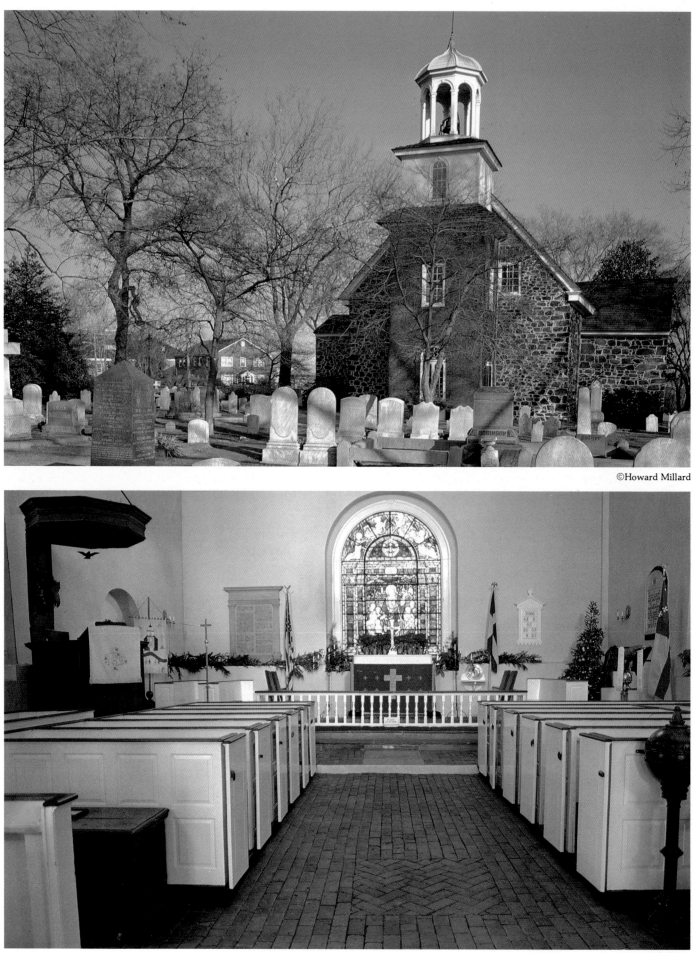

©Howard Millard

©Howard Millard

HOLY TRINITY CHURCH (OLD SWEDES CHURCH), Wilmington, Delaware, 1699

Holy Trinity Episcopal Church was erected near Wilmington, Delaware, in 1699 by Swedish immigrants to serve a congregation of nearly a thousand. The church, nicknamed "Old Swedes," is remarkable not only as a rare example of Swedish architecture in America, but also because it is the oldest surviving Lutheran church in the United States.

The original granite walls of the structure still stand (between Church Street, Church Lane, and Seventh Street) in a simple rectangle supporting a "jerkinhead" roof. This missionary church was at the center of a colony conquered first by the Dutch and then by the British, who later adapted this cottage shape from the Swedes to make small Anglican houses of worship of their own, common in the Delaware Valley and in New England.

Holy Trinity's steep A-frame, shingled roof forced the thick walls apart, so in 1750 two north arched porches were added to act as buttresses; now enclosed, they serve as the vestry and the sacristy. A south porch was also added in 1763. In order to accommodate the growing congregation, a gallery was added in 1774 with room for twenty-five extra pews, which can be reached by an exterior staircase in the same porch.

The belfry, designed by Thomas Cole in 1802 and constructed in that same year, was built to house a bell that had been purchased some thirty years before.

Inside, the aisle and chancel are paved with bricks and lined with box pews. A simple, flat, octagonal sounding board is suspended above the original black walnut pulpit of the "wine glass" type. The original iron hinges, decorations, and fittings—wrought by a member of the congregation, Mathias de Foss—accent the heavy doors and walls. The silver communion cup, paten, and wafer box, sent to the parish from Sweden in 1718, are still in use. Portraits of three Swedish pastors line the gallery front.

The masons and carpenters for the buildings came from Philadelphia, as did the glazier, Leonard Osterson, who made clear glass panes, replaced in the late nineteenth century by stained glass. The cost of the building was £91 . Legend says that the women of the parish saved money by carrying mortar in their aprons to help with the construction.

After the British conquest, relationships were generally cordial between the Swedish Lutherans and the Anglicans. By 1742, the church began to hold two services: one in English and one in Swedish. Following the American Revolution, the king of Sweden ceased to support the Swedish Lutheran churches in the United States. They quickly became Americanized, in part because the Swedes held to the common eighteenth-century religious precept that heresy or schism in ecclesiastical affairs meant treason or rebellion in political matters. Thus, after their pastor sailed home to Sweden in 1791, the congregation voted to join the newly founded Protestant Episcopal Church.

Victorian row houses—built to house English, Irish, and Polish mill workers—were constructed around "Old Swedes" in the 1840s and thereafter. The population of Wilmington largely shifted away from the East Side during the nineteenth century, so much so that the parish constructed both a chapel and another church in "better locations" for the convenience of the congregation. However, the church has been used since then by those who prefer the older church. Though the neighborhood has undergone changes of fortune and population, the church remains a stable element and a reminder of the roots of Wilmington.

TOURO SYNAGOGUE OF CONGREGATION JESHUAT ISRAEL, Newport, Rhode Island, 1759–63

Touro Synagogue was begun in 1759 and dedicated on the first day of Hanukkah, December 2, 1763, by Doctor Isaac de Abraham Touro. It is the oldest existing place of Jewish worship in America. A synagogue had been built in New York in 1730, but it was demolished when the city expanded. In this hemisphere, only Mikueh Israel Synagogue in Curaçao (Dutch West Indies), consecrated in 1732, and Zedek ve Shalom Synagogue in Paramaribo Surinam (Dutch Guiana), dedicated in 1737, antedate Touro Synagogue.

Touro is the work of Peter Harrison, who was born in England in 1716, settled in Newport in 1740, and prospered there as a merchant (see also p. 174).

Sephardic Jews came to Rhode Island because of the religious freedom promised to them by Roger Williams, who, like William Penn, had made it clear that "all men may walk as their conscience persuades them, everyone in the name of his God." In 1677 Jews in Newport purchased a plot of land on Bellevue Avenue to serve as a burial ground. Religious services were conducted in private homes. The ancient Hebrews and later the Sephardic Jews of Spain and Portugal had led a nomadic existence; their architectural monuments were few. When the Sephardic Jewish community acquired a lot on Griffin Street in 1759 (now named Touro Street), Peter Harrison had no easy recourse to architectural models of the Jewish faith. He did receive requirements arising from the religious practices of the Sephardim and some suggestions based upon the Sephardic synagogue in Amsterdam from Rabbi Isaac Touro, who came to Newport in the late 1750s from the Rabbinical Academy in Amsterdam. The building he designed is a brick cube, painted tan, with an added ell where unleavened bread was baked in the early years.

In the center of the interior is a raised deck used for the reading of the Torah, surrounded by a heavy balustrade. The Ark of the Covenant, containing the Torah, is housed in a great panel based on the design of William Kent. Five large candelabra and a lamp of perpetual light before the Ark hang from the ceiling. Twelve Corinthian columns, symbolizing the tribes of Israel, run laterally through the main hall. In accordance with custom, the seats are not arranged to face the Ark, but at right angles to it. Around the ground-floor perimeter is seating for the male congregation, while the balcony seats are reserved for women. Against the north wall is a seat designated "banco," for the presiding officers.

Following the Revolution, Touro Synagogue was closed. A small congregation remained but was not able to hold regular services. When General George Washington visited Newport in 1781, it was being used as the town hall. From 1781 to 1784, both the General Assembly and the State Supreme Court used the building for their meetings. Today, Touro Synagogue is still used as a place of worship by the Jews of Newport.

On March 5, 1946, Touro Synagogue was declared a national shrine.

©Howard Millard

KING'S CHAPEL,
Boston, Massachusetts, 1749–54

King's Chapel, at Tremont and School streets in Boston, was the first established Anglican church in America and was also the first Unitarian church in America.

In May 1686, the Reverend Robert Racliffe, who was later to become King's Chapel's first rector, received a letter from Joseph Dudley, the Puritan president of the Massachusetts Bay Colony, stating that the king had commissioned an Anglican church to be built in Boston. Initially, Anglican services were held in the Town House, while the Puritans had three churches (a reversal of the Anglican-Puritan relationship in England).

In 1688 the first church building was begun. It was called Queen's Chapel during the reign of Queen Anne, but was later changed to King's Chapel. By 1710 the parish had grown quite large, and by 1741 plans for a new church had been started.

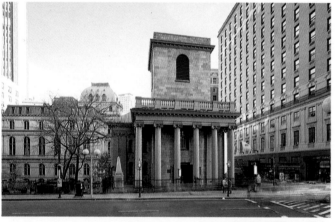

©Bruce T. Martin/Picture Cube

©Bruce T. Martin/Picture Cube

The architect for this new King's Chapel was Peter Harrison, formerly of Yorkshire, then of Newport, Rhode Island. Harrison was a merchant and an amateur architect, but since he was paid to design such buildings as Christ Church in Cambridge, the Redwood Library, and the Touro Synagogue in Newport, Rhode Island, he might be called—loosely—America's first professional architect, though that appellation really belongs to Robert Mills (see p.237).

King's Chapel (briefly renamed the Stone Chapel after the Revolution) shows Harrison at his most elegant and his most derivative. (American architecture had to await the arrival of Benjamin Latrobe, fifty years later, to find a genuinely original talent (see p.256). King's Chapel is the first large granite building in America. It is rectangular in shape, with a hipped roof. Harrison's original design called for a spire, but that enterprise was beyond the exchequer of the church.

The interior is based upon James Gibbs's St. Martin-in-the-Fields in London. Two rows of Corinthian double columns support a range of plaster vaults and galleries. The walls have a lower row of short windows and an upper row of high rounded windows, in a familiar Wren-Gibbs pattern. The ceiling is flat and supported by twin columns. At the end, behind the altar, is a Palladian window. The carved and gilded altarpieces are believed to be original. In the real gallery, enriched with crown and miters, is an organ, built in 1964. One of the most spectacular features of King's Chapel is the "three-decker pulpit," the pulpit itself being the only original part, built in 1717 for the earlier church. It was from this pulpit that Bishop Berkeley and Charles Wesley marched within five years of each other, in 1731 and 1735.

The colossal Ionic portico made of wood and painted gray, was added between 1785 and 1787. In 1814 the original bell cracked, and in 1816 a new one was cast by Paul Revere in Canton, Massachusetts.

From 1686 to 1776 King's Chapel served the Church of England. In 1785 the congregation ordained Reverend James Freeman, who was twice refused ordination by the Episcopalians. In 1787 King's Chapel became the first Unitarian church in America.

FIRST PRESBYTERIAN CHURCH (OLD WHALERS'),
Sag Harbor, New York, 1843–44

©Michael Habicht

The present building (its third) of the First Presbyterian Church on Union Street, Sag Harbor, New York, was built in response to a great religious revival in 1842, which had crowded the previous church building to overflowing. The early 1840s in Sag Harbor was a time of great prosperity. Sixty-three whaling ships were based there and over 1,800 men were employed in the whaling industry. The village of 4,000 was larger than it is today.

Minard Lafever, one of the nation's leading architects, designed the building, which was dedicated on May 16, 1844. The facade is one of the most important examples of Egyptian revival style in the United States today. The massive central tower, tapering upward, and the similar but smaller winged pylons, one on either side, are reminiscent of the Temple of Philae. A delicate cornice design of blubber spades, a whaling tool, tops the towers and is an appropriate symbol of the occupations of many of the church members of that day. Until the 1880's, an unusual 8-foot "obelisk fence" lined Union Street, reinforcing the Egyptian imagery.

The steeple, lost in the hurricane of 1938, stood 185 feet high and was a landmark for returning whaling ships. It was designed in three sections: the lowest, an octagonal colonnade in the Greek revival style, contained the bell; the second section, of carved panels with alternating rosettes and the ancient key motif, had four clock faces at the base; and the slender, tapering top section ended in a weathervane.

The stately interior of the sanctuary, seating about 800, is in the Greek revival style, with fluted Corinthian columns, a coffered ceiling, galleries, and box pews. The organ, built by the master organ builder, Henry Erben, and installed in 1845, is the oldest organ in a church on Long Island, and the case is a replica of the church facade.

The building remains the same as when it was built, except for the loss of the steeple and the addition of electricity. The Greek revival interior, Egyptian exterior, and whaling motifs are joined in a confident synthesis.

GOVERNMENT STREET PRESBYTERIAN CHURCH, Mobile, Alabama, 1835–37

Henry Hitchcock, a client of genius, and Charles Dakin, a carpenter turned architect, rebuilt the tropical city of Mobile, Alabama, during the bonanza decade of the 1830s into a gleaming white Classic revival town. Not much is left of their work, but, fortunately, the Government Street Presbyterian Church remains at 300 Government Street.

James Gallier and Charles Dakin were partners in both Mobile and New Orleans, where James Dakin later joined them. Sorting out which buildings can be attributed to which is impossible, although it was apparently Charles who worked most closely with Hitchcock in Mobile. That association had only three years to sustain its frenzied pace before it was ended in the panic of 1837.

Henry Hitchcock's life began on a small farm near Burlington, Vermont, in 1792. His grandfather was Ethan Allen, the leader of the Green Mountain Boys who seized Fort Ticonderoga from the British early in the Revolutionary War and later grew very rich and very miserly. Allen's deist religion, as articulated in the tract *Reason the Only Oracle of Man*, was Henry's major inheritance; one which would haunt him the rest of his life.

Henry Hitchcock was a stern, proud man who was accounted "benevolent" but "strongly opposed to warm-hearted piety . . . especially to all religious excitement." He said of himself in this period that it was "too much my pride to act with scrupulous honor" without acknowledging his frailties, believing he had "nothing to confess to man."

In the end he did confess his religious feeling, and in 1836 called Dakin to Mobile to design the Government Street Church. It was built after Hitchcock recognized that although he had been "too proud to be saved," one early morning he "fell on his knees . . . and spoke . . . of conscious guilt, of long cherished pride, of agonizing struggle and of comfort and joy resulting from . . . accepting salvation bought with blood." That comfort and joy resounded in the interior of the church he caused to be built.

Charles Dakin's father died when he was thirteen, and he learned the carpenter's trade in order to support his mother and his younger siblings. In 1833, at the age of twenty-two, he was apprenticed to his older brother James, who had entered the great firm of Town and Davis in New York City. There he met James Gallier, with whom he set out for New Orleans in 1834. They designed scores of buildings; the Government Street Church is one of their best.

The church has to be experienced to be appreciated: prose is unavailing to describe its clear white light, the originality of its use of Egyptian and Greek forms, its sense of antiquity, of intelligence, and, most of all, of passionate belief. It follows a pattern of reconsidered Grecian temple forms which began in the office of Ithiel Town and A. J. Davis and was employed earlier by Charles and James Dakin in Brooklyn and in New York City. Henry Hitchcock was the prime mover; the church is one of two great monuments to his conviction that learning and religious fervor both required containers to shield and protect them and that these containers should be sufficiently grand to be set at the center and summit of the community. (The other is the Barton Academy, also designed by Dakin.)

After the financial collapse of 1837, Charles Dakin's financial affairs were in such disarray that his brother James was only able to stave off the bankruptcy of the firm a little longer by finding work in New Orleans. Charles, seeking business, or perhaps seeking escape, went off alone to Europe. Two months after he returned in the spring of 1839, he suddenly became ill and died. He was twenty-eight years old. He was buried obscurely in a section of a Louisiana cemetery for fever victims at the end of July 1839.

Hitchcock was struck by yellow fever and died six days later. He was followed to his grave by "the largest concourse of sorrowing citizens that we ever witnessed," reported the *Mobile Advertiser*, but we do not know where that grave is to be found. For his epitaph we must turn to that inscribed upon the tombstone of Charles Dakin by their favorite mason, which can serve for them both:

'Tis ever thus, with all,
Always the first to go,
The dearest, noblest, loveliest are,
He went amid these glorious things of earth
Transient as glorious.

©Mike Thomason

©Thigpen Photography

FIRST PRESBYTERIAN CHURCH
(DOWNTOWN PRESBYTERIAN CHURCH),
Nashville, Tennessee, 1849–51

Nashville, Tennessee, was the beneficiary of a group of large public buildings designed by William Strickland, who was one of the two students of Benjamin Latrobe who could rise to the standards set by that great man (the other was Robert Mills). The Tennessee state capitol is the largest, but it is rivaled by the splendid First Presbyterian Church.

From Fifth Avenue, the First Presbyterian Church (now the Downtown Presbyterian Church) seems to be another relatively conventional, Neoclassical building: rectangular, brick, with a twin-towered, pedimented façade, though the details—window and door frames, entablatures, and columns—are gently Egyptian in character.

Upon entering, however, one is jolted by the polychromatic Victorian auditorium. The walls and half columns are vivid with Egyptianesque motifs in brilliant hues: winged suns, serpent heads, zigzags, stripes and lotus leaves, papyrus capitals, and battered moldings. The interior is not the work of Strickland, though he was the least inhibited of the late Neoclassicists. It was "redecorated" in the 1880s; to see an Egyptian interior of Strickland's own time, one would have had to visit his Philadelphia synagogue of 1825 or visit Charles Dakin's Government Street Presbyterian Church in Mobile, Alabama (see p. 176).

The First Presbyterian is one of the relatively few Egyptian revival buildings that date from before the Civil War. During that conflict, the auditorium was used by the federal army as a hospital, and horses were stabled in what is now the church's dining room. Seven thousand five-hundred dollars were given to the church by the government for the damage after the end of the war.

Between 1880 and 1887, a major remodeling was undertaken. The "amen corners" were enclosed, decreasing the size of the auditorium; clear glass windows were replaced by stained glass with palm-tree designs; two columns were added to the west façade; the frescoes of columns and sky (in perspective) were painted; the balcony was shortened; and vivid colors were applied to the formerly gray walls.

Victorian America was fascinated by Egyptian architecture for its evocation of the eternal, as well as for its solidity and seeming indestructibility. Its association with death, however, generally restricted its use among Christians to mausoleums, prisons, and memorials. Churches in this style were rare. See page 162 for a discussion of the relationship of Egyptian motifs and the architecture of synagogues and temples.

©Richard Reep

Overleaf left: St. George's Ukrainian Church, New York, New York. ©Don Hamerman

Overleaf right: Riverside Church, New York, New York. ©Howard Millard

pp. 182–183: Church of the Assumption of the Blessed Virgin Mary, Ferndale, California. ©Nicholas Foster

p. 184, left: Green Farms Congregational Church, Green Farms, Connecticut. ©Andrew Stewart

p. 184, right: a Catholic church in Newport, Rhode Island. ©Howard Millard

p. 185, left: West Parish Church, West Barnstable, Massachusetts. ©John de Visser

p. 185, right: St. Michael's Russian Orthodox Cathedral, Sitka, Alaska. ©B. Crader/Tom Stack & Associates

5
The Exiles

Now, finally, the Pilgrim fathers—among other religious exiles—appear upon the stage. We have glanced at them, from time to time, as we dealt with those whose primary motivation in immigrating to America was for commerce or for proselytizing. Now we focus upon those exiles who came to be with their God, not primarily to convert others but to attempt a religious way of life they were denied at home. They came relatively late, after the Catholics, the Anglicans, and the Jews. But because their progeny have included many historians, they occupy a disproportionate place among American chronicles. The Irish may be great tellers of tales, but the Massachusetts Puritans have been great writers of history. To be fair, the Puritans claim our attention not merely because of the ceaseless flow of books from Cambridge; because the Puritans and Separatists had their priorities right, they have been influential far beyond their number, wealth, or primacy in time.

The term *Pilgrim fathers* may be harmlessly extended to include both the Puritans and the Separatists, neighboring settlers of Massachusetts who formed their lives around what they took most seriously, their religion. They did not live out their time accumulating trivial satisfactions or pursuing other people's opinions. If they sometimes seemed grim, if, indeed, they were nasty and intolerant, they did live in a grim time and did not wish to be distracted from what they believed to be at the core of life. Their communities were centered upon the meeting house, which was not coincidentally the church. It was a meeting house *because* it was a church. They came together and worshiped together because they had come from a country that had been torn by fratricidal violence and sectarian murder for more than a century. They preferred the modulated tranquillity of a peaceable kingdom to the discord they had left behind.

The orderly design of the New England village is liturgical, and so, too, is the choreography of its daily life, its goings and comings about the church/meeting house. Such a village presents almost the order and choreography of a monastic community. There is a wholeness in such a place. And, as the New England migration began at the end of the eighteenth century to spread across New York, across the Great Lakes states, and finally to Oregon, that wholeness reappears constantly. Villages grow around the green and can be identified by the steeple. Later, when the church moves to the side street, and is replaced by the bank and the county courthouse, we know the peaceable kingdom has faded into ancestral memory.

The Puritans' architecture has already received some attention here, juxtaposed to others. New England churches of this tradition and their progeny are so well known that very little more needs to be added beyond a

"Old Ship" Meetinghouse in Hingham, Massachusetts—the shape of the ceiling resembles the inverted hull of a ship. ©John de Visser

Mennonite meeting house in Lancaster, Pennsylvania. ©George A. Tice

straightforward statement that the Puritans elevated the sermon liturgically and the place where the sermon was delivered (the pulpit) physically. They took the auditory, one-room church of Wren and transformed it into a true auditorium. While the eye was deprived of color and images, the ear benefited from a succession of blessings. These began with congregational singing of the Psalms and swung on to the full theatrical apparatus at the end of the nineteenth century of a stageful of preachers, readers, and choir. We had come a long way from the mystic gloom of the Romanesque and the thick, thronging light of the Gothic. Yet all are ways to seek the Mystery, whether the chief means is the eye or the ear, the intellect or the heart.

The assault of the religious emotions upon the cool, self-confident religious intellect began, it might be said, with the Great Awakening, an evangelical outburst in the early eighteenth century a century after the exiles first landed. After 1750, revivals swept the South and West and even raised the temperature in New England, although it was not the center of the new movement. Before we examine the architectural expressions of the nineteenth century, which has been called the "Evangelical century" (or, more particularly, the "Methodist century"), we should be certain to suggest that even in the South and West, even at the height of emotional evangelism, Puritanism was very much alive among people who do not immediately come to mind when we say "Puritan."

The Moravian Protestants who came to Pennsylvania and North Carolina, the Puritans of East Jersey who centered around the little market town of Newark, the German Pietist sects like the Mennonites and Dunkers—and, later, the Shakers—the Baptists of Rhode Island the second- and third-generation descendants of Massachusetts Bay who immigrated to New York and Connecticut, all built and worshiped in similar, simple struc-

Vermont. ©Steve Rosenthal

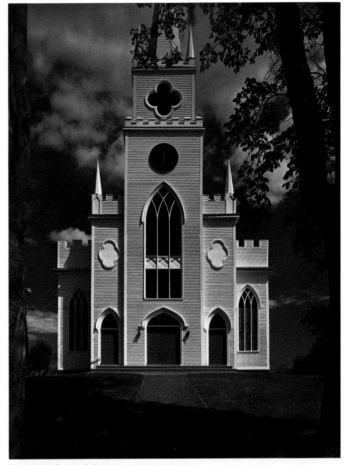

East Machias, Maine. ©Steve Rosenthal

York, Maine. ©Steve Rosenthal

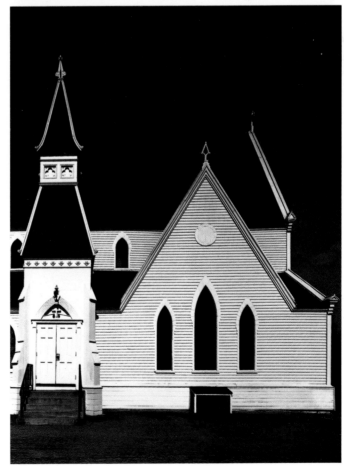

Westford, Massachusetts. ©Steve Rosenthal

The Greenfield Hill Congregational Church, Inc., Fairfield, Connecticut—from light to light.
©Andrew Stewart

tures. The interiors focused upon the pulpit, or the Communion table, or the baptismal font to differing degrees; music was important to some, disdained by others. But the absence of elaborate visual symbols and the austerity of the setting united them all.

Those radical Puritans, the Quakers, demonstrated how a community could come together to share its religious concerns without any impedimenta or, as they might put it, "distractions." For Quakers, like the later Christian Scientists, even a sermon was a distraction. Their architects had no occasion to lavish their skill upon the design of pulpits, which, for Quakers, had come to seem overelaborate, like ornate book bindings on a grand scale. The sermon was exposition of the Book: architecturally, the elaborate pulpits of some Catholic and Anglican churches seemed to Quakers, who needed no sermons, to be like the gem-encrusted covers placed upon the Bible in the Middle Ages. Other denominations of a Puritan orientation gave pulpits their own appropriate treatment: Congregationalists were proud of their learned clergy, and gave them solemn, massive pulpits, but not costly or elaborate ones. Baptists stressed Baptism; Congregationalists stressed Communion, but in the early churches they all avoided expensive visual symbols, not completely—like the Quakers—but almost so. Their symbols were actions, not objects.

190

In medieval days, some might recall, the symbols in a religious space were not felt to be impedimenta or distractions: icons had been transparent surfaces, windows to another world, the crowded light of the Gothic church invited the worshiper to join the heavenly throng. But the Puritans were ready to look directly into the face of the Mystery without the intercession of symbol or clergy. They were bold indeed.

Other settings for worship were simple, not necessarily by intention, but by necessity. From the time of the Great Awakening in the early eighteenth century, temporary structures for revival meetings have provided arenas into which great preachers invoked the presence of a redeeming spirit. Revivals have sustained into our own day those public confessions of faith that, long ago in Boston and New Haven, had been a requirement for inclusion in the congregation. Tents, where there was canvas at hand, "brush arbors" where there was none, provided shelter to keep off the sun or rain. These were all the evangelists needed, if the spirit came.

Despite eighteenth-century revivals, however, the nineteenth century opened at a low point in the life of organized religion in America. It has been estimated that not more than 10 percent of the population of the British colonies were members of churches at the time independence was declared. Circuit-riding preachers served a larger population, perhaps, but by far the greatest number of Americans were untouched by the experience of religious architecture. The Revolution itself disrupted matters even further. Many English soldiers of the French and Indian War and many of the French who served as the saviors of the military fortunes of Washington's army were no longer Christian in any sectarian sense, but deists. So were many of the leaders of the Revolution, like Thomas Jefferson. Ties of history and of financial support had bound the Anglicans and the Methodists to the mother country, and the Revolution resulted in severing those ties. That temple of Anglicanism, King's Chapel in Boston, went over to the Unitarians.

But the religious impulse was seeking new means of expression. In 1784, the Methodists reorganized to form a national church in the United States, and the Protestant Episcopal Church was founded in 1789. As the new nation began its independent life, 40 percent of its church-affiliated people were Presbyterians or Congregationalists, many of them tough Scotch-Irish pioneers who had entered America through the tolerant portal of Pennsylvania, had swept southwestward down the long central valley of the Appalachians, and were standing upon the last ridges looking out upon the plains of the Ohio and Tennessee valleys. In the north the villages of the Puritans still held firm and cloned themselves out across the upper Hudson. Baptists and Anglicans each accounted for about 15 percent; the great age of the Evangelical sects was dawning.

OLD SHIP MEETINGHOUSE (now CHURCH), Hingham, Massachusetts, 1681

Old Ship Meetinghouse is located nineteen miles southeast of Boston, in the town of Hingham, Massachusetts, an important maritime center of the seventeenth and eighteenth centuries.

Old Ship Meetinghouse is patterned upon English medieval precedents, older than the Classic revival of Sir Christopher Wren and James Gibbs, which dominated much of the religious architecture of colonial America. It is Gothic, as well as Puritan. It represents not only a breaking away from the liturgical practice of the Church of England, but also an effort to create a simple, direct gathering place, where secular activities were permeated by religious conviction.

Originally built in 1681, "Old Ship" was enlarged and remodeled in 1731 and in 1755, and finally was restored in 1930.

"Old Ship" derives its name from the shape of the framed roof, which resembles the inverted hull of a ship. It was the practice in the seventeenth century to appoint a "committee of three men" to examine meeting houses of other towns and to select the design that was appropriate for the town's needs. This is exactly what the men of Hingham did; their meeting house is built in the tradition of others in New England—Dorchester (1677), Ipswich (1653), and Concord (1667). It was roughly square, 55 feet long by 45 feet wide with a height of 21 feet to the eaves. At present, its dimensions are 75 feet by 55 feet.

The original roof was pitched from all four sides, carried by three "Hingham" trusses, with 45-foot tie beams resting on the main vertical frame of the building. Later the belfry was replaced by a cupola.

In the original interior, each side had seven oak benches; nine to ten persons were assigned to each bench. Nine shorter seats were located on the north side of the house at right angles to one another. A gallery went around three sides of the perimeter. Originally, no plaster was used; the walls were of exposed native pine clapboards.

In 1730, the east wall was pushed out 14 feet to provide more interior space; in 1731 a new belfry was erected; in 1734 the interior was plastered for the first time; in 1755 the west wall was pushed out 14 feet and changes were made on the roof on the north and south sides, making it more gentle in pitch; a new pulpit was placed on the north wall, with a double pulpit window opening behind it. The main entrance was on the south side of the meeting house.

From the first service, held on January 8, 1682, and given by Reverend John Norton, the Old Ship Meetinghouse served both the needs of the church and the town. Samuel Lincoln, ancestor of Abraham Lincoln, worshiped here regularly. Married men sat on the "northward" side, married women on the south, young men and "maids" in the galleries. Front seats in the church were reserved for the town elders (in the literal, not the Quaker, sense of the word) together with the deacons, one of whom was the church scribe. A Communion table, curved and shelflike, hinged in front of the deacon's seat, still remains.

In the late eighteenth century, boxed pews were constructed and sold at a public auction—a change of great significance from the earlier hierarchy. In 1869 curved Victorian pews were inserted.

Thanks to a gift by Eben Howard Gay, the parish was able to restore the church to an earlier form. The boxed pews were put back, modernization of the pulpit was removed, the ceiling covering the auditorium was removed, and the posts, trusses, and beams were restored.

Today the church stands in the same place as it did in 1681. It has weathered remodelings and the modern age. Old Ship Church is indeed a survivor.

ST. PAUL'S CHURCH (OLD NARRAGANSETT CHURCH),
Wickford, Rhode Island, 1707

"Old Narragansett"—St. Paul's Church—is the oldest Episcopal church in New England. Originally it was located southwest of Wickford, Rhode Island, on Shermantown Road, which, it was hoped, would become a link in the Boston-to-New-London route. The Church was half a mile west of what later became the Post Road; an early highway between New York and Boston. The original church was built of oak and plaster; bricks, of the sort used in King's Chapel, Boston, and lime for cement were expensive, and skilled masons were only available in major cities like Boston.

The church, built in 1707, received the support of the Society for the Propagation of the Gospel in Foreign Parts (SPGFP) of London. It was patterned after Christopher Wren's small parish churches in London, built after the Great Fire of 1666. Wren's plans were compatible with the Puritans' meeting-house design and, in American fusions of the two, often took a form indistinguishable from a detached home or small county courthouse.

St. Paul's is rectangular, under a gable roof with a double door, ornamented with pilasters and broken pediment made of pine. Constructed in a four bay form, the building has four palladial windows on each long side, and two on the short; the upper win-

©Bruce Whyte

dows are close under the eaves. The frame is split oak, and oak planks form the side clapboards. St. Paul's once had a belfry, added in 1811, and a bell, installed in 1820, but on a windless night in 1868, the bell and belfry collapsed, never to be rebuilt. A wooden, "wine glass" pulpit served the preachers.

St. Paul's thrived from 1721 to 1757 under the aegis of the "Apostle at Narragansett," the Reverend Doctor James MacSparran. MacSparran preached and baptized Indians and slaves as well as the slaveholders and congregation members; and it was for MacSparran that the reading desk was enlarged in 1721, as he weighed over 300 pounds at the time. John Smibert painted the MacSparrans during a visit to Wickford; Gilbert Stuart was baptized by the preacher in 1756.

During the Revolution the church was closed (because prayers had been said for the King) and used as a barracks for the colonial soldiers. St. Paul's never functioned dually as church and meeting place, as did its Puritan counterparts. And though it was reopened in 1784, St. Paul's, like many other American Anglican churches, lost the financial support of the "venerable society," which was dedicated to supporting churches in British colonies. Then in 1799, the elders of the congregation voted to move it to Church Lane in Wickford, a rapidly growing seaport five miles to the north. There, in a broad, open field donated specifically for the purpose, St. Paul's was rebuilt. Although the new Church was finished in 1800, it was not consecrated until May of 1820, due to an absence of bishops during the colonial and war periods.

There were changes. The square pews were reinstalled, but the original "wine glass" pulpit was replaced. The altar was moved to the east wall, with the pulpit and reading desk facing the entrance.

In 1848 another building, a new St. Paul's Church, was consecrated, and the older building was neglected until the late nineteenth century, when a movement to restore it gained popular support.

FIRST CONGREGATIONAL CHURCH,
Old Bennington, Vermont, 1804–5

The First Congregational Church of Old Bennington sits on a hill above the present town of Bennington, Vermont. Surrounded by beautiful houses from the same era, it faces the old town common.

From 1790 until 1800, Congregationalism spread throughout New England and westward with the great Yankee migration of the period. Vast areas of agricultural land were abandoned; New Englanders exchanged their old rocky hillside farms for the deep soil of the Midwest. As New England Congregationalists moved westward, they took their church architecture with them. The ensemble of buildings around the church in Old Bennington presents what they left behind; similar groupings in Taylors Falls, Minnesota, or Atwater, Ohio, exemplify their efforts to reconstruct those scenes from memory.

There are many reasons why New England can boast of beautiful town churches like First Congregational. It was the most prosperous region in the United States at the turn of the nineteenth century, with plenty of good lumber, able designers and craftsmen, among them Asher Benjamin. Born in Greenfield, Massachusetts, in 1772, he was a country carpenter who turned to design. In 1797 he published what is reputed to be the first "how to" handbook published by an American, *The Country Builder's Assistant*. It was reprinted many times and used throughout New England. Among its designs was one which Lavius Fillmore, the local builder of the First Congregational, used as the starting point for his church.

As a result, First Congregational in Old Bennington is, in a literal sense, a typical New England church of its time. It is of frame construction, covered with clapboard, built upon an above-grade masonry foundation. An entrance tower marks one short side. Characteristic "Federal" motifs, dainty and repetitive, mark the classical elements.

Lavius Fillmore did not merely reproduce Benjamin's model; he was an important designer in his own right. The transition in the tower from the square base to the top is quick, producing a stately structure topped with a dome. Fillmore's greatest contributions, however, are the graceful belfry with arched openings and the round tops of the upper rows of windows and the doors.

Within the church, the vaulted ceiling is groined and supported by six tall columns. The raised pulpit is supported by four columns and is reached by two stairways rising before a Palladian window, vastly "overscale" by classical standards and vastly effective in its present use. Traditional New England wooden pews line the front of the gallery, while the ground floor and rear of the gallery are graced with enclosed square box pews, allowing seating on three sides.

During research leading to its restoration in 1937, it was learned that two pews with sides 7 feet high were set apart at the rear of the church gallery for black people. The unmarried women sat in the south gallery, the unmarried men in the north, where extensive jackknife carvings give witness to their boredom with Puritan sermons.

People from all over the state contributed funds to restore First Congregational Church in Old Bennington, which has been made Vermont's colonial shrine. Robert Frost read the following lines at the dedication of the restored church in 1937:

Most of the change we think we see in life
Is due to truths being in and out of favour.
As I sit here, and oftentimes, I wish
I could be monarch of a desert land
I could devote and dedicate forever
To the truths we keep coming back and back to.

Mr. Frost and members of his family are buried in the old graveyard behind the church, the oldest in Vermont.

FIRST CHURCH OF CHRIST, Lancaster, Massachusetts, 1816

The masterpiece of Charles Bulfinch, "architect of Boston," is not in the capital of Massachusetts. It is approximately forty-five miles away in the little town of Lancaster: the First Church of Christ Unitarian. Built in 1816, the monumental brick structure exem-

©Bruce T. Martin/Picture Cube

plifies the imaginative possibilities within the Federal style.

Charles Bulfinch, born in 1763 into a prominent Boston family, graduated from Harvard in 1781, and then embarked upon a grand tour of Europe. Although he served as chairman of Boston's selectmen and as superintendent of police, Bulfinch had no head for business; his land and development ventures twice led to bankruptcy. After the second debacle, he turned seriously to architecture. His reputation rests upon a series of splendid exercises for Harrison Gray Otis, buildings for Harvard, Phillips Academy at Andover, Massachusetts, the Boston State House, improvements to the national Capitol in Washington, and the Lancaster meeting house.

Lancaster, one of many theocracies that existed in Massachusetts until 1830, commissioned the meeting house in 1815, as the church's fifth building since its founding in 1653. Square and open in plan, the auditorium is preceded by a narrower vestibule, which provides a vertical accent to the generally low massing of the building. The square tower is topped by an open Doric colonnade and dome. The cornice unifies the whole, and the simplicity of the exterior suggests an almost modern austerity. The local master builder, Thomas Hearsey, is reported to have added the curved corner pieces (volutes) to the tower and to have altered Bulfinch's plan to make the central archway higher than its left and right partners. Bulfinch intended a carved swag panel on the sides, but Hearsey made all the arches uniform.

The most striking interior feature is the vestibule staircase, which is quietly elegant. Bulfinch placed the pulpit in the center of the shorter wall, an unusual arrangement. Although the ceiling and walls of the interior have been redecorated since Bulfinch's time, the basic form—a large auditorium space with a balcony curving around the perimeter—is typical of New England meeting houses.

FIRST CHURCH OF CHRIST, New Haven, Connecticut, 1814

"Don't these damned Yankees do anything but build churches?" Tradition reports that these were the words of Commodore Hardy, commander of the British blockade on the Connecticut River during the War of 1812, upon allowing the passage of three shipments of oak timbers for the construction of churches. There were, indeed, three churches built in New Haven during the War of 1812. The oldest, the First Church of Christ, built in 1814, is also known as the "Center Church" because of its position on the New Haven green. The two other churches on the green are the United Church and the Trinity Episcopal Church, both built in 1815.

Many of the Congregational churches being built in New England were influenced by the handbook published by Asher Benjamin, *The Country Builder's Assistant*. These churches evolved directly from the colonial patterns based upon the Wren-Gibbs prototypes in England, the most influential of which was St. Martin-in-the-Fields in London. But Benjamin's "Federal" style brought into play a freer American variety of Neoclassicism, which appeared in a multitude of clapboard churches with towers and spires containing many classical features not deployed by Christopher Wren or James Gibbs.

Ithiel Town was the architect for this building, working from a plan purchased from Benjamin, with whom Town had worked in Boston.

The congregation goes back to the very early days of the settlement, when New Haven was a theocracy and town and church were one. It is a fully developed, Classic revival church of the Federal style, with a rectangular nave and frontal tower. Taking a cue from the refinements of Periclean Athens, the tower columns lean inward slightly. Popular history holds that the builders constructed the entire spire on the ground before inserting it through the tower to its final position. The pedimented portico with Doric colonnade gives the First Church of Christ its distinctiveness. The frieze is ornamented with styl-

ized bull skulls, symbols that reach back to a more primitive era.

Since its original construction, the pulpit and gallery have been lowered and the original pews removed. More recently, the stained-glass windows, except for the chancel window, have been replaced by clear glass. The existing edifice, built to the rear of the third church building, was erected over part of the town's first burial ground. As a result, its crypt contains 135 headstones. Yale University commencements were held in the church until 1895.

FIRST CONGREGATIONAL CHURCH,
Old Lyme, Connecticut, 1817

©Bruce Whyte

The Congregational Church in Old Lyme, Connecticut, designed by Samuel Belcher in 1817 and reconstructed to his designs in 1907, stands on the main street of the town. With its elegant Ionic portico and graceful steeple and spire, the church epitomizes the beauty inherent in the Federal style. Like many other churches in New England, it is constructed of wood and is painted white. It is composed of a rectangular nave, approximately three bays wide and five bays long. The design of the early New England meeting house is apparent in the simple main body of this church, as in many other Congregational churches. It presents a square clock tower, a square belfry, an octagonal stage, and an octagonal spire, all delicately ornamented with pilasters and columns. A projecting portico, supported by four Ionic columns and topped with a simple pediment, marks the entrance to the church.

The Congregational Church of Old Lyme recalls the larger Center Church in New Haven, built three years earlier than the original church building, and, in turn, the much larger St. Martin-in-the-Fields in London. Yet, in its setting, amid ancient trees and houses of the same style and feeling, Old Lyme has long seemed to epitomize the New England of the opulent shore, so different from the harsh New England of the mountains. It has been much beloved by painters, of whom the American Impressionist, Childe Hassam, is probably the best known. Lesser-known figures, too, are often to be seen moving their easels about before it, seeking that perfect patch of shadow which appears to be purple upon the gleaming white façade.

FIRST CONGREGATIONAL CHURCH, Hancock, New Hampshire, 1820

UNITED CHURCH, Acworth, New Hampshire, 1820

SOUTH CONGREGATIONAL CHURCH, Newport, New Hampshire, 1823

CONGREGATIONAL CHURCH, Atwater, Ohio, 1838–41

In three small New Hampshire towns—Hancock, Acworth, and Newport—architect Elias Carter left prominent marks of beauty in the form of churches. Born in Auburn, Massachusetts, in 1781, Carter designed and built many churches in New England, including the Federated Church in Templeton, Massachusetts (1811). The Federated Church served as a model for many others, including those in Hancock, Acworth, and Newport. All display a vertically elliptical window in the pediment and a row of downward-pointed brackets below the cornice.

Built in 1820, the portico of the First Congregational Church in Hancock carries pilasters, not the columns of Templeton. Like its predecessor, the church features a common lintel for its three entrance doors and a steeple composed of a square, open-arched belfry topped by two octagonal stages and a spire. In 1851, the town divided the church into two stories and moved it across the road to its present site. The lower level is used as a town hall, the upper level as the church auditorium.

Farther north is the United Church in Acworth, also built in 1820. It faces the common, flanked by the town hall and local school. Unlike its contemporary in Hancock, its three entrance doors are separate and arched. Its steeple, however, reproduces that of the Templeton church except that a dome has replaced the spire. The Acworth church was constructed in the pastorate of Phineas Cooke, called the "Apostle of New Hampshire," an early leader of the temperance movement. The church presently uses both stories of the building.

The South Congregational Church in Newport, built in 1823, is the farthest north of the three. Its steeple is almost a reproduction of that at Acworth. But brick, not wood, composes the main body of the church, with a course of light stone at the level of the tops of its windows. The three entrance doors are again separate but are surrounded by blind arches, which include the upper windows. These windows are much simpler than those on the Hancock and Acworth churches.

The three churches, expressions of the Wren-Gibbs tradition that persists in rural New England, serve as meeting houses at the center of their small communities. Their towers, of course, are also ex-

Nantucket, Massachusetts. ©Steve Rosenthal

201

©James Kittle

©James Kittle

First Congregational Church, Hancock, New Hampshire.

United Church, Acworth, New Hampshire.

South Congregational Church, Newport, New Hampshire.

©James Kittle

Congregational Church, Atwater, Ohio. ©Frank Aleksandrowicz

pressions of the much older tradition, which began in the campaniles along the Adriatic in the tenth and eleventh centuries and continued in the Gothic spires of the Île de France and the Renaissance churches of London.

The Gothic sometimes reasserted itself; spiky towers had appeared even in the work of Wren himself; and as the Yankee migration moved across New York and into the Midwest, it encountered the Gothic revival of the 1830s. In Atwater, Ohio, between 1838 and 1841, the Congregationalists, a generally conservative lot, made about as much of an adjustment to the new fashion as might be expected.

Atwater lies in that portion of northern Ohio occupied by Yankees—some of them came to receive land as compensation for losses suffered in British raids during the War for Independence. In its general form, it is a church that might have been built amid the New Hampshire cluster, but it is not so traditional (in one sense) and more traditional in another: it breaks away from the Yankee form of the white, severe, rectangular meeting house/church by adding pointed windows and doors, which unite it, by a very restrained reference, to the cathedrals of Europe and to the early Gothic revival buildings the Anglicans were building at the same time.

Nantucket, Massachusetts. ©Steve Rosenthal

6
The Great Century

The nineteenth century has been called the "Age of the Great Revival," the "Evangelical century," and, more narrowly, the "Methodist century." It was all these and more.

The nineteenth century presented the first opportunity in two thousand years for the Jews to deploy large physical resources upon their own synagogues. A few early congregations, like those at Charleston and Newport, had been able to do so earlier, but only after 1800 were many rich enough and safe enough to do so. In 1820 there were only about 5,000 Jews in the United States, and though they had been powerful intellectual and commercial forces in Charleston, New York, and Newport, they had not yet made much of a physical impact upon the American landscape. But nearly one hundred times that number emigrated from central Europe in the next three decades, and 2 million more, largely from eastern Europe, by the end of the century. Their places of worship, like the Jews themselves, were almost exclusively urban, where their presence made an indelible impression upon American aesthetic and intellectual life.

Alongside the appearance of Jewish religious practices in the cities came a remarkable resurgence of the old sacramental churches, the Catholics and Episcopalians especially. Vast numbers of immigrant Roman Catholics, who are not generally described as "evangelicals" came into America, and during several decades they probably grew more rapidly than did the Methodists. An important aspect of the Anglican resurgence was symbolized by the Gothic revival.

Among historians of religion, however, the revival that counts is not one affecting the forms of buildings but the forms of worship, not the crockets and finials but the spirit. The resurgence of the Anglicans and the Roman Catholics is important, and so is the first palpable appearance of Judaism in the great new cities. But the nineteenth century was most obviously the century of the evangelical churches. We have good reason to use the term "Great Revival" for this phenomenon, because it occurred most vehemently in the folded valleys of the Appalachians and in the great flat river basin west of those mountains. To focus attention there is useful because this may balance a picture that otherwise might be distorted by the persuasiveness of those Yankee historians who tend to depict American history as if it all occurred within easy commuting distance of Cambridge, Massachusetts. They are interested in the second Great Awakening, which was very important in New England and involved some great prose writers, but was only a small part of a larger upsurge of renewed Christianity.

During this extended evangelical period churches did, indeed, achieve extraordinary gains. Twice as large a proportion of Americans were church members in 1850 as had been in 1800. The Methodists, in particular, had

An Episcopal mission church in Lauder, Wyoming. ©William Felger/Grant Heilman

grown from a tiny offshoot of Anglicanism, organized only in 1784, to more than a million in 1844, by far the largest single group of Christians in the country at that time. The magnitude of this feat can be comprehended when we recall that the total population of the nation was only 4 million in the 1790s, and these people were spread over half a huge continent.

John Wesley, the spiritual guide to Methodism and the man who developed its "method" (its extraordinarily successful mode of organization), did not make it easy. Wesley taught that people could be improved, but that they had a long way to go. They were not hopelessly depraved, but they had need of a clergy to lead them and Sacraments, including frequent Communion. These were not facile doctrines, nor, on the other hand, were they forbiddingly Puritan. Repentance was as much the heart of his ministry as it was of the Baptists, originally Puritans, who also enormously increased their following in those years. Nineteenth-century evangelism was seldom casual or vacuously optimistic. Rather its power came of a willingness of the churches to go out to the people without patronizing them or asking them to defer to a clergy educated in a literary way—and a capacity to organize on a grand scale in a very raw country.

Peter Cartwright, the circuit rider, explained how the farmer-preachers of the Baptists and the circuit riders of the Methodists filled the vast spaces left open by what he called the more finiking and expensive (and we might call architectural) requirements of the Episcopalians and Presbyterians. They "used to contend for an educated ministry, for pews, for instrumental music, for a congregational or stated salaried ministry." He and his colleagues "opposed these ideas; and the illiterate Methodist preachers . . . set the world on fire . . . while they were lighting their matches!"

The tinder was dry. Blacks and whites alike were unmoved by the desiccated rationalism of deism and lonely for religious life in a community of people who confessed to the same temptations and troubles and fears as they.

Though people of all sorts might assemble in a love feast, this was a time of intense theological competition among preachers, who were free from the embracing constraints of the old mainline denominations and could each create a sect of his or (often) her own. A fissiparation into a multitude of sects ensued. The hardening of a spiritual experience into a doctrinal shell occurred quickly, and the West accumulated as many theological crustaceans as a west Florida beach. This process was exacerbated by the very seriousness of religious life. Large questions, like slavery and temperance, and complex symbolic and theological issues newly rediscovered cut cruelly across the great churches and divided them North from South, synod from

Lovely Lane Methodist Episcopal Church in Baltimore, Maryland—a center of Methodist evangelism.
©Robert C. Lautman

synod, hard and soft, wet and dry.

We will not here attempt another compendium of histories of the pro-liferating sects of the period. There are a number of excellent books of that sort already, and since we are presenting some selected examples of churches, not even an encyclopedia of church architecture, we can move on to allude to the phenomenon that distinguishes this period from any other in religious history. This was the presence of vast new material resources (the country was getting rich very quickly) and vast accumulated good will in an open arena. These coincidences led to the formation of voluntary groups of like-minded people to achieve secular objectives from a religious point of view. The uniquely American charitable and fraternal "sector" came to life.

Missionary societies (domestic and foreign), Bible societies and tract so-cieties, Sunday schools—innumerable colleges, seminaries, high schools—temperance and moral societies, abolition societies, and societies for the protection of the deaf, the dumb, the blind, children, animals, homeless women, working women, seamen, and the generalty of the destitute—filled the land. All, or nearly all, required buildings. All are, in a sense, religious buildings, but not in the narrow sense we are employing. So we shall turn aside from recording them here. (We can also turn away from the vexed question of whether the new asylums and prisons, based upon industrial models, actually achieved the purposes of their humanitarian sponsors bet-ter or worse than had those they replaced.)

This was the time, in short, when people felt with Emerson that "in the history of the world the doctrine of reform never had such scope. . . . we are to revise our whole social structure—the state, the school, religion, mar-riage, trade, science, and explore the foundations of our own nature." Exploring the foundations of human nature! People were engaging in the restoration of the universe from the damage done by that nature, probing within it for what was good, sometimes with excessive hope in what Emer-son called the "infinite worthiness in man." The evangelicals set about rebuilding the cosmos, though they had few illusions that the work would be easy. They worked to clean up the debris of humanity's errors, in the "conviction . . . that all particular reforms are the removing of some impediment."

This time is not yet over. Its architecture is continuous with ours. Since our own ecclesiastical history is sufficiently familiar as to require no more extended a description here, it remains for us to sketch out the important parts of that history which expressed themselves in architecture.

German Gothic at St. Mary's in the Mountains, Virginia City, Nevada.
©Mirko J. Pitner/After-Image

CHURCH OF ST. JOHN CHRYSOSTOM,
Delafield, Wisconsin, 1851–53

©John de Visser

"Without fitness of arrangement and adaptation to the end proposed, no structure—however elaborate and costly—can be pronounced truly beautiful—and with these qualities the simplest and plainest edifice may claim the praise." So wrote Richard Upjohn in an advertisement for his book of church designs entitled *Rural Architecture*. He had been deluged by requests from needy parishes for simple, low-cost plans for churches, so Upjohn published the book as a manual for unskilled builders, translating into wood the stone lineaments of the Gothic.

A design for a wooden church very closely resembling St. John's appears in *Rural Architecture*. It is probable that Upjohn sent the parish the plans prior to their publication, since the book was published in 1852, the year after the church was begun.

It was built on a frontier, on ground taken not long before from the Indians, in Black Hawk's War, and a decade before the Sioux War broke out not far to the west. Constructed of oak timbers in the "board and batten" method (wherein planks are placed vertically and their joints covered with thin strips of wood), the church has a vertical emphasis, reinforced by the extremely steep pitch of its gable roof. The bell tower stands apart from the church. Both buildings are trimmed with a sort of "gingerbread," created not with a jigsaw, as in later buildings, but by traditional methods of carpentry.

It is the interior that reveals the full beauty of the design: somber dark wood, small stained-glass windows, and muted lighting. The altar, the primary liturgical center, is located in the sanctuary. The chancel is partially hidden from the view of the laity by a rood screen, so named because of the large cross, or rood, that surmounts it. The woodworking is carefully and smoothly finished, unlike the rough appearance of the exterior; the open-beam ceiling, which rises steeply to the ridge beam, completes the effect.

Hundreds of such "carpenter Gothic" buildings sprang up across the country, melding the general "feel" of the Gothic basilica to the vernacular traditions of American building; but there is none more beautiful and appropriate to its setting than St. John Chrysostom.

UNITARIAN CHURCH, Charleston, South Carolina, 1852–54

NEW TABERNACLE FOURTH BAPTIST CHURCH, Charleston, South Carolina, 1862

Unitarian Church, Charleston, South Carolina. ©Tom Jimison

Unitarian Church, Charleston, South Carolina. ©Ron Anton Rocz

In the middle years of the nineteenth century, the Gothic revival increasingly replaced Classical forms as "the only proper style" for Christian churches. Older buildings were often remodeled in the Gothic mode.

The Unitarians of Charleston presented a difficult problem of Gothicizing to Francis D. Lee, their architect. Their building at 8 Archdale Street was a High Georgian structure built between 1774 and 1784. Rectangular in plan and of squat proportions, it was ill-suited to the proposed remodeling into "soaring" Gothic. Lee began by applying buttresses and finials to the exterior; the tower was sheathed in a Gothic shell and given a few extra feet of "aspiration." The windows, which had been round-arched and double-hung in typical Georgian style, were extended upward to add pointed arches and given stained glass with elaborate tracery.

On the interior, Lee produced a hung ceiling of lath and plaster in a marvelous free adaptation of the stone fan-and-pendant vaults of the Chapel of Henry VII in Westminster Abbey. The Charleston interior is well described by William H. Pierson as "an exquisite masterpiece of fakery which is visually delightful but structurally illogical."

Concessions were made to accommodate the size of the congregation by retaining the side galleries, which were not characteristic of the Gothic style. The interior is spacious and open, calling attention to the complexity of the curved, intricate ceiling and away from its proportions.

In 1885 a hurricane blew down the spire of the tower; the following year, an earthquake produced further damage.

Lee's masterpiece in the Gothic style, however, is across town at the corner of Charlotte and Elizabeth streets. Originally to have been St. Luke's Church, designed for a congregation of Episcopalians, it was wholly Lee's creation, with no concessions required to accommodate an earlier building. Even though it was left unfinished, like the Brooklyn Bridge and the Washington Monument, it is far more handsome in its raw, expressive state than it could have been with its structure stuccoed over and its design made fussy in accordance with the original plans.

The church, constructed in 1862, was a grand brick structure, containing a huge single room in the shape of a Greek cross, 100 feet by 80 feet. A cluster of Gothic windows, 37 feet high, graces each side. Tudor arches spring from the interior columns to the ceiling, which is 55 feet high. During the Civil War, shells damaged the exterior and federal troops stripped the church, which was further injured by the hurricane of 1885 and earthquake of 1886. Now the church is alive again, repaired and improved, with a new altar, a new organ, and a new congregation. In 1950, the New Tabernacle Fourth Baptist Church bought the St. Luke's church buildings for $55,000. A new cornerstone was laid in 1952, bearing its new name. On Sunday mornings it is one of the great religious spaces in America.

Unitarian Church, Charleston, South Carolina. ©Ron Anton Rocz

214

New Tabernacle Fourth Baptist Church, Charleston, South Carolina. ©Ron Anton Rocz

FIRST UNITARIAN CHURCH,
Philadelphia, Pennsylvania, 1883–86

©Walter Smalling, Jr.

Few more dramatic reversals in critical opinion can be found than those which have eddied about Frank Furness and his architecture. Furness dropped in public esteem in the early twentieth century, and only recently has his reputation begun to revive. The consequence of such abrupt changes in "taste" was the wholesale destruction and alteration of what were later recognized as irreplaceable works of art.

Furness's First Unitarian Church on Chestnut Street in Philadelphia has suffered from these shifts of fashion. Although still distinctive and recognizably a Furness building, its character has been weakened by alterations meant to modulate a robust, eccentric Victorian into something more suitable to the anxiously classicist 1920s and 1930s.

Furness drew from north Italian prototypes for his design. Following the publication of John Ruskin's *Seven Lamps of Architecture,* many architects designed buildings with Ruskin's motley features: restless varieties of texture and color, out-of-scale ornament, complicated and irregular plans, and intricate massing. Furness managed to create his own style out of the Ruskinian Gothic, a style that elicited strong reactions, both positive and negative. Furness was at his most aggressive in 1883 in his design for First Unitarian, where his father had been minister. It is an assemblage of gently pointed arches and what was originally rusticated masonry. It is "picturesque," "brutal," and, to some, of "perverse originality."

Like most meeting houses, Furness's church has a broad, open plan, best described as a Greek cross with a shortened transept. The walls are divided by a chair rail, below which is wood paneling and plaster above. The stained-glass windows (which were originally clear leaded glass) are large and simple in shape, while above them a wood-and-iron trussed ceiling adds drama. Before it was modernized, there were openings in the roof to permit light to break through down from the ridge, and the roof was of red fish-scale terra-cotta tiles. After nearly seventy years of the same dull colors, the interior was repainted in 1982, in its original design of bright blue and red with gilt lilies.

The architect's father, William Furness, spoke prophetically in 1870 to the American Institute of Architects of the problem the First Unitarian Church was to encounter in the twentieth century: "With all our freedom," he said, "we do not tolerate oddness. We insist, in this country, upon everything's being cut to one pattern.... It is an adventurous thing... to set before us anything of which we cannot at once tell what to think. We resent it... take... the law of taste into our own hands, and condemn it."

Even in its crippled state, Furness's First Unitarian can run rings around most American architecture of succeeding years. It is fortunate that its congregation now appreciates it.

TRINITY CHURCH,
Boston, Massachusetts, 1872–77

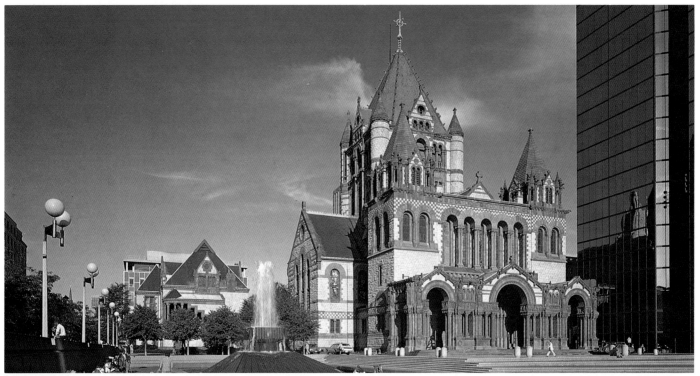

©Richard Cheek

Henry Hobson Richardson's first great architectural success was Trinity Church in the City of Boston. Phillips Brooks, its rector, said at Richardson's funeral in 1886: "Whoever came in contact with his works felt the wind blew out of an elemental simplicity, out of the primitive life and qualities of man. . . . It was that which made his work delightful."

Richardson attended the University of Louisiana, Harvard, and the École des Beaux-Arts and began his career in 1865 in New York City. His style (which is sometimes called "Richardsonian Romanesque") deployed monumental stonework, massive low arches, bulky towers, brightly colored brick, stone, and terra cotta.

Trinity Church was erected on Copley Square in the period 1872–77. The original site, changed to a larger truncated triangular one after six architects were invited to submit competition drawings and Richardson was chosen, permitted the exterior to be designed to gladden the eye from several approaches. The use of Dedham granite, left rough from the quarry, with Longmeadow sandstone trim shows Richardson in his most eclectic mode (which can be compared on p. 220 to his clear, serene, "modern" mode).

Richardson's delight in bits and pieces of ancient buildings, recreated with archaeological accuracy, and in the French Romanesque in particular, appears in the detailing and polychrome decoration of the apse. The design of the dominant central lantern-shaped tower was derived from one of those at the Cathedral of Salamanca. The elaborate porch was added in the mid-1890s by Richardson's successors, Shepley, Rutan, and Coolidge.

The interior is a large, open auditorium with a huge semicircular chancel completely remodeled in 1937 by Charles D. Maginnis. The choir stalls and rector's chair were added in 1902, and the elaborate pulpit in 1916.

Henry Hobson Richardson and Phillips Brooks were not the only powerful figures whose influence is felt at Trinity. The whole vast space bears the imprint of the decorative genius of John La Farge, whose superb stained glass is the glory of the west front. But he also oversaw all the mural decoration, doing the more important figures and the two large paintings himself; and the three other windows in the nave and transepts are his work. In the north transept, as well as one in the baptistry, are windows by William Morris and Burne-Jones. Trinity was conceived as a brilliant statement of the unapologetic opulence and confidence of nineteenth-century Boston.

217

ST. MARY'S-IN-TUXEDO, Tuxedo Park, New York, 1888
ST. GABRIEL'S CHURCH, Chicago, Illinois, 1887

St. Mary's-in-Tuxedo, Tuxedo Park, New York. ©Colin Chambers

Though H. H. Richardson and Frank Furness were unrivaled among the architects of American churches on a grand, picturesque, ceremonial scale in the nineteenth century, there were many splendid monuments to the skills of others in developing that American idiom. Nothing in Britain, still inhibited by the Gothic revival, could match the heft and rock-and-shingle freedom of American church building in the 1880s and 1890s, just as nothing in America, except perhaps some of the work of Tiffany Studios and the Bryn Athyn Cathedral (see pp. 102–105), could match the final glories of the "Arts and Crafts" chapels of Britain in the subsequent Edwardian years.

One can find "Richardsonian" churches (build-ings that show how gladly other architects responded to Richardson's challenge to work without inhibition in shingles and boulders and broad, beefy expanses of brick) wherever congregations could afford to employ these architects and these materials. Two such examples will merely suggest the exuberant variety.

St. Mary's was built in Tuxedo Park, New York, in 1888. Tuxedo Park was conceived by Pierre Lorillard, a tobacco magnate who had an excellent eye for real estate, as a community of estates to be served by railroad. The land is magnificent, amid the high granite ridges of the Ramapo Mountains, with deep lakes, streams, great pines, and hemlocks. The Episcopal church at Tuxedo served a congregation that included the Astors and Emily Post. In 1900, according to a contemporary report, their vehicles made quite a spectacle as they wound down the hill to the church: ''surreys, landaus, phaetons, yellow basket Victorias with parasol tops, watchmen, and grooms dressed in livery...behind the wire fence the deer were silent spectators.''

The architect for St. Mary's was the fashionable William A. Potter, son of one bishop and brother of another. Potter was trained as a chemist, but he soon showed great skill in the Richardsonian use of rough masonry, round arches, shingles, and asymmetrical plans. Richardson had shown the way in libraries, town halls, and gatehouses for similar enclaves in Massachusetts.

The interior, originally a dark, richly paneled room with a heavy diaphragm-arched ceiling of timber, was remodeled some time after 1910. Today it is lighter and more open; much of the woodwork has been removed. The effect is different than that originally intended, though not unpleasant. It is an elegant survivor of its time; so is Tuxedo Park.

St. Gabriel's in Chicago was designed by the hugely successful firm of Burnham and Root (and its successor), best known for their work on such early skyscrapers as the Rookery and Monadnock Buildings of Chicago; for the planning of Manila, the Philippines, San Francisco, and the Chicago Lakefront; and for commercial buildings in London, New York, Duluth, and scores of other cities. When St. Gabriel's was built in 1887 at 4500 S. Lowe Avenue, it was considered a suburban church serving an Irish Catholic community. Chicago, in the intervening years, has grown to the point of engulfing the neighborhood of St. Gabriel's. The parish has remained active since its founding.

Alterations include the addition of an entrance porch, the removal of a section of the bell tower, and remodeling of the vaulted interior. However, the basic forms and configuration remain as they came from the drafting boards of Daniel Burnham and John Root in 1887.

St. Gabriel's Church, Chicago, Illinois.
©Gary Milburn/Tom Stack & Associates

EMMANUEL EPISCOPAL CHURCH,
Pittsburgh, Pennsylvania, 1883–86

©Jack E. Boucher/HABS–courtesy of Library of Congress

The building committee of Emmanuel Episcopal Church commissioned H. H. Richardson's office for designs in August 1883 for a church to be constructed on the corner of Allegheny and West North avenues in what is now Pittsburgh's north side. Richardson was already at work upon the competition designs for a vast complex of Allegheny County buildings in Pittsburgh. The original plans for the church, submitted in 1884, were for a stone building under a dome, resembling the architect's earlier success, Trinity Church in Boston. The design called for the typical Richardsonian Romanesque building with heavy, low massing, rusticated masonry, rounded arches, a steep gable roof topped by a peaked tower, and a cruciform plan. The building costs would have been four times greater than the congregation could afford, so the building committee requested "other plans for a much plainer church building to cost, say, $12,000 or $15,000, . . . complete and ready for use, but so constructed as to permit enlargement." The final product is a fresh, clean Richardson design with a smooth brick façade, an abstraction of a Romanesque form, under a dominating gable roof that cost close to $25,000.

The entrances are cut into the smooth façade, with no carved ornament. The interior is also straightforward, with exposed rafters and unadorned beams, giving one the same sense of power one feels in Old Ship Meetinghouse (see p. 193). Allegheny Avenue wall began to lean outward within a year of the building's completion, but has remained stable in this condition for nearly a century, earning the local moniker, "The Leaning Wall of Pittsburgh." In its once fashionable neighborhood, full of down-at-the-heels architectural survivors of the eclectic 1880s, it may look (in the words of James Van Trump) "like a mastodon at a fancy dress party" (the garish red sign it bears makes it look more like a stuffed mastodon in a natural history museum). But it is now "going again" as an interracial church catering to the poor with a ministry of the gospel and social action to serve inner-city needs.

FIRST CHURCH OF CHRIST, SCIENTIST,
Berkeley, California, 1909–11

The Christian Scientist Church at 2619 Dwight Way in Berkeley is a reflection of the genius of Bernard Maybeck and the receptivity of its congregation to that genius.

Maybeck was an "original." He was also, perhaps, the last of America's great Victorian architects, of the unrepentant line of H. H. Richardson and Frank Furness (see pp. 216 and 217). Though educated in the rigors of the École des Beaux-Arts in Paris, he managed to combine old forms and new materials to create the Maybeck style. The Christian Science Church displays, quite candidly, industrial materials and a modern concern for structural articulation, yet makes free use of motifs from traditional sources, including the Japanese, the American vernacular, and the Gothic. Maybeck rejected any archaeological reuse of historical precedents, but he felt quite free to doff his hat in various directions.

Impressed by the sincerity of his clients (who insisted that he was the architect they wanted, having considered the matter prayerfully), Maybeck began his design as if he were a twelfth-century craftsman with access to modern technology. Confusion often resulted from his use of industrial materials for the church; in fact, one company which manufactured steel sash refused at first to tender an estimate because it felt its product inappropriate for a church. When the estimate finally came in, Maybeck noted that the "inappropriate" material was also noticeably inexpensive. In addition to steel factory sash, he employed cement asbestos board, poured-and-cast concrete alongside rough-sawed Douglas fir, stained and leaded glass, and redwood. Turning adversity to advantage, he used the accidentally wrinkled finish on the concrete lecterns to create a floral pattern.

The church is essentially square in plan, with a clerestory and cross-gable roofs. The seating was designed so that the members of the congregation could see one another when they rose to speak. The open ceiling exposes the structure of the roof, which is a trusswork of wood and structural steel. Vivid stenciling provides a contrast to the colors of wood and concrete.

Maybeck believed in "total design," and took responsibility not only for the building but its fittings as well: windows, chandeliers, seating, and lecterns. He coordinated the ornament with the structure and orchestrated every detail for total effect. The result, with massive beams and shifting perspectives, has been described (with Vincent Scully's usual flair) as "fluid with energies running through it." Maybeck and Scully—the most ingenius and elegant architectural writer of our era—deserve each other.

©Julius Shulman

ST. JAMES' EPISCOPAL CHAPEL,
Grosse Ile, Michigan, 1867–68

©Robert D. Beard

In 1858 Gordon Lloyd, a young Englishman raised in Canada and trained at the Royal Academy, arrived in Detroit to begin an architectural career. While working in his uncle's architectural office in London, Lloyd had learned the English Gothic style as revived by Augustus W. Pugin. He may also have been influenced by Sir George Gilbert Scott, who was then lecturing at the Royal Academy. Lloyd's sketches from a tour of Continental Europe before his immigration to the United States reflect a romantic interest in the Gothic as well.

Lloyd received several important commissions in Detroit, all of which provided an opportunity for exercises in the Gothic. Since many of the builders could not afford the expensive stone construction, Lloyd was allowed to be very original in the use of arcades, shortened naves, semioctagonal transepts, and a multiplicity of other forms.

St. James' Episcopal Chapel is on Grosse Ile near Detroit. It is one of several of Lloyd's churches that refer not only to English Gothic but also to the work of Richard Upjohn (see p. 211). Lloyd learned from Upjohn how to create handsome Gothic churches of wood. A bell cote of vertical battens broken by wood buttresses like those of the roof surmounts the façade. It is pleasant to see how St. James' Chapel compares to Upjohn's great churches in Wisconsin (see p. 211) in scale, in style, and in materials.

CHURCH OF ST. JAMES THE LESS,
Philadelphia, Pennsylvania, 1846–48

Spurred on by the English *Ecclesiologist*, many American Anglicans in the middle of the nineteenth century attempted to revive the liturgy of the Gothic age. St. James' stands in America as an earnest effort to reconstruct a medieval church in a rural English parish. It was successful, and it influenced the architecture and liturgy of many subsequent churches.

The Ecclesiologists were Anglican reformers. Reacting against the cold rationality of the unadorned Protestant churches that were built after the Reformation, they hoped to see the rituals of the church return within a highly symbolic Gothic style. They asserted that only within a proper medieval church could the Sacraments be properly administered.

In Philadelphia, Samuel Farmar Jarvis heeded the Ecclesiologists, especially the Cambridge Camden

Society, from which he requested plans for St. James the Less. These plans were sent by George Gordon Hall of Nottingham in October 1844. Jarvis remarked that "the chancel...should always be a separate building from the nave." The separation, of course, was of the clergy from the laity.

St. James the Less was modeled after the Church of St. Michael in Longstanton, Cambridgeshire. St. Michael's was one of three thought by the Cambridge Camden Society to be "correct" in size, shape, and character for the colonies. (They recommended the simpler Norman style for New Zealand, a province they deemed more primitive than the North American "colonies.") Cruciform churches like St. Mary's, Burlington (see p. 225), remind one of great cathedrals; they could not possibly have been built in rural towns. Instead, St. Michael's and St. James' have a one-story nave with a high, steeply pitched roof and a small, similarly shaped chancel, and south porch. They have no frontal tower and spire, but instead, a bell gable rising from the plane of the wall.

Robert Ralston directed the work, paying meticulous attention to the Society's drawings. The vestry originally allotted $3,000 for construction, but as their enthusiasm for the project grew, they added $27,000 more. Even the Cambridge Camden Society was pleased with the work.

Earlier American Gothic revival churches had had plastered interiors, but when instructed that exposed granite was more authentically Gothic, the Philadelphians left theirs unadorned.

A high stone wall and nineteenth-century cemetery now isolate St. James the Less from urban Philadelphia. Once inside its cool stone walls, the sounds of traffic dim, and one can feel a strange sense of stepping into another time, place, or world. Within St. James the Less, one could almost be in a village church waiting for the vicar, or perhaps in another medieval basilican church, like Acoma, across the continent in New Mexico.

ST. MARY'S EPISCOPAL CHURCH,
Burlington, New Jersey, 1846–48

St. Mary's in Burlington, New Jersey, is Richard Upjohn's masterpiece in stone, as St. John Chrysostom in Delafield, Wisconsin, shows his genius in wood (see p. 211).

The English followers of Ecclesiology, in reaction to the secularization of Anglicanism during the eighteenth century, sought to restore a liturgy of reverence and to encase it in appropriate architecture. The Gothic, said the Cambridge Camden Society, pamphleteers of Ecclesiology, was the only "true" Christian architecture. In the hope of spreading Ecclesiologically "correct" architecture to "the colonies," measured drawings were published in the 1840s and 1850s which could serve as patterns even for unskilled builders. Richard Upjohn, a man of broad education and of many skills, chose a Gothic model when, in 1846, he began to design a church for Burlington. He chose as his model drawings of the fourteenth-century parish church of St. John the Baptist in Shattesbrooke, Berkshire, England. The drawings had been published by a rival group at Oxford University, so the Cambridge-based pamphlet, *Ecclesiologist*, expressed alarm at what it saw as a poor choice.

For the exterior, Upjohn chose New Jersey freestone, which could be precisely carved and provided variety of texture and color. He used the cruciform plan of the drawings (in contrast to most American Protestant churches of the time, which were rectangular) and its central tower. Yet he was not slavishly reliant upon his model. He provided a graceful transition between the tower and the steeple, curving the walls inward, a juncture clumsily handled in the original. The nave was lengthened to double the size of the chancel; slender buttresses alternate with lancet windows on the exterior. Inside, a tunnel effect provided additional focus on the altar through the horizontal sequence of the windows, paneling, and sills. The nave is plain, but its lighting fixtures and rood screen are magnificent. There is no doubt that this is a High-Church Anglican building. In accordance with Ecclesiological theory, the chancel (and the clergy) are emphatically separated from the nave (and the laity) by four massive chamfered piers at the crossing, which support the tower. Above, an exposed trussed-wood ceiling, now reconstructed after a fire and left to show the natural color of the wood, contrast with the white plaster walls. The exterior was relatively untouched by the 1976 fire; its plain, unornamented quality is the result of the architect's intentions rather than any subsequent "modernizations."

Although in general form the church of St. Mary's follows its British antecedents quite closely, its austerity of ornament and starkness of finish reflect an American idiom. So, too, does its setting, with its seventeenth-century predecessor on the corner and one of the nation's few remaining street railways trundling along its front.

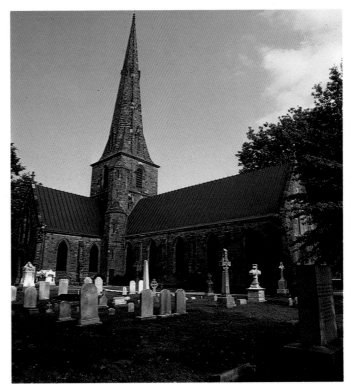

©Mark Sherman/Bruce Coleman

PART THREE
The Forms of Worship

1
Axes and
Symbols

If one reflects very long upon religious buildings, not just in America but everywhere, they come together in groups in which each is built along the same sort of axis of attention. The axis, in each case, falls along the line where the light takes the eye. In this way our physical attention is attracted toward a physical focus, which has a symbolic role in attracting our theological focus upon one way of perceiving the Mystery. These axes suggest metaphorically that God is

OUT THERE

UP THERE

WITH US

WITHIN ME

The long axis leading to the rose window in the Washington Cathedral. ©Fred Ward/Black Star

In Jewish and Christian churches, certain central symbols attract our gaze (and sometimes our motion) and thus reinforce or countervail the "directional signals" given by the primary axes. In Jewish places of worship, these symbolic objects are the bimah, or raised platform with a reading desk, where the Scriptures are translated, read, and explained, and the ark, a container for the Scriptures. Among Christians they are the Communion or Eucharistic table (which sometimes becomes an altar), a container of water for baptism, and a pulpit (sometimes supplemented with a reading desk).

These are the key symbolic objects in these two traditions. Other elements may have to be juggled by architects, including the furniture implied by decisions as to whether the congregation will stand or sit, whether the clergy will stand or sit, whether the choir will sing with or to the congregation, and whether or not this singing will be accompanied by an organ, an orchestra, a procession, or a loud-speaker system, and, finally, whether the congregation itself is expected to move about the space during the liturgy. But these are relatively minor questions once the axes are established and the symbols placed. Architects who have had the experience of contending with these "minor matters" of course may long for a group of Quakers or Amish, among whom there is an intentional liturgical absence of sacramental furniture.

The final sections of this book will suggest the interplay of the axes of attention (the four "directions" stated above) and the placement of primary three-dimensional symbols (the objects of furniture described above).

The baptismal font, set below floor
level, in St. John's Abbey Church.
©Father Hugh Witzman/courtesy of Marcel
Breuer Associates

The altar at the center of things—St.
John's Abbey Church in Collegeville,
Minnesota. ©Lee A. Hanley/courtesy of
Marcel Breuer Associates

©Dan Beigel

©Regina Kuehn

©Regina Kuehn

©Regina Kuehn

The bimah in Touro Synagogue, Newport, Rhode Island (p. 232, top left). ©Bruce Whyte

The iconostasis in St. Mary's in Dobro Woods, Saskatchewan (p. 232, top right). ©John de Visser

Sometimes the light itself may be sufficient (p. 232, bottom). ©Dan Beigel

©Regina Kuehn

Material means, inviting the immaterial (above).

233

A mandala in mosaic at Ascension
Church in Oak Park, Illinois.
©Regina Kuehn

2
Mandalas

Everything tries to be round.
BLACK ELK

Everything points toward the center.
C. G. JUNG

Mandala is a Sanskrit term for a symbol, most often a circle or a sphere, less often a square or a cube, which signifies wholeness. It appears throughout the world. The similarity of its meaning to very dissimilar people is a staggering fact of spiritual life. So is the ubiquity of the theme of light with which the mandala is associated. A glance at the Great Medicine Wheel or at Stonehenge is sufficient explanation of the association of circles and light—an association that is likely to hold so long as the moon revolves around the earth and the earth around the sun.

Among the builders of the cathedral of Chartres, the square was the symbol for Christ. Plato, in the *Timaeus*, found in "squares and cubes . . . the same proportions that also determine the composition of the world soul," which "is in unity and concord with itself." The Holy of Holies in Solomon's Temple, as was noted earlier, was formed as a cube. The Roman architect Vitruvius observed that a well-proportioned person, arms and legs extended, fits into "the most perfect geometrical figures, circle and square." And the Renaissance architects, who rediscovered Vitruvius, pursued the goal of churches, which interrelated the cube and the sphere, the square and the circle.

They were employing a form considered holy from the time the pre-Socratic philosophers Empedocles and Parmenides called God "an infinite sphere." Throughout the millennium and more that followed, they found agreement from the Roman philosopher Plotinus, the medieval theologian, Meister Eckhart, and other mystics. Later, philosophers and scientists like Johann Kepler and Gottfried Wilhelm von Leibniz thought in much the same imagery, speaking of God as being at the "psychic center" of the "infinite circumference of the universe."

The Renaissance architect Andrea Palladio, who has been called with some justice "the most influential architect who ever lived," was fascinated by these concepts. He followed Leonardo da Vinci, Michelangelo, and Bramante in working with the idea of a circular church because it would be "enclosed by one circumference only, in which is to be found neither beginning nor end. . . . every part being equidistant from the centre, such a building demonstrates extremely well the unity, the infinite essence, the uniformity and the justice of God."

When applied with the skill of a Breuer or a Saarinen or a Palladio, the concentric church also makes it easy for all worshipers to see and hear each other, and to focus "with us." The term *concentric* is not here used to mean revolving around a point exactly at a geometric center, but to denote a space that has a central focus rather than a focus at the end of a linear sequence of spaces. If the central object is an altar, as it had been in German Baroque masterpieces like the Lutherans' Frauenkirche in Dresden, at St. John's

The communion table in North Christian Church in Columbus, Indiana—the centerpoint. ©Balthazar Korab

Abbey, or in the medieval churches of the Knights Templar, it becomes the focus. So, too, does a simple Communion table, as at North Christian in Columbus and in the Swiss and German churches influenced by the theology of Karl Barth. Sometimes the central object is the bimah, and then, as at the Touro Synagogue, a Jewish structure seems quite like a Puritan meeting house. Finally, when there is no central object, as in the houses of the Amish or a Quaker meeting house, it is circumference that is the center. The circles of worshipers turn to each other.

The symbolism of the mandala is at the core of religious observances seeking to reconcile opposites and find growth toward unity. It also serves to represent the more limited objective of a coming together of serious people to discuss serious subjects, including certain aspects of the Mystery. Christ in Majesty is depicted in an elongated circle above the sculptured Dies Irae, the separation of the saved from the damned, at the portals of medieval churches. This is the same form in which the Buddha reposes in much Eastern iconography, and the floor plan of the basilica at Lourdes. It is among the most powerful images experienced by humankind.

When Carl Jung, who was then still resisting the theological, found it, in 1916, he ''knew that in finding the mandala as an expression for the Self (the archetype of wholeness) I had attained what was for me the ultimate. Perhaps someone else knows more, but not I.''

As one surveys American churches and synagogues which turn in this fashion inward to the center, directing attention to a single unifying point and also outward from the center to all the people present, one can recall the

236

Quakers face each other in a meeting house in Philadelphia. ©Cary Wolinsky/ Stock, Boston

long history of this form. From the time the Emperor Constantine erected the Church of the Holy Sepulchre and before, when Christians adopted the circular forms of Roman baths and mausoleums for baptistries and martyria, the round church was a frequent alternative to the long church, adapted as it was from Roman courthouses. There are, therefore, innumerable predecessors for the round church in Richmond, Vermont, or the essentially concentric arrangements of most early meeting houses.

Not only were there many circular or octagonal structures in the early centuries of Christianity, but the first set of Protestant buildings, especially those of the very influential French Huguenots, were concentric. There is a tale told in Charleston, South Carolina, that in 1804—when the city was still largely ruled by the progeny of Huguenot refugees—Robert Mills was given the plan for the "Circular Church" by a parishioner. It is a pleasant thought that a Huguenot lady was still proselytizing the architectural ideas of her ancestors—of which little had been seen for a century or more—as late as 1804! We are not required to accept the tale or the thought; we do know that Mills went on to perfect the form in his Monumental Church in Richmond, Virginia, which became the model for a series of Methodist and Baptist buildings.

Mills's succession of four circular churches show the variety of uses to which the form could be put: his Sansom Street Church in Philadelphia for the Baptists was genuinely concentric. It placed the font in the center, as an operating amphitheater would place the surgeon's work. His octagon church for the Unitarians of Philadelphia is not truly concentric. It arranged

237

seats to afford easy attention to the teacher, who is on stage, no altar being necessary. His first experiment in the form, that of 1804 in Charleston, and his largest, the Monumental Church of Richmond, were likewise intended to house large congregations in a comfortable auditorium with good sight lines and curved pews. This relieved the parishioners from the need to cant their bodies in rectilinear pews toward the minister at the focal point, standing on a preaching platform along one wall.

One can see in this arrangement, however, a distortion of the circular or cubic form: it pulled the focus out of the center. While the lines of energy of the congregation did converge on a single point—as they had in the Greek theater—they did not engage with each other. It was not much of a step from this to the Akron plan, which distended the cube by adding another rectilinear space next to it, placing the stage, with the minister and the choir (and below them, the sacramental table) at the corner of the first cube, where it can be opened for overflow crowds to the second. This plan, which first appeared at the Methodist Episcopal Church in Akron, Ohio, became the model for many churches in the Mississippi Valley and the Far West. The second cube could house a variety of meetings, each in a separate space with sliding doors between. The whole congregation could join together to hear the preacher by sliding back the grand divider between the first cube and the second. Members of the congregation could also use the combined double cube for athletic contests, church suppers, or town meetings.

In one way the Akron plan returned the church to the meeting-house function it had had in the early days of New England, thereby bringing the community together in mutual affirmation. But discouraged by the sheer size of these auditoriums and the difficulty of distinguishing their uses from those of a high-school auditorium or even gymnasium, few congregations have built Akron-plan churches in recent decades. One cause of the decline of huge auditoriums was the much-lamented decline of preaching from the days in which the evangelist George Whitefield could bring tears to the eyes of listeners by merely intoning in his marvelous voice the word *Mesopotamia*—according to the slightly envious actor David Garrick, who could not do quite so much with a single word. For many, however, even when the preaching was eloquent, the theatricality of these places had become embarrassing. For others, however, "church" meant televised stages full of stars, ingenues, and casts of hundreds.

This is not to say that the wisdom of the theater cannot be applied to the arrangement of churches retaining their intimacy and a central focus. The theater has always been a part of religious ceremony, as it is of any gathering. One need only think of the liturgy as a kind of performance, however modest or even silent it may be, to recognize it as an architectural problem.

It is not necessary to invoke the memory of mystery plays and feast-day processions. The church taught the theater once, and then the theater taught the church: some churches were built like opera houses with good sight lines and acoustics; some churches were built like concert halls; and, finally, drawing upon the mid-twentieth-century revival of "thrust" or "apron" stages, some churches arranged their seats around a central focus either in an actual or implied circle.

(Acknowledging that one group may learn from another and that a sacred purpose can consecrate even what some people once described as "the wicked stage," many of the greatest and most liturgically effective modern churches have arisen because those who used them were unafraid to benefit from all human knowledge, wherever gained. For example, Louis Sullivan's partner, Dankmar Adler, was the son and the son-in-law of rabbis, and when the congregation led by his father was seeking architects for their new synagogue, Kehileth Anshe M'Ariv in Chicago [the title means "Congregation of the Men of the West"], they were delighted to make use of a man who had developed a genius for acoustics in a series of great theaters and would later work on New York's Carnegie Hall.)

It was not the wisdom of the theater, but that of a religious community examining its liturgy, which shaped the design of the church at St. John's Abbey, in Collegeville, Minnesota. There, priests, monks (who may not necessarily be priests), and laity face each other in a circular, unifying form. Michelangelo and Bramante had laid out such plans for St. Peter's in Rome. Leonardo da Vinci had endorsed the view that the "altar should be placed . . . at the center," where, in Jung's words, "everything points." Protestant architects have been as powerfully drawn to the mandala as a symbol of a uniting impulse and have produced small circular churches like Eero Saarinen's chapel for St. Stephen's College in Missouri, his MIT chapel in Cambridge, Massachusetts, and his concentric plan for North Christian Church in Columbus.

Protestant theologians have given considerable impetus to this plan. Though they differed in their views of the role of symbolism, Karl Barth and Paul Tillich concurred in their preference for the concentric plan around a Communion table. Said Barth severely: "Images and symbols have no place at all in a building designed for Protestant worship," but "the principle of a 'circular place' seems right to me." Tillich's view was that "churches can be filled with symbolic objects of all kinds" if this were done "under the criterion of the manifestation of the transcendent God in Jesus as the Christ," and that the best plan "for the Protestant purpose" would be "a central one in which the members of the congregation look at each other, and in which the minister is among the congregation for preaching and leading the liturgy."

Both of these august figures in twentieth-century theology were enthusiastic about the search for "new forms" to achieve "an honest expression of their faith." Tillich explicitly embraced the view that diversity of forms would be a desirable consequence of searching after a diversity of ways to approach the Mystery. "An element of risk is unavoidable in the building of sacred places, just as a risk must be taken in every act of faith."

The monks of St. Louis Priory in St. Louis, Missouri. ©Tom Ebenhoh

OLD ROUND CHURCH, Richmond, Vermont, 1813

©Gary Bressor

©Grant Heilman

The "Old Round Church" on the Round Church Common in Richmond, Vermont, is an extraordinary exception to the ubiquitous Wren-Gibbs model for New England churches, as adapted and popularized in the carpenter's guides of Asher Benjamin and Minard Lafever. Perhaps its unitary form arises from the fact that five denominations built it jointly in 1813: the Congregationalists, Baptists, Methodists, Universalists, and Christians. Designed by William Rhodes, it is of wood framing covered with clapboard. It is not exactly round; there are sixteen sides and three doors. Two windows adorn each side. Inside, the church remains as it was built, with square pews and a gallery that extends three-quarters of the way around the auditorium. The entire interior is painted white save the fine pine pulpit, which is painted a walnut grain and is supported by four columns. Religious services were discontinued in 1880. Since then the town has owned the building and has used it for town meetings and other purposes.

It is beguiling to consider the fact that Robert Mills's famous Monumental Church, of a similar shape (see p.243), was only built in the previous year and is often described as setting a new precedent. Were the five denominations of Richmond, Vermont, aware of what was being done in Richmond, Virginia? Or were they and Mills and his clients all moved by the same unconscious impulse toward the form of the mandala?

242

MONUMENTAL CHURCH, Richmond, Virginia, 1812

He called himself "the first native American who directed his studies to architecture." Robert Mills, America's first professional architect, launched his career with three churches. The most impressive is the Monumental Church in Richmond, Virginia. Built in 1812, the building commemorated seventy-one people who had died in a theater fire in Richmond. Mills introduced to America the rotunda shape and severe Grecian detail, thus breaking from the eighteenth-century Wren-Gibbs "colonial" plan and its successors in the Federal era, which were still predominant in America in 1812. The church shows how Mills had learned from his mentor, Benjamin Latrobe, to make uninhibited use of Classical ideas in association with function and pure geometry.

Mills went beyond Latrobe's planning for the spaces of the Baltimore cathedral, the consummate masterpiece of rational Neoclassicism, (see p. 256), and adapted church design to the changing character of American practices. Puritans and Anglicans had been joined at the end of the colonial era by growing numbers of evangelical sects, which placed a much greater emphasis upon emotional preaching. Amid a proliferation of denominations, buoyed by the heady prospects of the new country, Mills began his career.

Mills had used the rotunda form in America with his Circular Church in Charleston, South Carolina, in 1804, but it was in Richmond that it assumed its full grandeur. A stucco-covered brick octagon, crowned with a plaster dome, makes up the main body of the church. A short lantern tops the oculus in the center of the dome. Two side doors in the octagonal main building are used as primary entrances to the church, each part of a short projecting wing which also includes stairways to the balcony. Free-standing Doric porticos front these wings.

But Monumental Church is more than an active place of worship—it is a memorial to the dead. Mills attached a memorial porch to the side of the main

©Katherine Wetzel

©Katherine Wetzel

243

building, built in stone masonry to set it apart from the octagon. In the center of this porch, which resembles a small Greek temple, stands a funerary urn on a pedestal, a memorial to the fire victims. A bare Doric frieze, decorated with lachrymatories (vases used by Romans to hold tears) lies above the heavy corner piers. The unorthodox, unfluted Doric columns that stand beside the piers and the unclosed pediment show Mills to be unafraid to redefine a traditional classical formula.

The interior of the main building mirrors its exterior's simplicity. The altar area, recessed behind piers and two Greek Ionic columns, is the focus. Its elevation is that of the memorial porch, which it faces. All pews on the main floor and gallery provide direct vision to the altar, a testament to Mills's belief "that convenience and utility were constituent parts" of beauty.

Robert Mills's aspiration was to be, as he put it, "altogether American in his views." As America's first American-born professional architect, he had many opportunities to express that aspiration, the most famous of which was the Washington Monument.

FIRST CHRISTIAN CHURCH, Columbus, Indiana, 1942
NORTH CHRISTIAN CHURCH, Columbus, Indiana, 1964

Our endeavor has been to design a church which could be lastingly appreciated rather than bring about a design which might effect momentary excitement and early indifference.

—Eliel and Eero Saarinen

Eliel and Eero Saarinen were organizers of building blocks to form aesthetically powerful compositions. In the formation of the complex of buildings for the First Christian Church of Columbus, Indiana (then called the Tabernacle Church of Christ), the Saarinens—father and son—had an opportunity as well to demonstrate the symbolic function of architecture, composing simple forms on a large scale simultaneously to represent and to serve a congregation highly conscious of the interaction of theology, community service, and aesthetics.

The building committee, addressing the architects, sought a building that would be simple yet large enough to accommodate the worshiping community of 1,600 in a town that only numbered 12,000 at the time; simplicity, they felt, was appropriate for people who were trying to "practice primitive Christianity and nothing else." But their definition of that primitive quality included an obligation to the larger community to create beauty.

The Saarinens followed the wish of the building committee that the structure be as straightforward as a theology based on the fundamentals of Christianity, by designing a church whose source was in the fundamentals of architecture. They wrote, "simplicity is the most lasting form of value," and presented a group of bold, rectilinear, but mutually reinforcing shapes.

The church complex is a group of blocks—the church proper, the tower, the educational wing, and the "bridge." The church proper is opposite the educational wing and is connected to it by the "bridge," an enclosure that houses more classrooms as well as offices, crossing the sunken terrace and forming a loggia. Unlike the church proper, which contains fewer windows, the educational wing and the connecting bridge have long, horizontal areas of glass across their walls, overlooking the sunken terrace.

The church buildings are of brick on a frame of steel. Indiana limestone is the primary decorative element on the exterior of the front of the church proper. The limestone is placed in a grid pattern on the façade, and the horizontal lines presented by the front steps leading to the main entrance offset the verticality of the church block and the campanile. A perforated design, once intended to provide a sounding chamber, runs up the west wall of the campanile.

The interior of the church is quiet and plain. The middle aisle is set off-center and the side aisles are of different widths; the Saarinens believed that forced symmetry created artificial and sterile conditions. The space deliberately avoids too obvious a focus upon any object; attention is subtly drawn, however, toward the cross. The pulpit extends over the chancel steps into the congregation, but not too emphatically.

Natural lighting illuminates the interior—softly in the morning in the nave, from side windows, and more strongly in the baptistry, from the east window. The whitewashed brick walls and the light wood of the pews, screening, and furnishings are consistent with the subtlety of the interior.

Some of members of the congregation, moved by differences in theology, turned again to Eero Saarinen, after the death of his father, to build for them a North Christian Church.

The church, completed in 1964, stands where the town dissolves into the flat, fertile Indiana cornfields. Eero Saarinen deliberately made use of the site to provide for the town a symbol—the spire. The church was meant to proclaim its mission, to invite attention, and then to provide shelter. Like a blockhouse, its hexagonal form appears the same from every side. Like a frontier fort, it is a rallying point. As Saarinen saw it:

On this site, with this kind of central plan, I think I

First Christian Church, Columbus, Indiana. ©Balthazar Korab

would like to make the church all one form: all the tower. There would be the gradual building up to the sheltering, hovering planes becoming the spire. The spire would not be put on a box or come up from the sides of the roof.

Saarinen translated his wishes into his design. Six steel spines spring from the steel arches upon the concrete foundation and move up the roof to connect above the skylight. At that point the spines unify to become a 12¾-inch-diameter column which forms the center of the 192-foot spire. Light gray copper-steel plates of gradually smaller sizes are attached to this column, eventually diminishing into a cross. The spines also are covered in copper, their light gray contrasting with the dark slate roof.

Saarinen had a more fundamental reason than visibility to elevate his church. He had worked with church building committees and knew they often wanted the architect ''to make everything on one level and easy, sort of inviting you to come in like a supermarket. But I don't think religion should be something easy. I think you should have to work for it and it should be a special thing.''

The sanctuary of North Christian is itself elevated. Concentric in plan, it is at the center of a totally self-contained unit, with no auxiliary buildings. Saarinen intended, he said, ''to put all the activity downstairs, far away, and put only the sanctuary above ground and make it the significant visual and architectural thing.''

The ground level holds the entry, classrooms, offices, a small library, and a baptistry-chapel featuring a grill over the baptismal pool. The underground level, lit by windows high on the wall, provides an auditorium, a lounge, recreational and music areas, a kitchen, and additional classrooms.

To get to the sanctuary, Saarinen required a journey:

> After the approach, there is the act of entering. There should be awareness of a changing environment, like a decompression chamber from the outside world into the church. Maybe you would go down and then up again into the sanctuary. The light, of course, would begin to change, too.

The sanctuary is worth the journey. It is what Saarinen hoped it would be—a "special, enclosed spiritual world." The six panels that make up the walls soar to the skylight high above the altar. The altar is composed of a group of twelve Communion tables representing the twelve Apostles and a taller one representing Christ, connected by silver crosses. The tables are set on a three-tiered hexagonal platform.

From the altar, five sections of mahogany-stained pews (the sixth area is reserved for the choir) spread out in the same hexagonal pattern. Four hundred sixty-five people can sit in the pews, with an overflow capacity of one hundred fifty more on a bench at the upper perimeter.

Direct light from above shines onto the altar, while a softer light is diffused throughout the sanctuary from glass panels behind the perimeter of the nave level.

Eero Saarinen never saw the North Christian Church. He died before it was completed.

North Christian Church, Columbus, Indiana. ©Balthazar Korab

CRYSTAL CATHEDRAL
(GARDEN GROVE COMMUNITY CHURCH),
Garden Grove, California, 1980

Robert H. Schuller at one time called his Garden Grove Community Church a "22 acre shopping center for Jesus." The Crystal Cathedral is the biggest, newest, and most expensive component of that shopping center. Schuller began his preaching from the rooftop of a drive-in refreshment stand. By 1954 his church had grown to a fourteen-floor tower with a 75-foot cross and large windows that opened to a congregation in parked cars; by 1970 services were broadcast on television. Television, in turn, attracted even more people, forcing Schuller to expand again. For a grand sanctuary he commissioned the grand architect, Philip Johnson, to design what he hoped would be a major attraction for drive-in, television, and walk-in worshipers. The Crystal Cathedral is Johnson's attempt to fulfill his client's needs.

The Crystal Cathedral responds to the ambitions of a masterful minister, but it also responds to the needs of a southern California area, where automobiles, shopping centers, and television are as integral to life as farms, meeting houses, and itinerant tinkers were in New England. Appropriately, the opening of the $18-million building was advertised in full-page ads in the *New York Daily News*, and a weekly TV show *The Hour of Power* has made it a southern California tourist attraction.

The structure is shaped like a four-pointed star, 207 feet by 415 feet. California's light and heat are admitted through the clear glass sides and roof of syncopated geometric shapes and planes that reach a height of 128 feet with no interior columns. The dimensions of the building are misleading because of the proportions—it has the same ground area as a 186-foot square.

The irregular floor plan is covered by a suprisingly uniform exposed truss work that appears to be a decorative ceiling rather than the structural support of the building.

Schuller had expressed the hope that the glass building would enable the congregation to observe nature and to be reminded of the Garden of Eden. As it turns out, parking requirements have turned the garden into pavement, except for a group of pools which, in the view of John Pastier of the *AIA Journal*, give the complex the look of "a splendid gymnasium for an enlightened band of 1920s European naturopaths devoted to sunbathing and hydrotherapy."

Many antecedents have been suggested for the Crystal Cathedral, especially Bruce Goff's plans for a Crystal Chapel at the University of Oklahoma. Johnson maintains that the church was designed starting "with structure and function. That is, we find out what the purpose of the building is, we find out what the best way of building it is, and we suit things to that purpose." There were some design considerations that vied with these purposes: the pulpit is set 50 feet off-center, but this means some worshipers are as far as 220 feet from Schuller. The acoustics are far from perfect. Yet, as a work of architecture, it is remarkably efficient in many ways: it needs no central heating or cooling, despite the southern climate; its operable strips of windows both ventilate and give the drive-in worshipers a view of the preacher.

For Christmas 1981, it was planned that the congregation could also see 250 actors and angels dangling from cables in "the world's largest Nativity scene." One is reminded of Anne of Austria.

©Gordon H. Schenck, Jr.

3
The Basilican Tradition

At the end of the great rectangular space, in his majesty, was the judge. Before him, only slightly less exalted, were the jurors or interlocutors, and then, in their own compartment, the members of the bar. In the body of the hall, coming and going, attending when they wished, gossiping and flirting, were the members of the crowd. This was the Roman basilica or courthouse. It exerted a powerful effect upon Christians, who emerged from the underground burial places, private houses, and secret lairs where they had worshiped. After they gained imperial sanction, Christians were delighted to be able to practice their religion in spaces that invoked the power of the law.

The longitudinal axis of the basilica, directing attention "out there," was reinforced by the reading by the early Christians of descriptions of Solomon's Temple. Though Solomon's Holy of Holies was a cube, that cube was set at the end of a long series of spaces. In descending gravity, the next space was that of the priests, then that of the lower clergy, and, finally, a space for the people.

The form of the basilican church was established by superimposing the Roman rectangle upon the Hebrew one. It has been a compelling model—sometimes, it seems, an irresistible model—for church architecture ever since. The ancients called the "royal path" the long progression from the door to the presence of emperor or judge (later the bishop, sitting upon his bench, which was called the "cathedra"). To later critics, the royal path was "the superstitious vista." Christian churches adopted as well the cruciform shape of such Roman buildings as the baths of Maxentius; and after the nave was elongated to accommodate larger numbers and to display processions, the shape of the cross became conventional—essentially, the basilica acquired transepts.

The basilica did imply a hierarchy; but unlike the later Gothic of the High Middle Ages (and the nineteenth-century Gothic revival in its High Church form), the basilica did not imply a separation of the laity from the clergy. The high altar, in classical times and as late as the Romanesque period immediately preceding the Gothic, was set in full view and accessible at the crossing of the two great spaces of the church (the long nave and the transept). With the Gothic there came an accentuation of the growing distinction between the laity in the nave and the religious community, arrayed in the choir initially behind the altar. Then, after the altar had been pushed to the far end of the choir—replacing the seat of the bishop—a low wall was interposed to cut off the choir, now full of meaning and of clergy, from the much larger and almost certainly more dangerous, more noisy, and colder area of the nave. Since that vast space was very seldom occupied by a congregation in any modern sense, but was generally intended for pro-

The basilican form at Temple Emanu-El in New York City.
©Nathaniel Lieberman

251

cessional purposes, this shift merely placed a small church—largely intended for the clergy—within a large church designed more for ceremony than for those activities we tend to call "worship."

The strange consequence of all this was that in Protestant countries like Holland the area of the choir was often sealed off completely after the dissolution of the religious communities whose members previously had occupied it. In some Dutch churches today bicycles are racked where the clergy once sat, while a very active parish life is conducted in what once was the nave. In Britain, the insertion of the wall—either complete, as in some British cathedrals, or in perforated form (often highly ornamental "rood screens")—has been perpetuated not by Catholics but by Protestants, whose movement of the altar back to the crossing rendered the choir almost as unnecessary as in Holland.

Over the millennia the sacred focus of basilican and Gothic churches moved forward and back. Its location has been moved by the gravitational force of the clerical community and the location of the altar. Mid-nineteenth-century Gothic revivalists selected, out of this switching, the location of the altar during only one interlude in that sequence, when they insisted upon pushing the Eucharistic ceremony back behind a rood screen and again lengthening the choir. They sensed a desire in that sometimes mechanical and hasty age for a renewal of enigmatic and solemn worship, for that sequence of ever more exclusive spaces that had appeared in churches of many forms, behind façades of Gothic or of Byzantine or even of Renaissance derivation. It is to that Gothic revival, to the middle years of the nineteenth century, that most American architects owe the inspiration for their subsequent work in this manner.

When it came time for it to be so renewed in America, the Gothic was not extinct; but it had been an endangered species for two centuries. Old churches in the North had been replaced by eager, white new ones; old churches in the South were crumbling or had been burnt out in one war or another. St. Luke's in Smithfield remained. One tower at Jamestown survived. Benjamin Latrobe, who had offered a Gothic design to Bishop Carroll in Baltimore, offered another in 1808 to the congregation of Christ Church, behind the Capitol in Washington. It was approved. His example had no immediate followers, nor did Charles Bulfinch's half-hearted Gothic exercise at Boston's Federal Street for his friend William Ellery Channing, a Congregationalist on his way to Unitarianism. The vestry of Trinity Church near the wall of old New York built three successive Gothic churches on the same site, the first in 1698—a rare instance of Gothic persistence in that period. They went about their building process without deference to the fashions of their neighbors until, as their final Gothic version was being completed in the 1840s, from its steeple one could look up Manhattan Island toward others of the new revival rising to greet it.

Richard Upjohn, the architect chosen to design the latest (and current) Trinity Church, was already the beneficiary of a flood of advice from English Episcopalians about how the vigor of Anglicanism could be restored by building new churches resembling English parish churches of six hundred years earlier. There were masterpieces of church architecture that closely followed this advice, among them St. Mary's in Burlington, New Jersey, and St. James the Less in Philadelphia. Anglicans expressed some chagrin, thereafter, when Unitarians in Britain and America quickly began building churches modeled on Trinity and its Gothic siblings. But Anglican murmurs failed to dull an appetite for the Gothic on the part of Congregationalists, Presbyterians, Baptists, and Methodists.

It did not seem to matter that the chief proponents of the Gothic revival at the beginning of the century, the Cambridge Camden Society, made it clear that they wished the "non-conformists" to keep their hands off the style. Nor did it matter that the American High Churchman Ralph Adams Cram—who was the architect for some of the grandest Presbyterian, Baptist, and Methodist churches—made no secret of his view that "there was something incongruous in using Catholic Gothic to express the ethos of that Protestantism which had . . . done its best to destroy architecture and other artistic manifestations." The triumph of the sequential basilican form was fairly complete in the nineteenth century, even if the final Holy of Holies was reserved for the pulpit or the stage rather than the altar.

It is very important to distinguish here between architecture built in the Gothic spirit, as that view of life has been described earlier, and architecture that merely adopted Gothic forms. The Gothic spirit was, of course, a medieval spirit that thought analogously and symbolically. It could be housed in a round space, under a dome, in a rectangular basilica, or in a white cube as long as the symbols of the faith were present and the spirit—especially the spirit—was present as well. The Gothic revival in architecture quickly spread into buildings like New York's Riverside Church, where thirteenth-century Gothic was used for a space in which, until very recently, there was a multitude of subtle symbols but no image of Christ. (Such an image, large and golden, can now be seen by the clergy, who look back beyond the congregation to the organ loft.)

It is no accident that almost the same set of architectural forms in almost the same size as those on Riverside Drive appeared at the same time at the equally beautiful Temple Emanu-El on Fifth Avenue in the same city. The temple is a very large synagogue; Riverside Church is of cathedral size, built initially for the Baptists. Both have adopted a basilican plan very far re-

moved from either Roger Williams's meeting houses or the Touro Synagogue. This does not imply that there is any greater virtue in the earlier than in the later, the smaller than the larger, but merely that the earlier structures are of a concentric form and the later, vastly larger ones are basilican and with very muted symbolic content.

Throughout the nineteenth and early twentieth centuries the associations of the Gothic with Catholic worship diminished, in part because few American Catholic congregations were drawn to the Gothic. More often they built in the Baroque, in sometimes so grand a scale as the Cathedral of St. Paul in St. Paul, Minnesota. Huge churches made meticulously like the Gothic, however, became hugely popular among all denominations of Protestants. This despite the view of Ralph Adams Cram (its most successful practitioner from the time he was asked to redesign the Cathedral of St. John the Divine in New York) that "it would have horrified Doctors Calvin and Knox in their day." Very large churches, Gothic and otherwise, were intended to convey a comfortable, vague "churchiness" in which fear and trembling, awe and dread were absent. The Unitarian architect Van Ogden Vogt, who vied with Cram for the Gothic market, was enthusiastic about its "intimations . . . not chiefly intellectual . . . but emotional and mystical," which could lead the imagination to find some communion with the "infinite unknown." Cram spoke of "mystery and devotion," and others of "worshipful atmosphere."

As an earlier portion of this book has attempted to make clear, there is a gulf between a rigorous theology that distinguishes among aspects of the Mystery (sometimes through the use of the categories of analytical psychology) and puts very heavy emphasis upon the deployment of consciousness and intellect and vague talk of "mystery and devotion." The "infinite unknown" is a concept that has exercised some of the best and most rigorous minds—not just the lazy imaginations—of two millennia. It is doubtful, however, that symbolic contemplation or earnest theology are well served by architects who deploy symbols merely as ornament and who are essentially hostile to the theological point of view of the clients they serve. This is not to say that a test oath would be a wise requirement for a church commission. But a willingness to enter seriously into the life of the professing community, to treat its religious aspirations as more than incidental to the shaping of a building, has been found present in the architects of every distinguished building in this book.

Another basilican-form church on a grand scale—Riverside Church in New York City. ©Howard Millard

THE BASILICA OF THE ASSUMPTION (BALTIMORE CATHEDRAL), Baltimore, Maryland, 1804–18

British law forbade any Roman Catholic congregation in the thirteen colonies from constructing a church, restricting Catholic worship to small gatherings in private homes. In 1789, after Independence, Baltimore was established as the seat of the national Catholic diocese, and John Carroll was named as its bishop. Carroll decided in 1804 that his position was sufficiently secure to consider building the first Roman Catholic cathedral in the United States.

Benjamin Latrobe was commended to Bishop Carroll both because he was acknowledged to be the most highly trained architect in America and because it was known that he would work for religious institutions without fee. At first, Carroll merely asked Latrobe to criticize another architect's proposal. Latrobe felt the design to be expensive and structurally doubtful and requested the honor of undertaking the project himself. As usual, he would accept no fee. Carroll gratefully agreed. (The architect of the first plan may have been Dr. William Thornton, whose subsequent libelous attacks on Latrobe landed him in court.)

At the time, the Catholic churches of Canada and Mexico were generally in the Baroque style, but Latrobe's training in British classicism made him disdainful of "Baroque ornaments." Nor were the prevailing "Wrennaissance" Protestant styles suitable, either liturgically or aesthetically. Instead, Latrobe (anticipating future trends) submitted a Gothic design as well as a "modern," Neoclassical scheme. Carroll and the trustees chose the Neoclassical design, and work was begun in March 1806.

Latrobe's work is distinguished by large open spaces, a delight in the play of large geometric forms, and restrained decoration. His conviction that the church must be permanent, clearly distinguishable from its humble domestic predecessors, reinforced his propensity for vaulting in stone. The Basilica of the Assumption provided him with his greatest opportunity to orchestrate these without concessions to elements already in place, like those that had hobbled his work at the national Capitol. There were limitations of site and budget; his original plan was altered three times during the course of construction. Relations between the architect and contractor were strained; the builders were not used to architectural drawings.

Latrobe was unaccustomed to such inexperience—possibly compounded by ill will. He was also almost as volatile of temperament as later architects Louis Sullivan and Frank Lloyd Wright. When one of the trustees proposed major alterations, he tried to resign. Carroll was a masterly client. Assuming the blame himself, vowing to keep the inept trustees away from the architect and the plans, he was able to mollify Latrobe and keep him on the job.

Latrobe came to have much the same feeling about Carroll that Sullivan felt for his greatest client, Carl Bennett, of Owatonna, Minnesota. In a letter that throbs with the same affection and despair as Sullivan's to Bennett a century later, the touchy, vain, splenetic genius wrote the kindly bishop that, for him, "the opportunity of becoming personally known to you . . . will always be one of the most pleasant circumstances of my life." But he feared the outcome: "Reverend Sir . . . [despite] . . . your good taste, your sound reasonings, your freedom from prejudice, or your knowledge . . . the pressure of general opinion, the perseverance of those who are honestly ignorant, is always an overmatch for the yielding disposition which belongs to such benevolence as yours."

But Carroll was crafty as well as benevolent. He saw the cathedral through, despite reductions in size from Latrobe's original plans. Together they commenced a masterpiece that was completed two generations later, when most of Latrobe's original ideas were ultimately executed. Along the way there were many doubters: Americans were not educated in vaulting in stone; they had settled, instead, for

dropped ceilings to simulate vaulting, or wooden trusses or beams. But Latrobe and Carroll built it in stone.

Latrobe felt the plan of a Latin cross to be liturgically necessary for a Catholic church, and he covered the lengthy nave with a succession of curved spaces: a barrel vault succeeded by a saucer dome and, finally, covering the crossing, a large dome. The size of the dome required large piers, diagonally placed and curved on their innermost surfaces to support the stone construction. It is these shapes that gladden the eye, not any brilliance of color or any assertive decoration. The domes are coffered, and moldings are painted in soft blues and golds. Almost all the decoration is high above eye level so that all sight lines converge upon the altar, beneath the saucer dome in the choir. The interior is a masterly composition of flowing lines, spaces, and light. (Or was, until the effect was partly spoiled by the insertion of colored glass in the windows.)

Remodelings in 1879 and 1890 lengthened the choir, in keeping with Latrobe's intentions; he had pleaded for just such a large choir. Except for the odd onion-shaped belfries added after his death, the cathedral, as it exists today, can be said to be the cathedral Benjamin Latrobe wished to see, as John Carroll assured him it would be built.

257

TEMPLE EMANU-EL, New York, New York, 1929

Temple Emanu-El, completed in 1929, lies in the heart of New York City, with a frontage of 150 feet on Fifth Avenue and 253 feet on Sixty-fifth Street, the site of Mrs. Caroline Schermerhorn Astor's famous mansion. The temple, one of the largest built in modern times, is derived from the basilicas of northern Italy in an admixture of Byzantine and Romanesque forms.

A great recessed arch on Fifth Avenue, which encloses a rose window with supporting lancets and three entrance doors, highlights the exterior. Ornament carved on the stone exterior is drawn from Hebrew symbolism. The east-west walls themselves are self-supporting, built of variegated limestone. They carry the transverse structural steel beams, covered in stone and plaster, which bridge the span of the great nave. The main auditorium is 150 feet long and 77 feet wide and has a seating capacity larger than that of St. Patrick's Cathedral, accommodating 2,500 people. Guastavino acoustic tile covers the walls of the auditorium; Siena travertine marble covers those of the entrance vestibule. Red, green, and yellow marble columns support the side galleries.

The sanctuary, which is 30 feet in depth and just over 40 feet wide, with a marble floor and marble wainscot on the sides, contains the most striking symbols of the temple; the Ark, most ancient of Jewish religious symbols, is found to the rear of the altar. In front of the Ark is the *Ner Tamid*, or Perpetual Light, symbolizing the eternal and universal truths contained in the Torah. The Shield of David appears frequently in the mosaics and windows of the temple. The architects were Robert D. Kohn, Charles Butler, and Clarence S. Stein. Visitors to their work may wish to compare it to Riverside Church, its contemporary in the Gothic, basilican form, of similar size and elegance, fifty-five streets to the north and ''across town.''

RIVERSIDE CHURCH, New York, New York, 1927

The Riverside Church building is conservative, even backward; the congregation is strikingly, unmistakably liberal. When Dr. Harry Emerson Fosdick was asked by the congregation to lead their parish in 1925, he agreed, under the following conditions:

First, affirmation of faith in Christ must be the only requirement for membership. Second, any Christian, regardless of denomination, seeking admission to the church, must be freely welcomed. Third, a new and larger building and a more expansive ministry should be planned in a neighborhood critical to the life of the whole city.

Accordingly, the church took on an ecumenical character, despite its historic connections to Congregationalism as well as the Baptist Church.

The site, on Riverside Drive in Morningside Heights at 120th Street, was acquired, and plans were drawn up in 1926. Designed by Charles Collens and Henry C. Pelton, the church was completed by 1930. It is very large, very handsome, very expensive, and stately. It is scholarly Gothic revival with a few Romanesque details. Though church architecture is often conservative, it does seem odd that such freethinkers as Fosdick and his parishioners would commission such a building at a time when Frank Lloyd Wright, Le Corbusier, Gropius,

and Mies van der Rohe were gaining international significance, and Barry Byrne was demonstrating how an ingenious architect could reinspirit the Gothic.

Known for their espousal of social services, pacifism, and general nonconformity, the congregation's inclusive perspective can, however, be noted in its choice of sculpture. Represented are not only the traditional saints of Christendom, but also Booker T. Washington, Michelangelo, Walter Reed, Leonardo Da Vinci, John Ruskin, Jane Addams, Hippocrates, Savonarola, Louis Pasteur, Socrates, and John Milton. Such choices are, perhaps, indicative of the idiosyncratic hand responsible for the columns near the phone booths: carved into the capitals are six grotesques—one a pig—holding telephone receivers to their ears. The *Visitor's Guide* assures us that "no symbolic interpretation is here attempted."

Providing relief during the depression, espousing pacifism during World War II, Riverside Church continued its liberal tradition when, in 1977, the Reverend William Sloane Coffin, Jr. was called to head the church. Riverside Church remains steadfast in its "belief that liberty of the individual is based not on the idea that what one *is* is unimportant, but that it is too important to be regimented and controlled by external authority."

4
Heavenly Spaces

The more splendid that mystery, the deeper it should lie in darkness. —TERTULLIAN

Roman Catholic, Anglican, and Protestant churches and the religious buildings springing from these three are familiar parts of the landscape throughout the settled portions of the United States. But occasionally, as one travels the streets of New York or Chicago or the central wards of St. Paul, Minnesota, or across the pine barrens of New Jersey or along the California Coast Highway, or sails through the Aleutians, one sees an onion dome bearing a cross of unfamiliar form and is reminded of another and very powerful tradition among Christians. This is the world of the Orthodox Churches, which come out of the Byzantine tradition. Their religious practices, though of vast antiquity and predominant in Alaskan history, came to the "southern forty-eight states" late in the American experience. The Orthodox are, in this narrow sense, the oldest of the young churches.

The fact that the presumably Orthodox "Martin the Armenian" traveled through Virginia in 1618 is as welcome as the record of the explorations of the Son of Islam "Istfan the Arab" in Arizona nearly a century earlier. Both bestow a therapeutic primacy upon groups thought by some Americans to be latecomers. But the real advent of the Eastern Orthodox to the area now encompassed by the United States came at about the time the Methodists began their swift exfoliation from a tiny rhizome of Anglicanism. In 1792 eight monks began the construction of the Eastern Orthodox Church on Kodiak Island, then within the North American extension of the czar's vast empire. Their successors, like the Spanish priests to the South, were immensely successful missionaries. By 1900 one out of every six Alaskans was a member of the Russian Orthodox Church. Emigration from the Balkans and Greece was largely a twentieth-century phenomenon and concentrated in the large cities, though some rural communities had been established in the nineteenth century. According to the 1970 Census, there were more members of the Eastern Churches in the United States (38 million) than there were Episcopalians (34 million) or Presbyterians (33 million).

Eastern Orthodoxy is one of the great streams of Christianity. After centuries of disputes about theology and ecclesiastical preference, the pope had a writ of excommunication laid upon the high altar of the patriarch of Constantinople in 1054, an event that presaged the sack and storm of that city by European Christians in 1204 and affected the division Catholic Christianity into its Eastern and Western branches.

Very old liturgies are still maintained in the Eastern churches. Whereas worshipers traditionally stood or knelt during the liturgy, they are now often seated. (Congregations have been seated in the West only since the late Middle Ages.) Feast days now often conform to a Western calendar, and

The Russian Orthodox Church at St. Michael, Alaska. ©Steve McCutcheon

263

The altar of an Eastern Orthodox
church in Phoenix, Arizona.
©Glenn Short/Bruce Coleman

musical instruments and mixed choirs join in services. But the close ethnic communities that express themselves in their own rites tend to retain a far closer identification of ethnicity and liturgy than is common among western Europeans and their American descendants.

This closeness of the communicant community has resulted in misunderstandings. Some Western Christians have forgotten that all Christian groups arising in the Middle East are not "Eastern Orthodox" in the same sense. During the first seven centuries of the Christian era, the Armenian, the Egyptian, and the Ethiopian churches, and the fabled Nestorians of the East had broken away. As late as the Second World War, a gulf of mutual antipathy and ignorance separated many Orthodox from Western congregations.

Eastern churches are sometimes served by married priests, many of whom do not earn their living by their religious work and thus have not separated themselves from the secular economy, as Western clergy, we now take for granted, "always have." Unfamiliar costumes, beards, and services that, when they are visited, seem very dark, very long, and very full of strange incense, have led Christians and Jews of a western European tradition to adopt a baffled stance toward their Orthodox neighbors.* Some such feelings have been mutual: a Russian theologian in the nineteenth century used his worst anathema to include all the progeny of the Fourth Crusaders: "all Protestants are Crypto-Papists," he said.

Those who remember what symbolic contemplation meant to medieval Christians in the West will have little difficulty in understanding how the Orthodox churches have been arranged. The place in which the Sacrament of the Eucharist ("Communion" among many Protestants) is performed by the priest is even more withdrawn than it was among Roman Catholics. Traditionally, the action takes place out of sight of the congregation, and the bread and wine are brought forth to them from a holy space. There are doctrinal reasons for the restoration of such a space of special significance. The long iconographic tradition of the Eastern church leads to the presence of many images near the doorways from the congregational space into the holy space.

The Orthodox clergy are not removed from life. There are, of course, monasteries, but, as noted earlier, the parish priest often works alongside his parishioners, and his wife and children (if he was married before ordination) are their neighbors. Though the basilican form, with its ascending order or mystery, tends to direct attention in the Eastern churches toward places, rather than persons, the real focus of attention is inward and upward. The Orthodox turn inward, using rituals like those of India and the Far East, seeking to quiet the noise in the head, to gain a tranquillity within

264

* Jews of an east European provenance, if sufficiently emancipated from the traditional prohibition of visiting non-Jewish places of worship, may be struck by the similarities between Eastern churches and orthodox Jewish synagogues of eastern Europe.

which the Mystery may better be apprehended. This practice—called *Hesychasm*—is a preparation for that process of looking through the aperture provided by the icon into the realm of the spirit.

The icon is not merely a work of art. If Hesychastic meditation or merely quietness is availing, the icon becomes transparent. Through it the worshipers turn upward toward figures in mosaic or painted on the curved surfaces above. Thus the congregation is induced to enter into the realm that those images suggest (or, as the word is properly used, "symbolize"), and, as a Greek patriarch said, a church becomes "the earthly sky in which God of the Heavens above lives and moves." William Butler Yeats wrote of what we may feel in such a place when our bodies hang heavily upon us:

> *O sages standing in God's holy fire*
> *As in the gold mosaic of a wall...*
> *Consume my heart away; sick with desire*
> *And fastened to a dying animal*
> *It knows not what it is.*

It may be that those who come from damp, cold northern countries can gain a better acquaintance with the enveloping darkness of many Eastern churches if we think of them as they must have felt in their original setting, which was, from our point of view, more Southern than Eastern. Though Orthodox churches have been built near the Arctic Circle and reached America first along the coldest immigration route of all those traversed by Europeans, they were first designed for the Mediterranean world. From that world, from its most ancient religious settings in cool caves and hidden underground sanctuaries, comes that love of shadow, of the enveloping darkness which seems so strange to those who have an aversion to the damp, an aversion deriving from millennial exposure to the sea winds of the North and Irish Seas.

But to the Orthodox, a religious environment is often one of flickering candles in a dark and indeterminate space, of strange visages hanging immobile overhead, of shimmering mosaics. Here one can find oneself environed where the scents, the sounds, and the visions are not those of any profane place, but, instead, of a sanctuary. Above, in the darkness—more intense than any image that must contend with light—glows the image of Christ Pantocrator, "ruler and center of the universe." Here the Mystery is invoked in darkness that yet contains a deep intensity of color, amid shapes as large as those in dreams, amid incense, gentle bells, and voices, low and measured, repeating, repeating hallucinatory sounds of ancient meaning.

American architects have approached the opportunity presented by

Within a Russian Orthodox church in Baltimore, Maryland. ©D. Lyons/ Bruce Coleman

The Russian tradition at Fort Ross, California. ©James Griffin/After-Image

this sort of liturgy in a number of widely varied ways. St. Sava Serbian Orthodox Cathedral in Milwaukee, which uses very traditional forms on a very grand scale, envelops its congregational practices convincingly. And so does the little St. Mary's Russian Orthodox Church, which is set amid the huge white pines and copper mines on the exposed south coast of Lake Superior, at Cornucopia, Wisconsin. Despite the recent loss by fire of St. Michael's in Sitka, there remain small but powerful reminders of the early Russian presence in North America, including the Orthodox Church of the Aleutians. Frank Lloyd Wright's virtuoso performance of the 1950s was his Annunciation Greek Orthodox Church at Wauwatosa, Wisconsin, and in the pine lands of New Jersey there is one of the most moving and expressive of America's small churches, the center of its community at New Kuban.

The architectural setting of the Eastern liturgy cries out for the hand of a master of the ornamental style, a man like Louis Sullivan or Henry Hobson Richardson in an association like Richardson's at Boston's Trinity Church with a designer of glass and mosaic of the skill of John La Farge. Sullivan's Holy Trinity Orthodox Cathedral in Chicago gives some sense of what he could do; but it, like his Kehileth Anshe M'Ariv Synagogue, had to be executed on a very small budget. We can only let our imaginations roam through his other work to envisage what he might have done for an Eastern Orthodox client as munificent and sympathetic as Commodore Ferdinand Peck (of the Auditorium Building) or a banker like Carl Bennett (of the Security Bank in Owatonna, Minnesota).

In his *Kindergarten Chats*, Sullivan spoke of the task of the architect in this way:

> That which exists in spirit ever seeks and finds its physical counterpart in form, its visible image. . . . there should be . . . a relation between the form . . . and the causes that bring it into that particular shape; and . . . the building, to be good architecture, must, first of all, clearly correspond with its function, must be in its image.

This is a much richer doctrine that the exegesis upon it made by writers who exerted little effort to understand the roots of Sullivan's ideas in German Neoplatonism, which was transmitted by his Grandfather List from the cathedral builders. (Some references to the sources of these ideas appeared in our discussion of the Gothic.) Sullivan tried to find the "spirit" of a building, its "form" in the Platonic sense. For him form did not "follow function" by exposing the plumbing or by becoming a giant billboard. That sort of thing, like the making of buildings that are mere museum reproductions, is, in Sullivan's terms, "dry, chilling or futile." Form, it can be

The interior of Holy Trinity Russian Orthodox Church in Chicago, Illinois. ©Regina Kuehn

argued, actually precedes function, but by so infinitesimal an interval that only a logician could put his razor between the two. Working architects report that they are thought about simultaneously, and their "solutions" seem to arise simultaneously from the frontier land between the conscious and the unconscious. This is especially true when the "form" is a church and the "function" is religious.

Traditional church buildings, as we have seen, often took the form of wholeness, the mandala. Often, too, they followed the shape of a basilica. Sometimes the space was open, sometimes a series of compartments. Round or rectangular or in the shape of a cube, great buildings have wrapped themselves about the liturgical functions they were intended to serve. Great architects have put themselves at the service of religious communities and also of the "forms" which, over the ages, have manifested the "spirit" of a church, a spirit that is an aspect—but not by any means the only aspect—of the Mystery.

RUSSIAN ORTHODOX CHURCH,
New Kuban, New Jersey, 1964

©Jack E. Boucher

In rural south Jersey, near the town of Buena, a bit of tsarist Russia survives today. The Russian Orthodox Church, in the center of the community known as New Kuban, is only the most visible manifestation of the character of the town, which was settled in the early 1950s. Its people are displaced Cossacks—White Russians—who resisted the Soviet Revolution, fought in the anti-communist Russian Army of Liberation in World War II, and still hope to return to the Caucasus—under a non-communist government.

The church was constructed in 1964 under the supervision of the Very Reverend Nikolai Nekludoff (or, as he's known locally, Father Nicholas). Built according to the design of Sergi Padukow, it is a manifestation of its congregation's allegiance to the old regime. In addition to the icons, Byzantine motifs, and onion-shaped cupolas, the interior displays tsarist imagery: a portrait of Nicholas II and the royal family, and an abundance of double-headed eagles, emblem of the Byzantine Empire and then of the Romanovs. The rector, Father Nicholas, wears a long black robe and a flowing beard; many people in the congregation still use English sparingly.

Though they have transplanted a culture intact to this little community, and have built a church meant to be permanent, there is an air of transience to New Kuban. The people worship here, but they pray for the restoration of a life they are separated from—by time as well as by space.

ST. SAVA SERBIAN ORTHODOX CATHEDRAL, Milwaukee, Wisconsin, 1956–58

St. Sava Serbian Orthodox Cathedral, constructed between 1956 and 1958, is a response to a powerful desire on the part of its Serbian congregation that their cathedral reflect its Eastern heritage as closely as possible. Drawing upon Byzantine antecedents, most particularly the monastery church at Gracanica (built in 1321), the building is a Greek cross topped by five domes in a typical Byzantine pattern.

The interior walls, as in fourteenth-century prototypes, are covered with marble, mosaics, and frescoes. The altar screen or "iconostasis" was designed by the Chicago architects Cambouras and Theodore, but the icons were painted by Serbians. A Serbian also designed and installed the stained-glass windows.

©Jack Hamilton

HOLY TRINITY ORTHODOX CATHEDRAL, Chicago, Illinois, 1900–03

Louis Sullivan is primarily remembered as a pioneer of modern architecture, producing a group of famous skyscrapers in the 1880s. Due to changes in public taste, economic depression, a separation from his genial partner Dankmar Adler, and his own cantankerous personality, from the late 1890s Sullivan's practice fell away. Although he was no longer commissioned to do great complexes like the Auditorium Building or skyscrapers like the Wainwright, Guaranty, or Chicago Stock Exchange buildings, he did execute some great works, especially his banks for small Midwestern towns like Owatona, Minnesota; Grinnell, Iowa; and Columbus, Wisconsin. Anything he touched, even in the nadir of his fortunes, bore the imprint of genius. Such a building is Holy Trinity, designed during the same period as his masterpiece at Owatona.

Based on Russian and Byzantine prototypes, Holy Trinity was commissioned by a working-class congregation of recent Russian Orthodox immigrants and could only be constructed with some help from Tsar Nicholas II. The structure, at 1211 North Leavitt Street in Chicago, is not elaborate, but it is a handsome, domed, central-plan church with a frontal tower and foyer. The hood moldings over the doors and windows, hexagonal drums on the dome and tower, and small onion-shaped finials relieve the simplicity of the façades. Unlike most Eastern churches, the interior of the dome was decorated not with a depiction of Christ Pantocrator, but with clouds and stars. It has been observed that the dome itself acts like a baldacchino over an altar, to bring the congregation to stand to worship together under a canopy; it is an intimate space in which one feels a roundness, a unity, missing in grander churches. Sullivan satisfied his clients' need for reminders of their heritage, and he made intimacy a substitute for the grandeur, which this working-class congregation could not afford.

©Gerald Mansheim

ANNUNCIATION GREEK ORTHODOX CHURCH,
Wauwatosa, Wisconsin, 1959

©Balthazar Korab

One of the last designs of Frank Lloyd Wright, the Annunciation Greek Orthodox Church in Wauwatosa is a sophisticated mutation of Byzantine prototypes into a thoroughly modern conception.

The plan responds to the requirements of the Orthodox liturgy; it is basically a Greek cross over which a circular dome is imposed. Drawing from the example of the Hagia Sophia in Constantinople, Wright (as was his custom) disavowed any direct quotations from the past: "It is never necessary to cling slavishly to a tradition. The spirit of religion is all that will live because it is all that is really significant as life changes and emerges." Writing in his eighty-ninth year, Wright continued, "The building is therefore not a copy of Byzantine architec-

ture—but better than a copy, it is in proper scale and feeling to reflect the beauty of . . . that ancient period without copying a single feature."

Under its shallow concrete dome, the interior receives the daylight through a variety of circular and paraboloid windows punched into the drum and through a circular clerestory under the overhang. Though predominantly of a cream color, the auditorium is enlivened by the gold-leafed dome above and blue and gold furnishings below. The dome's exterior, following Byzantine tradition, is tiled in blue. Though the exterior appearance is vehement, the interior is quiet and shadowed, in accordance with the Orthodox tradition.

5
A Final Note

History has made it impossible for us to depict buildings arising out of one of the most important religious traditions in America, that of the Africans. These people, perhaps as many as 9 million, were brought across the Atlantic as slaves. After slavery of Africans had lasted for three hundred years, the United States was among the last of the nations of the Western Hemisphere to abolish it; but even then African Americans were only slowly brought into a full participation in American society. They had supplied the labor by which many of the buildings in these pages were constructed but were able to build only a few of their own.

Since it is virtually impossible to identify religious buildings specifically representative of black religious practices, and since this is a book about buildings, some churches can be presented here that are largely used by African Americans, but none designed entirely by them. (The association of Paul Rudolph with the community at Tuskegee is the nearest approximation we can offer.) However, we can note the importance to the continuity of their religious practices of forms of architecture we cannot present. Like the ''brush arbors'' of mesquite or bushes where Native Americans and frontier whites assembled to worship, plantation slaves gathered in ''hush arbors.'' In such places they could sustain not only their own forms of liturgy, but also find Scriptural consolation in the similar experiences of exiled Jews in Babylon or Egypt or of early Christians huddled to worship in the days of their persecution. But none of these buildings survive.

Nor did the poverty of black people make it possible for their early churches to be built of the durable materials that have permitted us to admire other buildings of the time. Blacks were members of many Southern churches, especially among the Baptists and Methodists, though they sat or stood in segregated places before 1830. They were discouraged or forbidden to gather at all for religious observance in most of the South after the ''great fear'' of the 1830s and before emancipation. (Even so far north as Hingham, Massachusetts, blacks were admitted to the meeting house but hidden behind a wall.) After emancipation there was a brief period during which they came into many white churches while organizing many of their own. This interlude in segregation came to an end in the 1890s with the advent of Jim Crow laws.

In the twentieth century large, prosperous black churches in the cities appeared at the termini of another enormous black migration to the cities, an exodus on a scale to match that from Africa. This time, however, their migration was voluntary. Three quarters of black Americans in 1900 had lived in the rural South; a century later, three quarters lived in cities. Half lived in the North. But their churches were nearly all purchased from whites, who had built them to accommodate religious practices that were

The full panoply of Victorian grandeur at Trinity Church in Boston. ©Richard Cheek not exactly the same as those of wholly black congregations. Some buildings, like the Kehileth Anshe M'Ariv Synagogue, now the Pilgrim Baptist Church in Chicago, and St. Luke's Episcopal Church, now the New Tabernacle Fourth Baptist Church in Charleston, South Carolina, are splendid buildings splendidly used.

This book also omits examples of hermitages and individual chapels, even though we have suggested that a fourth axis for religious architecture would be "in me." There are monasteries that carry forward into our own time the solitary life that began in Egyptian deserts with people like Saint Anthony the Anchorite. *Monk* in its original meaning meant one who dwelt alone. Hermits and cenobitic holy ones are to be found in America today. Some inhabit places of remarkable beauty. But it is a fair guess that none of them would welcome inclusion in this book. So we have refrained from doing so.

We have, however, included an example of a form that cannot narrowly be described as a church, although it is representative of a type demonstrating the best and the worst in the American architectural response to large religious themes. This is a funerary chapel, the Wade Memorial of Cleveland, Ohio. Its inclusion permits us to explore along the frontiers of this book itself.

If Louis Sullivan's masterpieces in funerary architecture, the Getty and Wainwright Tombs, had been intended to be entered and used for religious purposes, we would have included essays upon them. But they are closed to the public, and one of our criteria for discussing buildings in this book has been that we would write of spaces that could be experienced, not just of places. There are magnificent mortuary places in America, like one of Henry H. Richardson's works, the Ames Monument, high on a barren pass in Wyoming. Finally, our insistence upon spaces intended to be entered also forces us to exclude great mortuary designs that were never completed, like Harvey Ellis's Burnes Memorial. But the accompanying illustrations can show some of these objects as a suggestion of the wealth of funerary architecture, which lies beyond our scope.

Naturally enough, we also exclude those sepulchral monuments that justify the anathema pronounced by Sullivan's biographer Hugh Morrison: "Such monuments as pretend to architectural distinction too often achieve merely an expensive notoriety—the pretension without the distinction. The word 'fashionable' is nowhere better applied: evidences of the Gothic fashion, the Romanesque fashion, the Egyptian fashion, the Classic fashion, and all other fashions, abound, as if architects hoped to celebrate the permanence of death through borrowing styles that have been dead for many hundreds of years . . . a cemetery resembles a kind of architectural morgue. The sentiment expressed in a majority of monuments is a preoccupation with death. . . . A different spirit animates Sullivan's tombs. They celebrate . . . the permanence of life; they express in terms of lyric beauty that a man or a woman has lived." Louis Comfort Tiffany designed several small chapels, the finest of which was temporary, to be shown at the Chicago Columbian Exposition in 1892. Its pieces survive, and someday the chapel may be reassembled. When it was first presented to the public, it was said that "entering the chapel may very well have been an experience similar to that encountered by the people of Ravenna when their own Byzantine mosaics were new." Tiffany asserted that he had used nearly a million pieces of glass, pearls, and semiprecious stones. There was, of course, a difference; in Ravenna this opulence was part of a scheme intended to suggest another world within a religious building. In Chicago, the intention was entirely secular and was an immensely skillful commercial venture.

To say that Tiffany's "chapel" had a commercial purpose implies no discredit to him. Like the work of Richardson upon a commercial warehouse for Marshall Field or that of Sullivan for his clients' banks—which are surely among the masterpieces of architecture in the world—Tiffany's exquisite craftsmanship justifies itself in a setting more like Disneyland than Ravenna. We would not be discussing the matter at all had not a pious Chicago widow sought to consecrate this commercial venture by donating it to the Cathedral of St. John the Divine in New York, where it actually served until 1911 as a religious space. The tragedy is that we cannot depict it here because the ubiquitous Ralph Adams Cram and his fellow Gothicists felt it to be out of keeping with their ideas for the building and permitted it to be dismantled.

While Louis Tiffany was himself an architect, he never completed a religious building, though the work of his firm in glass, metal, mosaic, and, it might be said, light is very widely distributed throughout America. His finest surviving funerary chapel was inserted into an undistinguished classic-revival building in the Lakeview Cemetery in Cleveland, Ohio. It was completed in 1899, in memory of Jephtha H. Wade. There are grand eight-foot-by-thirty-two-foot glass mosaic panels on the ceiling and marble walls, and a central window designed by Tiffany himself representing the "Consummation of the Divine Promise." All this work is, indeed, a consummation of nineteenth-century taste. Tiffany had assembled a group of craftsmen who could, without embarrassment, be compared to any the world has seen in Ravenna or in Rome or in Florence. The Wade Chapel is open to the public by appointment and does serve as a place of religious contemplation, though not of an active liturgy.

The most comprehensive surviving example of Tiffany's church work was, again, inserted into a building of perfectly acceptable but uninspired quality. The architect of St. Michael's Church in New York City was the versatile Robert W. Gibson. Gibson turned to a bland, gray Romanesque for this building after he had done an exercise in romantic Helvetian for his nearby Collegiate Church, and apparently with no greater effort than that required for the polished Renaissance style he employed for the Fifth Avenue mansion which has since become Cartier or for the classical utilitarian of his main building at the Bronx Zoo. But the miracle at St. Michael's is Tiffany's interior. The entire region of the altar, its railing, the windows behind it, the walls about those windows, the magnificent pulpit, the lighting fixtures, and an elaborate and very effective mosaic mural in a side chapel, together with two other entire ranges of windows, are by the Tiffany studios.

When the sun is setting and the light presses into this room from across the Hudson, St. Michael's blazes into one of America's great church interiors. The church itself, once in a fashionable district, now serves a polyglot neighborhood with a vigor justifying all the energies and all the genius of Louis Tiffany and his colleagues. His opulent craftsmanship illuminates the work of a living religious community, perhaps even more powerfully than it did for a congregation that might have taken such things for granted when it was shiny and new.

It is difficult for architectural historians to keep their imaginations from wandering back to the association of Louis Tiffany and Byzantium, to the glittering mosaics of which he was America's master, and to the surviving masterpieces of that art form in the mortuary chapels of Ravenna. They remind us again of the ancient tradition of churches built in association with cemeteries: St. Peter's in Rome is the largest funerary chapel in the world, and the Church of the Holy Sepulchre in Jerusalem was probably the most influential in form. The custom of using the tombs of saints and martyrs as places to perform the Sacraments commenced very early in the life of the church. The presence of death has been brought to the attention of worshipers in the great cathedrals, where the medieval "cult of death" has remained enshrined in thousands of macabre reliquaries. Death, like life, is an aspect of the Mystery. We do not know how to define either, death or life, despite our best and our worst efforts to try.

So the Wade Chapel, the only surviving temple of Tiffany's mortuary work, belongs in this book, in part because it is beautiful, in part because it is representative, and in part because it brings to a close this book, which, I hope, has been like a good life, just long enough.

278

Tiffany's great memorial chapel, the
Wade Chapel in Cleveland, Ohio.

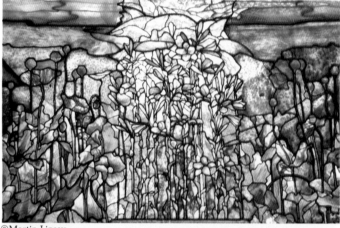

©Martin Linsey

©Martin Linsey

©Frank Aleksandrowicz

©Frank Aleksandrowicz

La Farge windows at Trinity Church
in Boston.

©Bruce T. Martin/Picture Cube

THE ROOFLESS CHURCH, New Harmony, Indiana, 1960

Philip Johnson, long-time advocate of Miesian architecture, broke with that style in the 1950s. Frankly concerned with aesthetics rather than structure per se, Johnson has been called the architect who restored "refinement and elegance" to the profession.

The church at New Harmony, Indiana, is an open-air, folded canopy of shingled curves, 50 feet high. It is "modern" in its lack of applied ornament, structural flamboyance, and concern with abstract geometry, while it is also reminiscent of Indian/Buddhist relic mounds or stupas. Having started his career as an art historian, Johnson admits to drawing from all sorts of precedents, Far Eastern as well as Western. "All great architecture is the design of space that contains, cuddles, exalts, or stimulates the person in that space," he said. The Roofless Church is an "embracing" space.

"I think to gather in Chartres Cathedral is an experience that makes all of us atheists want to be Catholics, just to enjoy it more. When I'm in Chartres, I wish that I could have been born and *brought up* a Catholic, I wish I could have had twenty years' background in the Catholic faith, because I think I would enjoy it more. But even as an atheist, or whatever the heck I am, not *that* bad, just the same, I have an overwhelming feeling that's almost unbearable, just walking in Chartres Cathedral. Well, that's to me what architecture does."

His New Harmony church does more: it represents an opportunity for quiet reflection upon the religious insights of people who did not build churches, or whose churches have not survived, people like the Rappites and the Owenites, whose powerful sense of what good will among humans might achieve led them to put their emphasis upon a community that might "redeem" itself.

ARCHITECTS' BIOGRAPHIES

Dankmar Adler (1844–1900) was born in Stadtlengsfeld, Germany, and emigrated to Detroit in 1854 with his father. He studied architecture there and in Chicago and served with the Illinois artillery regiment in the Civil War. He returned to Chicago after the war and in 1881 formed a partnership with Louis Sullivan. Being the more personable of the two (and a superb designer), Adler drew in most of the business. Adler and Sullivan's Chicago buildings included the Auditorium Theatre, the Transportation Building at the World's Columbian Exhibition (1893), the Gage Building, and the Kehileth Anshe M'ariv Synagogue. Their Wainwright Building in St. Louis (1890) is often described as the first skyscraper designed as a unit, from pavement to cornice. After the partnership broke up in 1895, Adler published technical papers until his death in Chicago.

Samuel Belcher of Ellington, Connecticut, was the builder of the Congregational Church in Old Lyme, Connecticut (1816–17).

George Frederick Bodley (1826–1907), a highly respected British gothicist, designed most of the 1907 plans for Washington Cathedral. Bodley was a poet and a musician as well as an architect. He received the gold medal of the Royal Institute of British Architects.

Marcel Breuer (1902–81) was born in Pecs, Hungary. He entered the new Bauhaus school in Weimar in 1920, where he designed the famous Wassily chair (named for Wassily Kandinsky, who purchased the first one) of leather straps across a tubular steel frame. In 1928 he began his own architectural practice in Berlin, where he designed his most famous work, the ''cesca'' chair, a dining chair of tubular steel with caned seat and back.

In 1937 Breuer joined his old Bauhaus associate Walter Gropius at Harvard University's School of Architecture and in 1946 began his own architectural firm in New York. His major works include the Paris headquarters of the United Nations Educational, Scientific, and Cultural Organization (1953–58); the IBM Research Center in La Gaude, France (1960–61); St. John's Abbey in Collegeville, Minnesota (1953–61); the Whitney Museum in New York City (1963–66); and many houses, including two for himself in New Canaan, Connecticut (1947, 1951). Breuer received various awards, including the American Institute of Architects' highest honor, its gold medal, in 1968. There have been major exhibitions of his work at the Metropolitan Museum of Art (1933) and the Museum of Modern Art (1981).

Charles Bulfinch (1763–1844), born into a wealthy, cultivated Boston family, began as an amateur architect and died a consummate professional. After graduating from Harvard in 1781, he took the advice of Thomas Jefferson and traveled through Europe from 1785 to 1787 to study architecture. Bulfinch began his career as a public servant, becoming a selectman of Boston and, later, superintendent of police. His first large-scale design

was for the Massachusetts State House in Boston (1793–1800), and gradually architecture became his career. Bulfinch's principal works are the Beacon Monument (1789), the Court House (1810), and the Otis Houses, all in Boston; the Connecticut State House in Hartford (1792); and the First Church of Christ in Lancaster, Massachusetts (1816–17). From 1817 to 1830 Bulfinch was the architect of the United States Capitol in Washington, following his predecessor Benjamin Latrobe's plans for the wings but redesigning the dome and rotunda.

The partnership of **Daniel Burnham** and **John Root** was one of the most successful and innovative of the late nineteenth century. Burnham (1846–1912) was born in Henderson, New York, and moved with his family to Chicago in 1855. Unable to gain admission to college, he worked as a draftsman in an architectural firm. He was a great salesman, organizer, and encourager of others. Root (1850–91), born in Lumpkin, Georgia, and studied in Liverpool, England, and at Oxford, then took a degree in civil engineering from the University of the City of New York in 1869. He moved to Chicago in 1871 where he formed a partnership with Burnham in 1873; however, Root was the chief designer of the firm.

The partnership's most important works were skyscrapers: the Monadnock Building in Chicago (1889–91), the Masonic Temple in Chicago (1891), and the Flatiron Building in New York (1902). The latter two were the world's tallest buildings at the time they were constructed. The team was chosen to design the grounds for the World's Columbian Exposition in 1893, and Burnham took sole control of the project after Root's death. Their more modest works include St. Gabriel's Church in Chicago. Burnham went on to concentrate on city planning, constructing plans for Washington, D.C. (1901–2), Chicago (1906–9), and others. He died in Heidelberg, Germany.

Barry Byrne (1883–1967) was born in Chicago. At the age of nineteen, without architectural experience or training, he went to work for Frank Lloyd Wright. Byrne worked in Wright's studio for six years and then entered into partnerships with Andrew Willatzen (1908–13) and Walter Burleigh Griffen (1913–16). Byrne designed many houses in the Prairie style until, after the 1920s, he developed his own freely Gothic style for ecclesiastical and educational buildings. Stylistically, he was not an easy architect to pigeonhole; his spaces are idiosyncratic and often very beautiful.

Little is known of **Samuel Cardy**, the designer of St. Michael's Church in Charleston, South Carolina (1752–56). He emigrated (probably) from Dublin to America some time before 1752, and died in 1774.

Ralph Adams Cram, (1863–1942), with his partners Ferguson and Goodhue, became the pre-eminent American gothicist of the late nineteenth and early twentieth centuries. He not only designed The Cathedral Church of St. John the Divine in New York and aided in the early planning of the Bryn Athyn Cathedral, but Cram was also supervising architect of the Princeton University campus between 1907 and 1927. A prolific writer, he is well remembered for his books *The Gothic Quest* (1907) and *My Life in Architecture* (1936).

Charles Dakin (1811–39) was born in the township of Northeast in New York State and lived to be only twenty-eight years of age; however, he left his architectural mark on the Deep South, notably Mobile, Alabama. He got his start in the New York firm of his famous older brother, James (Town, Davis and Dakin). He apprenticed there until 1833, when he and an Irish-born associate, James Gallier, departed for New Orleans. All of Charles Dakin's major works were executed in partnership with Gallier or with James. It appears that in 1835 Charles Dakin headed the Mobile office, James and Gallier the New Orleans office. Their work includes the two largest hotels in the United States, both of which have burned down: the St. Charles Hotel in New Orleans (Gallier and Dakin) and the United States Hotel in Mobile (Dakin and Dakin). Other designs include St. Patrick's Church in New Orleans (designed by Dakin and Dakin, completed by Gallier); Barton Academy in Mobile, the first permanent public school building in Alabama; and the Government Street Presbyterian Church in Mobile. After yellow fever, fire, and financial ruin beset Mobile, Dakin closed the office and traveled briefly in Europe. Two months after his return in 1839 he died, probably of yellow fever or cholera.

William Drummond (1876–1946) was born in Newark, New Jersey. He attended the University of Illinois Department of Architecture for a year, worked for Louis Sullivan, and then in Wright's studio between 1899 and 1909. He was a skillful Prairie school architect; among his designs in that style is that for the First Congregational Church of Austin, which he completed in 1908.

Lavius Fillmore (1767–1805), a cousin of President Millard Fillmore, was born in Norwich, Connecticut. He designed Congregational churches in New England; his most celebrated church is the Congregational Church in Middlebury, Vermont (1806). Others include the Congregational Church in Bennington, Vermont (1805), and the Congregational Church in Norwichtown, Connecticut (1801). There is evidence that Fillmore may have also designed the Congregational Church in East Haddam, Connecticut (1794), which suggests that he may have anticipated some of the church designs of Asher Benjamin, generally described as the chief author of New England Congregational church designs.

Frank Furness (1839–1912) was born in Philadelphia. He worked in the New York atelier of Richard Morris Hunt (1859–61) before joining the Union cavalry in the Civil War. (Many years later, he received the Congressional Medal of Honor for bravery.) After the war's end he began his architectural practice in Philadelphia as a partner of the firm Fraser, Furness and Hewitt. With Hewitt he designed the Pennsylvania Academy of Fine Arts (1871), perhaps his most famous work and typical of his noticeably picturesque style. During the last twenty years of his life, popular taste shifted toward more restrained architecture; as a result, many of his buildings (including Philadelphia's First Unitarian Church) have been "toned down" by later remodeling. His death went largely ignored by the fashionable architectural critics.

Hugh M. G. Garden (1873–1961) was born in Toronto. He lived first in Minneapolis and then Chicago, the center at that time of architectural innovation. As a draftsman, Garden often prepared drawings for other architects, including Frank Lloyd Wright and Louis Sullivan; but he was an adept designer in his own right. His early buildings, many of them commercial (but including the First Church of Christ in Marshalltown, Iowa), were in the "Chicago school" idiom. After 1907 he worked in an increasingly historicizing vein.

Bertram Goodhue (1869–1924) was born in Pomfret, Connecticut, and moved to New York City in 1884. He encountered the Gothic revival in his work as a draftsman in James Renwick's architectural firm. In 1889 he joined Ralph Adams Cram in Boston in a firm which in 1896 became Cram, Goodhue, and Ferguson. Goodhue opened a branch office in New York for the firm in 1903 and from 1913 focused on ecclesiastical architecture. His New York churches include St. Thomas's (with Cram), St. Vincent Ferrer, and St. Bartholemew's. His later work moved away from the Gothic toward a "style" of his own as evidenced in the Nebraska State Capitol and the National Academy of Sciences Building in Washington, D.C.

Peter Harrison (1716–75) was the most celebrated architect of the colonial period. Born in York, England, he emigrated to America in 1740 and settled in Newport, Rhode Island, as a farmer and trader. He was self-taught in architecture and learned how to deploy the elements of style then current in England. English Palladianisms abound in his first work, the Redwood Library in Newport, Rhode Island (1749–58). Thereafter, his buildings moved against the tide of British fashion, toward the influence of Wren and Gibbs at King's Chapel, Boston (1749–58), and Congregation Jeshuat Israel Synagogue (1759–63), then even further back toward the example of Inigo Jones in works such as the Brick Market, Newport (1761–72), and Christ Church, Cambridge, Massachusetts (1760–61). Harrison moved to New Haven, Connecticut, in 1761 and became collector of customs there in 1768.

Philip Hooker (1766–1858) was born in central Massachusetts and became the favorite architect of Martin Van Buren's "Albany Junto," the ruling politicians of New York State. As city architect of Albany, Hooker designed at least seven churches, three banks, three municipal markets, the chief school buildings, and a theater. His significant works include the Hamilton College Chapel in Clinton, New York (1827), and Hyde Hall near Cooperstown, New York (1833).

Philip Johnson, born in Cleveland in 1906, was an art historian and critic before becoming an architect. A vigorous proponent of Meisian modernism, he helped to organize and write the catalogue for the landmark 1932 exhibit at the Metropolitan Museum of Art entitled "The International Style." He attended Gropius's Harvard School of Architecture, building himself a house for his thesis project. A student, friend, and biographer of Ludwig Mies van der Rohe, he assisted in the design of the Seagram Building. Johnson's all-glass house in New Canaan, Connecticut, seems to epitomize the machine aesthetic, yet he has for years criticized the International style for its chilliness and mannered rejection of the past, saying, "you cannot not know history." In the 1970s and '80s, he is among the most flamboyant of the postmoderns; his AT&T Tower, under construction in New York City, has been likened to a Chippendale grandfather clock. This historicism, though not explicit, can be discerned in both his New Harmony, Indiana, Roofless Church (1960) and in the

285

Garden Grove Crystal Cathedral (1980, with his partner John Burgee).

E. Fay Jones, born in 1921 in Pine Bluff, Arkansas, received his Bachelor of Architecture degree from the University of Arkansas in 1950 and his Master of Architecture degree from Rice University in 1951. He served as an apprentice to Frank Lloyd Wright in 1953 before assuming a professorship at the University of Arkansas in 1954. Since then, Jones has combined teaching at the university with his architectural practice, which has concentrated on residential buildings, the most noteworthy being the Shaheen-Goodfellow House on Eden Isle, Arkansas (1967). The Thorncrown Chapel (1981) is his masterpiece.

Louis Kahn (1901–74) was born on the island of Saarama in the Baltic Sea and came to the United States in 1905. He graduated from the School of Architecture at the University of Pennsylvania in 1924, where he received rigorous Beaux-Arts training. In 1941 Kahn went into partnership with George Howe. From 1947 to 1957 Kahn taught at Yale, where he designed his first celebrated building, the Yale University Art Gallery (1951–53). His later commissions included the Richards Medical Research Building at the University of Pennsylvania (1957–61), the Salk Institute at La Jolla, California (1959–65), the Kimball Art Museum in Fort Worth, Texas (1966–72), the First Unitarian Church in Rochester, New York (1964), and the new capital at Dacca, India. He taught at the University of Pennsylvania and received the gold medal from the AIA and the Royal Gold Medal from the Royal Institute of British Architects.

Minard Lafever (1798–1854) began as a carpenter in the Finger Lakes region of New York. He was an associate of Charles and James Dakin and of James Gallier and is best known as the author of manuals for carpenters and builders, including *The Beauties of Modern Architecture* (1849) and *The Architectural Instructor* (1856). His architectural works include the Holy Trinity Church, Brooklyn, New York, and the Old Whalers' Church, Sag Harbor, New York.

Benjamin Latrobe (1764–1802) was born in Fulneck, England, to an American mother and a British father. After his education at Leipzig, he worked in the office of the London architect Samuel Cockerell. After the death of his wife in 1795, Latrobe set sail for America.

Thomas Jefferson's influence gained Latrobe the commission for the Virginia State Capitol. In 1798 he designed the Bank of Pennsylvania in Philadelphia, the first Greek revival building in the United States. As America's foremost architect, he was called upon to design the Philadelphia Waterworks (1801), the United States Capitol (1803, with Thornton), and the Baltimore Cathedral (1804–18). Although Latrobe was an important architectural designer and engineer, he never found a secure place in America. He was constantly on the move, seeking business and engineering ventures and architectural commissions.

After his son succumbed to a fatal attack of yellow fever while overseeing the construction of the New Orleans waterworks, Benjamin Latrobe took over the commission; he, too, died from yellow fever. His students included Robert Mills and William Strickland.

Francis D. Lee (1826–1885) was the premier architect of Charleston, South Carolina, in the mid-nineteenth century. His two major churches in Charleston were the Unitarian Church (1852–54) and St. Luke's Church (1859–61), now the New Tabernacle Fourth Baptist Church. Lee worked in a variety of styles and was a pioneer in the use of cast iron, which he often used in commercial buildings. Lee served as a major of engineers in the Confederate Army.

Robert C. Long, Jr. (1776–1849) contributed to church architecture in the city of Baltimore in the 1840s. Trained by his father, Long began his career by completing the work of Robert C. Long, Sr., after the latter's death in 1833. His first major commission was St. Alphonsus' Church in Baltimore, (1842). This was followed by two other Baltimore churches, the Franklin Street Presbyterian Church (1844) and the Mt. Calvary Church (1844–45).

All that is known of **Thomas McBean,** designer of St. Paul's Chapel in New York (1766), is that he was Scottish. It is said that he studied under James Gibbs.

Bernard Maybeck (1862–1957) was born in New York City where his father, a woodcarver, had emigrated from Germany. Maybeck went to Paris to learn furniture design, became interested in architecture, and enrolled in the École des Beaux-Arts. Upon returning to the United States, he moved to the San Francisco–Berkeley area, where his most important works were built. They include the Palace of Fine Arts (1915, rebuilt in 1960) and the First Church of Christ, Scientist (1909–11). Though his most noted commissions were completed before 1920, he continued to design until his retirement at the age of eighty. Resurgent interest in his picturesque, eclectic, and technologically ingenious work resulted in the gold medal in his honor from the AIA in 1951.

Ludwig Mies van der Rohe (1886–1969) was born in Aachen, Germany, and was exposed to the craftsman tradition by his father, a stonecutter and mason. He was apprenticed to a draftsman, worked with a furniture designer, and, later, studied under Peter Behrens. He established his own office in Berlin at the age of twenty-seven. His German pavilion at the Barcelona exhibition of 1929 was acclaimed internationally. Mies was director of the Bauhaus from 1930 until it was closed in 1933. Modern architecture was not favored by the Nazis, and Mies had few commissions in the mid-1930s. In 1938 he emigrated to the United States, where he taught at the Armour Institute of Technology (now IIT) in Chicago. He was regarded with the utmost respect by American architects, as can be seen from the fact that he was awarded the commission for the entire Armour Institute campus, including the chapel. The "glass box" is his trademark; it appears in such residences as the Farnsworth House, Plano, Illinois (1950), high-rise apartments on Lakeshore Drive in Chicago (1951), and in the building that has been regarded as "the Parthenon of modernism," the Seagram Building in New York (1956, with Philip Johnson). Mies became a naturalized citizen in 1944 and died in Chicago.

Robert Mills (1781–1855) was the first Native American to prepare for a professional career as an architect. Born in Charleston, South Carolina, Mills began his career in Philadelphia; he designed residences, churches, the Washington Hall (1808), and rebuilt Independence Hall. During this period he also was responsible for the Monumental Church in Richmond, Virginia (1812), and the Washington Monument in Baltimore, Maryland (designed 1815, finished 1829). His later works include many government buildings in Washington, D.C., all of classical design, including the Treasury Building (1836–49), the Patent Office (1836–40), and the Post Office (1839). His most famous work remains the Washington Monument in Washington, D.C., designed in 1836 but not completed until 1884, and then only in a reduced version of his design.

William A. Potter (1842–1909) was a fashionable architect of the High Victorian Gothic. His father and one brother were bishops. His half brother, Edward T. Potter, was also an architect, and it was to Edward's office that William was apprenticed in 1867. In 1875 he opened his own practice with Robert H. Robertson and was appointed the supervisory architect of the United States Treasury. He worked largely for prestigious clients—his designs include that of St. Mary's-in-Tuxedo—until his retirement in 1902. He then moved to Rome, where he died.

James Renwick, Jr. (1818–95) was born in New York City, the son of a brilliant engineer. After graduating from Columbia at the age of seventeen, he started out his career as an engineer but gained fame as a scholarly, eclectic architect. Among his best-known buildings are St. Patrick's Cathedral in New York (1853–57), the Smithsonian "Castle" (1846), and the Corcoran Gallery of Art (now the Renwick) in Washington, D.C. (1859), essays in the Gothic, Romanesque, and French Renaissance revivals, respectively. He was successful until his death in New York.

Born in St. Thomas Parish, Louisiana, **Henry Hobson Richardson** (1838–1886) attended schools in New Orleans before graduating from Harvard in 1859. After studying architecture at the École des Beaux-Arts in Paris (1858–62), he first practiced in New York. In Boston, he established himself by winning the competition for the Brattle Square Church (1870) and the Trinity Church (1877). In 1882 Richardson traveled to Europe to study the Romanesque style, which he freely transformed into his "Richardsonian" Romanesque style. Many of his works feature architectural and engineering innovations. The works include the libraries of North Easton (1877) and Quincy, Massachusetts (1870); two buildings for Harvard University, Sever Hall (1878) and Austin Hall (1881); the Emmanuel Episcopal Church, Pittsburgh (1883–86); the Marshall Field Warehouse Building in Chicago (1887); private houses, such as the Stoughton House, Cambridge (1882–83), and the Glessner House, Chicago (1885), completed the year before his death. Richardson's influence continued into the twentieth century through his students, Charles F. McKim and Stanford White, and through his impact upon Louis Sullivan, John W. Root, Frank Lloyd Wright, and a whole generation of romantic and picturesque designers.

Paul Rudolph was born in 1918 and later attended the Harvard School of Architecture under Gropius and Breuer. He began his career designing Florida residences, but gained larger commissions in the late 1950s. In 1958 he became dean of the Yale School of Architecture, designing a new building for that school in the same year. Rudolph went on to design other fresh, forceful, and often beautiful buildings, including the Tuskegee chapel. He left Yale in 1965, and has been in practice since then on a variety of projects.

Eero Saarinen (1910–61) was born in Kyrkslatt, Finland, and emigrated to the United States in 1923 with his architect father, Eliel. He later studied in Paris (1929–30), at Yale (1931–34), and in Finland (1935–36). His chief works were designed after World War II and include the General Motors Technical Center in Warren, Michigan (1948–56), the St. Louis Arch (designed 1948, built in 1964), the Kresge Auditorium and the chapel at the Massachusetts Institute of Technology (1953–55), the Ingalls Hockey Rink at Yale (1958), the TWA Terminal at Kennedy International Airport in New York City (1956–62), and Dulles Airport in Chantilly, Virginia (1958–63). Saarinen died in Ann Arbor, Michigan.

(Gottlieb) Eliel Saarinen (1873–1950) was born in Rantasalmi, Finland. His first famous design was the Helsinki railway station (1905–14). His influential design placed second in the competition for the Chicago Tribune Building in 1922, and he emigrated to the United States in 1923. His works in the United States include the buildings for the Cranbrook School in Michigan (1925, 1929, etc.), the Tabernacle Church of Christ in Columbus, Indiana (1942), and the Christ Lutheran Church in Minneapolis, Minnesota (1950). He worked in a partnership with his son, Eero, until his death in Bloomfield Hills, Michigan.

Skidmore, Owings & Merrill is one of the largest and best-known architectural firms in the United States, with branches in many cities. Perhaps their most influential designs to date are Lever House, a steel-frame skyscraper built in New York in 1952; the Air Force Academy, including its chapel (1956–62); the Chicago Circle Campus of the University of Illinois (1966); and scores of skyscrapers.

William Strickland (1788–1854) worked as an apprentice to Benjamin Latrobe in Philadelphia before coming into his own. He did some early Gothic revival work, but Strickland is best known for his Classic revival houses, churches (including two in Nashville, St. Mary's Catholic Church and the First Presbyterian Church), as well as public buildings (the Custom House and Merchant's Exchange in Philadelphia, for example). He was given a hero's burial in the crypt of the Tennessee State Capitol Building, his most famous design.

Commonly recognized as one of the pioneer figures of modern architecture, **Louis Sullivan** (1856–1924) was born in Boston. Educated at MIT and the École des Beaux-Arts, he was apprenticed to the prominent Philadelphia architect Frank Furness for one year. He gained early success and fame for his work with Dankmar Adler's firm in Chicago. During the 1880s and early '90s, Sullivan designed over one hundred buildings, among them the Chicago Auditorium Building, skyscrapers such as the Wainwright and the Guaranty buildings, the Kehileth Anshe M'ariv Synagogue, and the Transportation Building for the Chicago World's Columbian Exposition of 1893. His progressive design for the exposition, unlike the Beaux-Arts Neoclassicism of the other architects, won him the sole award for architecture given at the exposition by the French. His work in the design of steel-frame multistory buildings is acknowledged as a prelude to the twentieth-century "curtain walls" of modern skyscrapers. For various reasons, including changes in popular taste, as well as the breakup of his partnership with Adler, he gained few commissions after the turn of the century. Even these were relatively modest; his small banks as well as the Holy Trinity Russian Orthodox Cathedral are quite unlike his grander works designed before 1900. His writings of this period include *Kindergarten Chats* and *Autobiography of an Idea*, the latter published in 1924, the year Sullivan died in a seedy Chicago hotel room.

Louis Comfort Tiffany (1848–1933) was born in New York City, the son of jeweler Charles L. Tiffany. He was a printer, designer, and marvelous organizer of the crafts of others. He began working with stained glass when he was twenty-seven, and three years later opened a factory that produced metalwork, glass, terra cotta, mosaic, and pottery. His techniques produced works of singular beauty, some of it in kinship with the European Art Nouveau.

Born in Shaftesbury, England, **Richard Upjohn** (1802–78) began his career as a cabinetmaker. He emigrated to America in 1829, settled in Boston in 1834 as an architect, and then moved to New York in 1839. Chiefly known as a proponent of the Gothic revival (though he did work in other styles as well), Upjohn established himself with the design for Trinity Episcopal Church in New York, built between 1841 and 1846. Numerous commissions followed, including Old St. Thomas's Episcopal in New York, St. Mary's Episcopal Church in Nashville (1846–48), the Church of St. John Chrysostom in Delafield, Wisconsin, and Trinity Chapel in New York (1853). In 1852 Upjohn published *Upjohn's Rural Architecture,* a manual designed to teach poor parishioners how to build simple churches at minimal cost. He founded the American Institute of Architects (AIA) in 1857 and served as its first president until 1876.

Henry Vaughan (1846–1917) was born in England and apprenticed there under George Bodley. He later emigrated to Boston, where he became a specialist in the Gothic. He was, therefore, the natural choice to assist Bodley in designing Washington Cathedral. Vaughan was the supervising architect of the cathedral from 1907 until his death.

Frank Lloyd Wright (1869–1959) was born in Richland Center, Wisconsin. His father was a peripatetic preacher. It is largely due to his mother's influence that he became interested in design at an early age. Because the University of Wisconsin had no school of architecture, Wright attended its engineering school for one year. Unsatisfied, he pawned his father's copies of *The Decline and Fall of the Roman Empire* and *Plutarch's Lives* and ran away from school to Chicago for architectural training. He obtained work with J. I. Silsbee for one year before being hired by Adler and Sullivan for five years, eventually becoming Sullivan's chief assistant. In 1893 he opened his own practice in Oak Park, Illinois, and designed residences for the most part; but these years did include his design for Unity Temple. Upon publishing designs for his free-flowing, "organic" homes in the *Ladies' Home Journal,* they became known as "Prairie homes," harmonizing with the flat terrain of the Midwest.

Wright moved back to Wisconsin in 1911 and there set up Taliesin, his new studio. During this time his residential designs were published in Germany and brought him European fame. In the United States, however, he was not so well appreciated. In the 1920s and early '30s, his commissions were few. He resumed a heavy outpouring of designs in the mid-1930s, including "Fallingwater," the famous Kaufman House (1936). Though his works include the Price Tower (1953), the Guggenheim Museum (1942–60), and the Johnson Wax Complex (1937 and 1946), he is primarily significant for his impact on American residences and churches.

SUGGESTIONS FOR FURTHER READING

This is not a book intended for professional scholars, so it has no scholarly bibliography and footnotes intended for researchers interested in pursuing their studies. I have included a section of references, beginning on p. 290, indicating the sources I used in preparing the commentaries on specific churches and architects. In a book of this kind, the reading of a lifetime has crept in, and as I have reviewed the piles of books to which I made direct reference during the course of my writing, some were such welcome friends by the time I was through that I wanted to have the pleasure of recommending them to readers who find the subject interesting. I could not hope to list all the standard references, or even all the sources I have read; so I present those that occur to me as having been boon companions in the process of construction of this book. I've broken them into very broad categories.

Religion in America

Sydney Ahlstrom's *Religious History of the American People* (New Haven, Conn.: Yale University Press, 1972) won the National Book Award in 1973. The award was well deserved; the book is beguilingly written and carries with it a wealth of information.

History of the Churches in the United States and Canada (New York: Oxford University Press, 1977), by Robert T. Handy, addresses the same material as Ahlstrom's book. But, as the title indicates, it covers a broader geographical area.

Catherine A. Albanese surveys not only "official" religion but also what she calls "cultural" and "civil" religion in *America, Religions and Religion* (Belmont, Calif.: Wadsworth Publishing Co., 1981). She writes carefully but forcefully, and she swings a wide sickle in 371 pages.

Psychology of Religion

Those studies on the psychology of religion that I have found most intensely helpful have been the following from the *Collected Works of Carl Jung* (Princeton, N.J.: Princeton University Press, 1966): *Volume 5: Symbols of Transformation; Volume 15: Spirit in Man, Art and Literature;* and part 2 of *Volume 9: Aion.* Two anthologies were also enlightening: *C. G. Jung: Psychological Reflections,* edited by Jolande Jacobi (Princeton, N.J.: Princeton University Press, 1970); and *Psyche and Symbol,* edited by Violet S. deLaszlo (Garden City, N.Y.: Doubleday, 1958). Not in Jung's collected work, but a very acceptable route into his thought, is *Memories, Dreams, Reflections,* edited by Aniela Jaffe (New York: Random House, 1965), from which the reference to the Mandala was drawn.

Architectural Histories

The indispensable standard texts are Henry Russell Hitchcock's *Architecture: Nineteenth and Twentieth Centuries* (New York: Penguin, 1958) and *Architecture in Britain, 1530 to 1830* by Sir John Summerson (New York: Penguin, 1953). I have turned as well to another volume in the same series, Kenneth John Conant's *Carolingian and Romanesque Architecture, 800 to 1200* (New York: Penguin, 1974).

Alan Gowans, in *Images of American Living* (New York: Harper, 1976), makes no pretense at being encyclopedic. However, the book is full of marvelously stimulating ideas, and it has an elegantly opinionated, annotated bibliography.

William L. Pierson, Jr., is the indefatigable and reliable architectural historian who supplied the first two volumes of the *American Buildings and Their Architects* series—*Volume I: The Colonial and Neoclassical Styles* (1976) and *Volume II: Technology and the Picturesque, the Corporate and Early Gothic Styles* (1980). William H. Jordy carries on the line of his somewhat less encyclopedic, but more detailed, study of a group of American buildings in the next number of the series, *Volume III: Progressive and Academic Ideals at the Turn of the Twentieth Century* (1972). This series is published in paperback by Anchor.

Dover Publications (New York) has issued reprints of two general architectural histories of early America that should be part of every basic library. These are Fiske Kimball's *Domestic Architecture of the American Colonies and the Early Republic* (1970), originally published in 1928, and Talbot Hamlin's pioneering *Greek Revival Architecture in America* (1975), originally published in 1947.

Hugh and Samuel Eliot Morrison have also done well for us. Hugh Morrison is the author of the sturdy *Early American Architecture from the First Colonial Settlements to the National Period* (New York: Oxford University Press, 1952). Samuel Eliot Morrison has provided a wealth of anecdote and interpretation in a series of books. I found *Maritime History of Massachusetts, 1783 to 1960* (1979) and *Builders of the Bay Colony* (1958) most useful in preparing this volume. Both these books were reissued in Boston by Northeastern University Press.

I have rejoiced in a little volume entitled *Architecture in Worship* by Andre Biéler (Philadelphia: Westminster Press, 1965), which has a miniscule but potent essay by Carl Barth. This is remarkably harmonious in its point of view to Harold W. Turner's more comprehensive study, *From Temple to Meeting House: The Phenomenology and Theology of Places of Worship* (The Hague: Mouton, 1979).

I have used *The Architectural Setting of Anglican Worship* by G. W. O. Addleshaw and Frederic Etchells (London: Faber and Faber, 1956) and *Outward and Visible* by Basil Minchin (London: Darton, Longman and Todd, 1961). The Methodists at Wesley Seminary introduced me to Otto Von Simson's *The Gothic Cathedral* (Princeton, N.J.: Princeton University Press, 1974), for which I am exceedingly grateful. It is a wonderful book.

There is remarkably interesting and useful text, written by

Henri Peyre, that accompanies Dimitri Kessel's extraordinary photographs of the *Splendors of Christendom* in the Lausanne edition of 1964. The three volumes of the *Illustrated Histories of Medieval and Modern Architecture* (London: Elek Books Ltd.) have all been stimulating in the preparation of this book: *Baroque and Rococo* (1978), edited by Anthony Blunt; *The Gothic Cathedral* (1969), edited by Wim Swaan; and *The Monastic World* (1974), edited by Christopher Brooke, with pictures by Mr. Swaan.

Regional Guides

For quick references to pictures and short bits of sprightly text, there is no better series than Wayne Andrews's set of regional architectural histories: *Architecture in Chicago and Mid-America* (New York: Harper & Row, 1973); *Architecture in New York* (New York: Harper & Row, 1973); *Architecture in New England* (New York: Harper & Row, 1973); and *Architecture in Michigan* (Detroit, Mich.: Wayne State University Press, 1967).

This brings us to some other quite splendid regional guides. My favorites are the AIA *Guide to New York City* (1968) and the companion *Guide to Washington, D.C.* (1965). While not an AIA guide, *Maryland: A New Guide to the Old Line State* (offered by the State Archivist of Maryland, Edward C. Papenfuse, and his group, in 1976) is every bit as good (Baltimore: Johns Hopkins University Press, 1976).

Some lucky readers may still have WPA guides to such states as Virginia, New York, and Maryland; however, most of these treasures are out of print. I have used the more current *Guide to the Architecture of Minnesota* by David Gebhard and Tom Martinson (Minneapolis, 1977) and Barbara Clayton and Kathleen Whitley's *Exploring Coastal New England* (published in Boston in 1979) with equal gratitude.

Other regional or local histories eminently worth reading are *The Buildings of Detroit: A History* by W. Hawkins Ferry (Detroit, Mich.: Wayne State University Press, 1968) and the magisterial *Architectural Heritage of Newport, Rhode Island* by Antoinette F. Downing and Vincent J. Scully, Jr. (reprinted in Cambridge by Harvard University Press in 1967). Also of interest is a book by Sheila Steinberg and Kathleen McGuigan, *Rhode Island: An Historical Guide* (Providence, R.I.: Rhode Island Bicentennial Foundation, 1976).

Economic History

For economic history, which is inevitably braided into the rest of this story, the most recent and useful volumes to which I have turned for help are the fourth edition of *History of the American Economy* by Ross M. Robertson and Gary M. Wilton (New York: Harcourt, Brace, 1979) and *A New Economic View of American History* by Susan Previant Lee and Peter Passell (New York: Norton, 1979). Nobody, of course, can approach this territory without making use of Douglas C. North's *The Economic Growth of the United States, 1790–1860* (New York: Norton, 1966). And the two volumes of *The Historical Statistics of the United States, Colonial Times to 1970* (published by the Department of Commerce in 1975) are a glorious compendium of useful statistics on every conceivable subject.

Architects

With respect to individual architects, there are now a number of large and important studies, many of which found their way into the essays on each church; but I also made use of some of them in considering the more general opening statements. These include Norris Kelly Smith's *Frank Lloyd Wright: A Study in Architectural Content* (Englewood Cliffs, N.J.: Prentice-Hall, 1966) and Talbot Hamlin's *Benjamin Henry Latrobe* (New York: Oxford University Press, 1955). Curious readers might also search out two autobiographies: Frank Lloyd Wright's *An Autobiography* (New York: Horizon, 1943) and Charles Édouard Jeanneret-Gris's (Le Corbusier) *When the Cathedrals Were White: A Journey to the Country of Timid People* (New York: Reynal and Hitchcock, 1947). I know of no more satisfactory book on Sullivan than *Louis Sullivan: Prophet of Modern Architecture* by Hugh Morrison (a 1971 reprint of the 1935 edition is available from the Greenwood Press in Westport, Conn.). And Sullivan's own work, *The Autobiography of an Idea* (New York: Dover, 1924), is a powerful and tragic work.

References

Abercrombie, Stanley. "A Building of Great Integrity," *American Institute of Architects Journal*, May 1981, pp. 148–155.

American Institute of Architectural Bibliographers. *Paradise Improved.* Charlottesville, Va.: University of Virginia Press, 1972.

Andrews, Wayne. *Architecture in Chicago and Mid-America.* New York: Harper & Row, 1973.

———*Architecture in Michigan.* Detroit, Mich.: Wayne State University Press, 1967.
———*Architecture in New England.* New York: Harper & Row, 1973.
———*Architecture in New York.* New York: Harper & Row, 1973.

Bach, Ira J. *Chicago's Famous Buildings.* Chicago: University of Chicago Press, 1980.

Bates, Charles D. *The Archives Tell a Story of the Government Street Presbyterian Church, Mobile, Alabama.* Mobile, 1959.

Brooks, Harold Allen. *The Prairie School: Frank Lloyd Wright and His Midwest Contemporaries.* Toronto: University of Toronto Press, 1972.

Brown, Milton W., Sam Hunter, John Jacobus, Naomi Rosenblum, and David M. Sokol. *American Art.* Englewood Cliffs, N.J.: Prentice-Hall, 1979.

Brumbaugh, Thomas B., ed. *Architecture of Middle Tennessee.* Nashville, Tenn.: Vanderbilt University Press, 1974.

Bush-Brown, Albert. *Louis Sullivan*. New York: Braziller, 1960.

Cardwell, Kenneth H. *Bernard Maybeck: Artisan, Architect, Artist*. Santa Barbara, Calif.: Peregrine Smith, 1977.

Christ-Janer, Albert, and Mary Mix Foley. *Modern Church Architecture*. New York: McGraw-Hill, 1962.

Churcher, Sharon. "The Intelligencer: TV Church Raids Broadway for Deluxe Nativity," *New York Magazine*, 24 August 1981, p. 16.

Cook, John Wesley, and Heinrich Klotz. *Conversations with Architects*. New York: Praeger, 1978.

Courtenay, Samuel G. *The Old and the New: Or, Discourses and Proceedings at the Dedication of the Re-Modelled Unitarian Church in Charleston, S.C., on Sunday, April 2, 1854 . . . etc*. Charleston, S.C.: Unitarian Church, 1854.

Danz, Ernst. *Architecture of Skidmore, Owings and Merrill, 1950–1962*. New York, Praeger, 1963.

Dorsey, Stephen Palmer. *Early English Churches in America*. New York: Oxford University Press, 1952.

Fairfax, Geoffrey W. *Architecture of Honolulu*. Norfolk Island, Australia: Island Heritage, Ltd., 1971.

Feller, Richard T., and Marshall W. Fishwick. *For Thy Great Glory*. Culpepper, Va.: Community Press, 1965.

Ferry, W. Hawkins. *The Buildings of Detroit: A History*. Detroit, Mich.: Wayne State University Press, 1968.

Gallagher, Helen. *Robert Mills: Architect of the Washington Monument, 1781–1855*. New York: AMS Press, 1935.

Gibbs, James. *A Book of Architecture*. 1628. Reprint. New York: B. Blom, 1968.

"Gothic Architecture—A New Church." *United States Catholic Magazine* 2 (May 1843): 303.

Hamlin, Talbot F. *Benjamin Henry Latrobe*. New York: Oxford University Press, 1955.

Hitchcock, Henry Russell. *Architecture: Nineteenth and Twentieth Centuries*. New York: Penguin Books, 1958.

Huber, Leonard Victor, and Samuel Wilson, Jr. *The Basilica on Jackson Square and Its Predecessors*. New York: Pelican, 1973.

Hunter, Sam, and John Jacobus. *American Art of the Twentieth Century*. New York: Abrams, 1979.

Jacobson, John M. *Philip Johnson*. New York: Braziller, 1962.

Johnson, Philip C. *Mies van der Rohe*. New York: Museum of Modern Art, 1953.

———*Writings*. New York: Oxford University Press, 1979.

Jones, Cranston. *Architecture Today and Tomorrow*. New York: McGraw-Hill, 1961.

Jordy, William. *American Buildings and Their Architects: Progressive and Academic Ideals at the Turn of the Twentieth Century*. New York: Anchor, 1972.

———*American Buildings and Their Architects: The Impact of European Modernism in the Mid-Twentieth Century*. New York: Anchor, 1972.

Landau, Sarah Bradford. *Edward T. and William A. Potter: American Victorian Architects*. New York: Garland, 1979.

Latrobe, Ferdinand C. "Benjamin Henry Latrobe: Descent and Works." *Maryland Historical Magazine* 33 (1938): 247–261.

Lilly, Edward G. *Historic Churches of Charleston*. Charleston, S.C., 1966.

Lobell, John. *Between Silence and Light: Spirit in the Architecture of Louis Kahn*. Boulder, Col.: Shambhala, 1979.

Meade, William. *Old Churches, Ministers, and Families of Virginia*. 1857. Reprint. Baltimore: Genealogical Publishing Company, 1966.

Morrison, Hugh S. *Louis Sullivan: Prophet of Modern Architecture*. 1935. Reprint. Westport, Conn.: Greenwood Press, 1971.

Neil, J. Meredith. "The Precarious Professionalism of Latrobe." *American Institute of Architects Journal*, May 1970, pp. 67–71.

O'Gorman, James F. *Architecture of Frank Furness*. Philadelphia: Philadelphia Museum of Art, 1973.

———*H. H. Richardson and His Office, A Centennial of His Move to Boston, 1874: Selected Drawings*. Cambridge, Mass.: Harvard College Library, 1974.

Perrin, Richard W. E. *Architecture of Wisconsin*. Madison, Wisc.: State Historical Society, 1967.

———*Milwaukee Landmarks*. Milwaukee, Wisc.: Milwaukee Public Museum, 1977.

Pevsner, Sir Nicholas. *An Outline of European Architecture*. 1943. Reprint. New York: Penguin Books, 1977.

Pierson, William Harvey, Jr. *American Buildings and Their Architects: Technology and the Picturesque, the Corporate and the Early Gothic Styles*. Garden City, N.Y.: Anchor, 1980.

———*American Buildings and Their Architects: The Colonial and Neoclassical Styles*. Garden City, N.Y.: Anchor, 1976.

Ravenel, Beatrice St. Julien. *Architects of Charleston*. Charleston, S.C.: Carolina Art Association, 1945.

Rifkind, Carole. *Field Guide to American Architecture*. New York: New American Library, 1980.

Rightmyer, Nelson Waite. *The Anglican Church in Delaware*. Philadelphia: Church Historical Society, 1947.

Riverside Church in the City of New York. New York: Riverside Church, 1978.

Root, Edward W. *Philip Hooker: A Contribution to the Study of the Renaissance in America*. New York: Scribner's, 1929.

Rose, Harold Wickliffe. *The Colonial Houses of Worship in America*. New York: Hastings House, 1964.

Rusk, William Sener. "Benjamin H. Latrobe and the Classical Influence in His Work." *Maryland Historical Magazine* 31 (1936): 126–154.

Scully, Arthur. *James Dakin, Architect: His Career in New York and the South*. Baton Rouge, La.: Louisiana State University Press, 1973.

Scully, Vincent. *American Architecture and Urbanism*. New York: Praeger, 1976.

Shinn, George Wolfe. *The King's Handbook of Notable Episcopal Churches in the United States*. Boston: Moses King Corporation, 1889.

Sinnott, Edmund Ware. *Meetinghouse and Church in Early New England*. New York: McGraw-Hill, 1963.

Stanton, Phoebe B. *The Gothic Revival and American Church Architecture*. Baltimore: Johns Hopkins Press, 1968.

Sturges, Walter Knight. "A Bishop and His Architect: The Story of the Building of the Baltimore Cathedral." *Liturgical Arts* 17 (1949): 53–67.

Sullivan, Louis H. *The Autobiography of an Idea*. New York: Dover, 1924.

Wedda, John. *New England Worships*. New York: Random House, 1965.

Wolfe, Tom. "From Bauhaus to Our House: Why U.S. Architects Can't Get Out of the Box." *Harper's*, June 1981, pp. 33–54, and July 1981, pp. 40–59.

Wright, Frank Lloyd. *Writings and Buildings*. New York: Horizon Press, 1960.

INDEX

The text was set in Palatino by TGA Graphics, Inc.,
New York, New York.

The book was printed and bound by Toppan Printing Company, Ltd.,
Tokyo, Japan.